I0814680

NICE GOIN', MICKEY! YUH CAUGHT 'IM SINGLE-HANDED!

WALT DISNEY'S

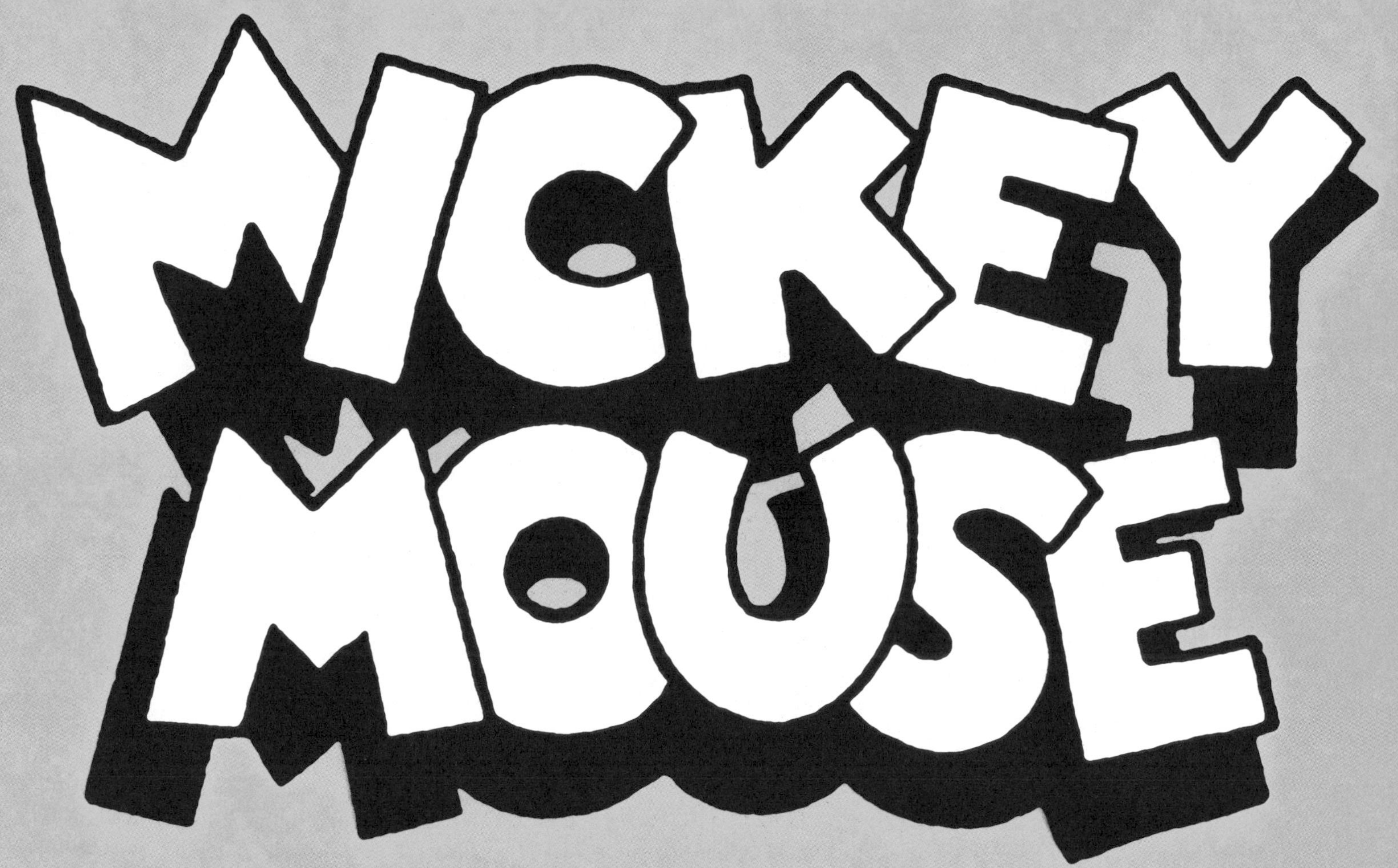

BY FLOYD GOTTFREDSON

WALT DISNEY'S

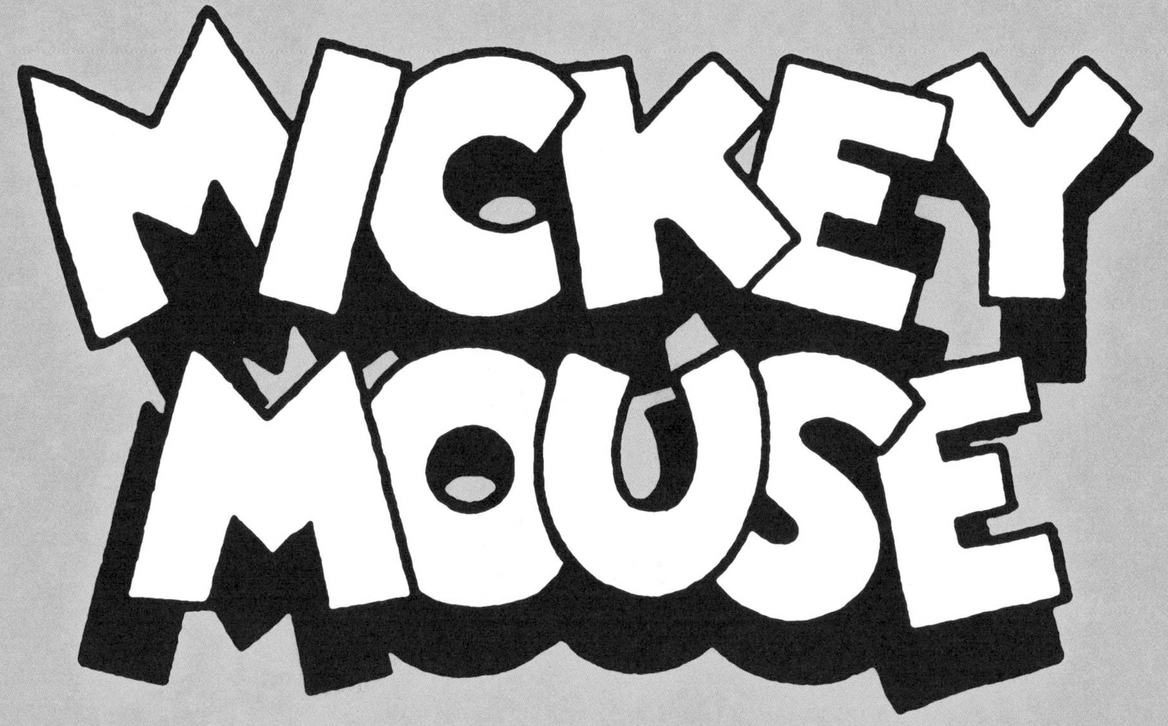

BY FLOYD GOTTFREDSON

"LOST IN LANDS OF LONG AGO"

Series Editors: David Gerstein and Gary Groth

FANTAGRAPHICS BOOKS

The Floyd Gottfredson Library

Series Editors: DAVID GERSTEIN with GARY GROTH
Series Designer: JACOB COVEY
Designer: DAVID GERSTEIN with KEELI McCARTHY
Production: PAUL BARESH
Associate Publisher: ERIC REYNOLDS
Publisher: GARY GROTH

Fantagraphics Books, Inc.
7563 Lake City Way NE
Seattle, WA 98115

Special thanks to:

Randall Bethune
Big Planet Comics
Black Hook Press, Japan
Nick Capetillo
Kevin Czapiewski
John DiBello
Juan Manuel Domínguez
Mathieu Doublet
Dan Evans III
Thomas Eykemans
Scott Fritsch-Hammes
Coco and Eddie Gorodetsky
Karen Green
Ted Haycraft
Eduardo Takeo "Lizarkeo" Igarashi
Nevdon Jamgochian
Andy Koopmans
Philip Nel
Vanessa Palacios
Kurt Sayenga
Anne Lise Rostgaard Schmidt
Christian Schremser
Secret Headquarters
Paul van Dijken
Mungo van Krimpen-Hall
Jason Aaron Wong
Thomas Zimmermann

ISBN 978-1-60699-782-6

First printing: November 2014

Printed in Singapore

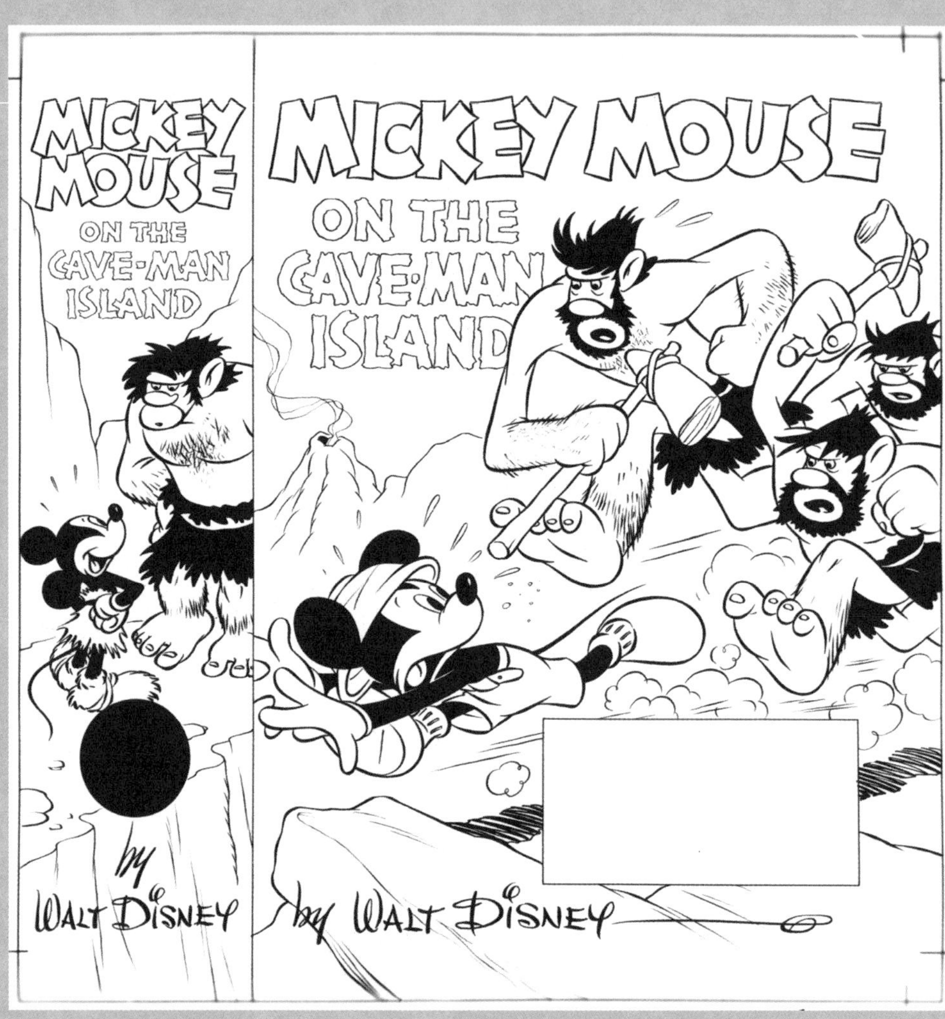

RIGHT: Original art for the front cover and spine of *Better Little Book* 1499 (1944), reprinting Floyd Gottfredson's "Land of Long Ago" (1940) under an alternate title. In print, the front cover's elaborate hand-lettering was replaced with a dull typeset font. Art by Hank Porter; image courtesy Walt Disney Photo Library.

THIS VOLUME OF *MICKEY MOUSE* DAILY STRIPS contains the final serials predating World War II—and nearly the final bunch that Floyd Gottfredson would plot singlehandedly. Our next few volumes will bring you wild new co-stars, Mickey's battles with the Axis, and Gottfredson's famous, long-standing teamup with writer Bill Walsh.

But then there's what our next volumes *won't* bring you. As it happens, wartime and postwar *Mickey* serials began to diverge from other Mouse media. No longer, after Pearl Harbor, would *Mickey Mouse* newspaper strips reflect—and be reflected in—quite as many *Mickey Mouse* cartoons and comic books. Up until now, our ongoing "Gottfredson Archives" section has offered tons of these tie-ins. After this book you won't see quite as many.

But what you *will* see is still good as gold! Like the classic *Mickey* strips themselves, supplied to me as usual for this volume by Ken Shue, Global Art Development, Disney Publishing, and Shue's secretary Iliana Lopez.

Numerous other scholars contributed artwork, knowledge, and archival items. I'm grateful to Director Rebecca Cline, Contractor Kevin Kern, and Archivist Steven Vagnini at the Walt Disney Archives, and Researcher Fox Carney at the Disney Animation Research Library. I'd also like to thank Thomas Andrae, Christopher Barat, Michael Barrier, Geoffrey Blum, John Clark, Stephen DeStefano, Byron Erickson, Arthur Faria Jr., Leonardo Gori, Thomas Jensen, Thad Komorowski, Roy Kooijman, Larry Lowery, Matteo Sonz, Francesco Spreafico, Frank Stajano, Joe Torcivia, and Malcolm Willits.

Others, too, have provided crucial support and encouragement. First and foremost come my parents, Susan and Larry Gerstein, and my brother Ben. Then come friends including Céline and Stefan Allirol-Molin, Nicky Barat, Alberto Becattini, Jerry Beck, Leo Breydo, Lana German, Didier Ghez, Colleen Gottfredson Toomay, Jan Gottfredson, Jonathan Gray, Joakim Gunnarsson, the Hake's Americana staff (including Alex Winter, Terence Kean, and Deak Stagemeyer), Andy Hershberger, Nelson Hughes, Lars Jensen, Mark and Cole Johnson, Vincent Joseph, J. B. Kaufman, Mark Kausler, Raquel Lopez, Mike Matei, Anne Marie Mersing, Geoffrey Moses, Floyd Norman, Martin Olsen, KaJuan Osborne, Jesse Post, Stefano Priarone, Tarkan Rosenberg, Travis Seitler, Warren Spector, Tom Stathes, Kwongmei To, Ted Toomay, Esther Torcivia, Fernando Ventura, Francois Willot, Germund Von Wowern, and Wilbert Watts.

What an army of Floyd Gottfredson fans! It's great to have you all on our side as we charge toward World War II—supplied, for the final time, with a prewar surplus of exciting extra features. Why? Because we like you.

—David Gerstein
May 2014

TABLE of CONTENTS

ABOVE: *Better Little Book* 1483 (1945), collecting Gottfredson's "Bellhop Detective" (1940) under an alternate title. Image courtesy Larry Lowery.

TABLE of CONTENTS

The Gottfredson Archives: Essays and Special Features

ABOVE: The spooks in Gottfredson's "Bellhop Detective" evolved from this animation design for the cartoon *Lonesome Ghosts* (1937). Image courtesy Walt Disney Archives.

ABOVE: Italian *Topolino collezione ANAF* 41 (1984), collecting "Love Trouble." Cover art by Romano Scarpa; image courtesy Leonardo Gori.

OF MOUSE & MAN

FLOYD GOTTFREDSON AND THE MICKEY MOUSE CONTINUITIES

1940–1942: SLIPPING INTO DARKNESS

» *Foreword by Thomas Andrae*

The Mickey Mouse tales in this book were published at a time when the Nazis were bombing England and invading other European countries. In an earlier era, Mickey had frequently fought foreign menaces, often on foreign shores. But now these nations were increasingly becoming battle zones. Not wishing to feature armed conflicts with which America was not formally involved, Gottfredson set his serials primarily in the United States. Yet most of Mickey's adventures registered the coming war, just the same. The stories became saturated with paranoia and confusion; no one and nothing is really as it appears.

"The Bar-None Ranch" (1940) reflects this confusion in its unusual mix of genres: it is both a science fiction saga and a Western. Gottfredson, long a fan of movie serials,[1] took inspiration for his story from the famous serial *The Phantom Empire* (1935), a similar genre combination. *Empire* was Gene Autry's first starring role, and the first major film featuring the singing cowboy as a hero. But its real interest lay in its sci-fi element: the underground, futuristic city of Murania, based on the legendary lost continent of Mu.

Besides a sci-fi story and a Western, Gottfredson's tale functions as a mystery. Pegleg Pete has been kidnapping women at a dude ranch, and Mickey tries to track him down. Just as Murania was hidden by a secret door in the side of a mountain, a similar door guards Pete's lair; the narrative hinges on Mickey's problems in trying to *enter* it. The hideout reflects Gottfredson's usual love of futuristic high technology: an invisible wall prevents planes from flying into the airspace over Pete's domain. The domain itself, once revealed, is a small underground kingdom: Gottfredson's take on Murania, with a high-tech electrical plant abutting ranch houses and a barn. The concept of a criminal "kingdom" leads us to our first war reference: the place is run for Pete by a bald-headed German scientist, reflective of Nazi villainy in Europe.

Returning to the story's Wild West themes, "Bar-None Ranch" parodies the unreal world of musical Westerns by subverting that world's conventions. Pete's love-starved captives view their kidnapping as a thrilling adventure rather than a danger, and Clarabelle—who is supposed to be trying to entrap Pete—has fallen for him, and is more interested in romance than in getting back home. Rather than playing a passive victim, however, Clarabelle becomes angry when she learns Pete is willing—in fact, anxious—to let her go.

Goofy, the comic sidekick, plays the role of Western hero more than Mickey. But his attempts to ape Hollywood Western he-men are more ludicrous than heroic. His macho posturing only makes him look like the naïve dude he is. He even warbles Western songs a la Gene Autry and Roy Rogers, but they are out of tune and their lyrics insipid. Gottfredson could not help but mock the artificiality of singing cowboys.[2]

"The Bar-None Ranch" contrasts a Hollywood America, lost in dreams—like Goofy—with unglamorous reality, as represented by Mickey's frustrated

ABOVE: Of cowpokes and cogwheels: *The Phantom Empire* (1935) inspired Gottfredson's mix of sci-fi and Wild West themes in "The Bar-None Ranch." Image courtesy Heritage Auctions.

RIGHT: Floyd Gottfredson with "Duck Man" Carl Barks at a commemorative Christmas dinner in 1982. Barks' 1941 cartoon *Timber* inspired this volume's "Mystery at Hidden River." Photo courtesy Malcolm Willits.

sleuthing. Mickey acts more like a detective than a Western hero, using brains to solve the mystery and bring the villains to justice. Mickey defeats Pete with good old-fashioned American fisticuffs, and the timely arrival of the sheriff. The foreign menace, meanwhile, is easily beaten; the German scientist's head is so fully in the clouds that he doesn't even realize Mickey—who helps him with his tools!—is really a dangerous invader. In effect, Germany is no match for pragmatic, levelheaded Americans and their tradition of frontier justice.

Gender conflict motivates "The Bar-None Ranch," but is marginal to it. The theme becomes central in "Love Trouble" (1941). The story was inspired by the 1936 cartoon *Mickey's Rival*, although Gottfredson greatly expanded its premise of Minnie's brief attraction to a city slicker. In "Love Trouble," Mickey returns from another adventure to find that—uncharacteristically—Minnie is not anxiously awaiting his return. She is no longer playing the role of surrogate wife, patiently enduring her boyfriend's protracted absences while he roams free. Instead, Minnie has acquired a new boyfriend, Montmorency Rodent: a gawky rat with a long snout, flashy clothes, and sleek sports car, whose big-city hipness makes the small-town Mickey seem boring and awkward by comparison.

Monty, a social climber who pronounces his surname "Rodawn," exemplifies one of Gottfredson's favorite targets of parody: the snobbery and the artificiality of the ultra-rich. He plays practical jokes on Mickey, humiliates him with derogatory remarks, and sweeps Minnie off her feet with his corny lines, parlor magic, and stylish dance steps. When he gracefully lifts her into the air, she coos "Oooo-oo... aren't you *strong*! I adore *masterful* men," much to Mickey's consternation.

The tensions in "Love Trouble" actually allude to events occurring backstage. Mickey was undergoing an identity crisis in animation at the time. In the cartoons he had begun to look a little staid and boring in comparison to the feisty troublemaker Donald Duck, who was displacing him in popularity. Even Pluto took over many nominal Mickey Mouse shorts. Walt Disney confessed that "Mickey's our problem child," and admitted that he had become so idealized and perfect on-screen that it was getting difficult to subject him to comedy.[3]

Luckily, such restrictions rarely hit the comics. With the aid of a new girl in town, Mickey fights back in "Love Trouble" by showing Monty up as a second-rate socialite—outclassed and outstyled by Mickey and his new paramour. When Monty receives his ultimate comeuppance at a high society ball, Minnie confesses that she never fell out of love with Mickey—but only pretended to be infatuated with Monty to make Mickey jealous. Keeping up with the Joneses is a fruitless enterprise, Gottfredson implies; one can always be temporarily outclassed by someone richer, flashier, and better-dressed. Thus, the goal of seeking such false status is fatuous and empty.

"Love Trouble" contrasts Mickey's authenticity with the superficiality of a social climber, whose acclaim is based on false appearances. Mickey's "new girl" is a genuine high society belle, while Monty proves not to be as wealthy as he seemed. These events reflect the illusions created by the consumer economy of the time, which enabled some show-offs to acquire the appearance of wealth without actually holding high-paying jobs. According to historian Warren Susman, the early 1940s witnessed a societal transition from character to personality: a shift from a producer culture anchored in an inner-directed, individualistic morality—and the Protestant work ethic—to a consumer culture grounded in fun, pleasure, and the desire to impress others.[4] Mickey represents the morality of the producers; Rodent, the superficiality of the consumers.

"Love Trouble"—inevitably—also reflects the burgeoning war: specifically, anxious male anticipation of being called to war overseas. Women were expected to maintain the home front and stay loyal to their men for the duration. But many men feared

ABOVE: Montmorency Rodent was a more refined version of Mortimer Mouse from the cartoon *Mickey's Rival* (1936). Art by Tom Wood; image courtesy Walt Disney Archives.

that when they returned home, they would discover they had been supplanted by someone else in their wives' or sweethearts' affections. "Love Trouble" resolves these tensions simply by whisking them

ABOVE: While outclassed by Montmorency in "Love Trouble," Mickey did boast a slick, updated design of his own for the story, adapted from this Fred Moore model sheet from *The Little Whirlwind* (1941). Image courtesy Walt Disney Archives.

away; but as Gottfredson's next story shows, it was too facile to assume that women would remain sutured in place.

"The Mystery at Hidden River" (1941) is perhaps the most important story in this collection. It is one of only a couple that have not previously been reprinted in modern times, in this case perhaps because of the dated Native American stereotypes it contains. But it is also unique in being the only Floyd Gottfredson continuity that was inspired by the work of future *Donald Duck* comics master Carl Barks.

Gottfredson had worked at the Disney studio for years before Barks became employed there. Barks was first an animation in-betweener, filling in the action drawn by the journeymen animators; but he soon became one of the Studio's key storymen. Barks and his partners—first Harry Reeves, then Jack Hannah—were responsible for creating the stories in the Donald Duck cartoons, tales they invented visually by drawing storyboards that laid out the plots in miniature. Barks and Hannah's first pairing of Donald with Pegleg Pete was titled *Timber* (1941). It concerned Donald becoming a northwoods lumberjack, oppressed by Pete as his brutal foreman.[5]

Gottfredson concocted a long Mickey mystery on the basis of this slim premise. Clarabelle has again been captured and Mickey goes for the FBI's aid. He learns that the logging company where she vanished has been losing valuable timber—and that only one-fourth of the lumber ever reaches the mills. Even more disturbingly, the G-men sent to investigate have also disappeared. When Mickey offers to help, the FBI refuses his aid, thinking he is not expert or competent enough to investigate.

When Mickey decides to investigate anyway, gender trouble again rears its head. Minnie demands to go with Mickey, a most unusual move for her in 1941, but reflective of the burgeoning war, in which women were called to various forms

of duty. Mickey chauvinistically rejects Minnie's offer—"this is a *man's* job! A girl couldn't be of any help!"—but the feisty female refuses to give in. Gottfredson's attempt at an anti-sexist sequence is notable; even if, when Minnie argues that "women have intuition," Gottfredson leans toward the problematic cliché of men as primarily rational, and women primarily emotional.

When Mickey arrives at the logging camp, he discovers that the foreman is his old nemesis Pegleg Pete, now assuming the French-Canadian-sounding *nom de plume* of Pierre de la Pooch. In the animated *Timber*, the comedy had derived from "Pierre" giving Donald dangerous jobs to make him pay off a stolen dinner. The situation is more serious in "Hidden River." Pete tries to eliminate the snooping Mickey by giving him a series of lumberjack assignments that threaten his life. However, it is not by dint of his usual heroism that the Mouse escapes death, but only by sheer luck. The extra-risky mood once again seems to owe something to wartime jitters.

"Hidden River" is the famous story in which Pete loses his peg leg. "I hav' replace heem weeth new model store leg!" he explains in fractured French. But the real explanation for the change was more prosaic. According to Gottfredson:

> When the animators first used Pegleg Pete they animated him like any other character, and he walked too naturally. Walt told them to get some weight on [his foot] and use it like a peg leg. They began to experiment and have so much fun that they overdid it to the point where it looked painful when Pete stepped on it. Walt said: "I've led you guys astray, so I think we'll just put a leg on him and forget it."[6]

Because Gottfredson was trying to mimic the look and spirit of animation, he followed suit. But when Pete faded out of the *Mickey* cartoons, Gottfredson

recalls, "we decided he was much more colorful with a peg leg, and [put it] back on him."[7]

A less realistic element in the story—and one that we acknowledge, today, as an unfortunate relic of the era—is "Hidden River's" ration of ethnic stereotypes and dialect. First and foremost comes Little Star, an Indian girl who looks remarkably like Minnie. She speaks in the pidgin English that was typical in the comics of this period, playing the role of Pocahontas to Mickey's John Smith. She is enamored of the "pretty white mans" and tries to save a Caucasian's life, as countless other Indian maidens have done in popular fiction and films.

In her attempts to help Mickey, Little Star is at times hindered by her seeming ignorance of modernity. But Little Star's aunt Rising-Full-Moon and an old "buck" character, are more ignorant

LEFT: Pete overbalances when walking on his peg leg in *Mickey's Service Station* (1935). Animation by Nick George.

ABOVE: Hank Porter's line art for a retitled *Better Little Book* edition of "The Bar-None Ranch." Image courtesy Walt Disney Photo Library.

still—as if they cannot understand the white man's culture, even in contemporary times. When an incidental Indian kid proves an exception to the rule, it is only to embody another invidious image: the child smart aleck, who offers Mickey information and then swindles him. This act, in effect, reverses the historical trajectory of Indian-white relations, in which the former have been exploited by the latter.

Toward the climax of "Hidden River," Gottfredson reverts to 1930s melodrama by bringing in Sylvester Shyster, a crooked lawyer who had been the brains behind Pete's schemes in many earlier Mickey adventures. Shortly after Shyster's appearance, on December 7, 1941, the Japanese launched a surprise attack on Pearl Harbor, and America declared war on the Axis powers. Gottfredson now openly references the wartime context in explaining Pete and Shyster's plot. Their hijacking of "molignumite" logs is undermining the defense program; that is why G-men were involved.

But Mickey's usual diligent sleuthing fails to expose the scheme. Instead, Little Star falls into the logging chute and Mickey must save her, accidentally discovering Pete's hideout in the process. When the Indian girl's makeup washes off, Mickey makes a second major discovery: that Little Star is really Minnie.

In an unusual ending, Minnie and Clarabelle take part in the final battle, pummeling Shyster with a broom and suitcase while Mickey defeats Pete with the usual male fisticuffs. It is a rare scene of sexual equality in a Mickey adventure, where—as in most adventure fiction of the period—the standard gender-division of labor more typically prevails. That said, in "Hidden River," neither Mickey nor Minnie fully triumphs through physical heroism. Mickey is only victorious through sheer luck: Pete accidentally knocks himself and Shyster out. In wartime, no one is completely in control, no matter how heroic.

The story's denouement wraps up its battle-of-the-sexes theme. A G-man congratulates Mickey alone for solving the case. Undaunted, Minnie claims she has a few congratulations coming too—but Mickey tries to reposition her back into a subordinate role, noting what he regards as her interferences. (Strangely, Minnie forgets to remind him that she and Clarabelle weakened Shyster during the mêlée, giving her a legitimate claim to heroism.)

It is striking to see a 1940s adventure in which Minnie refuses to assume her "proper" place in the domestic sphere, demanding to participate in the action like her boyfriend. But her gesture, once again, reflects World War II. It prefigures the coming of the real-life Rosie the Riveters, who took over men's jobs on the home front—and shook up gender roles that had been in place for years. The Rosies, WACs, and other female recruits altered the sexual division of labor much like Minnie challenges it here.

ABOVE: Donald takes orders from "Pierre" in *Timber* (1941). Storyboard art by Carl Barks; image courtesy Walt Disney Animation Research Library.

OPPOSITE TOP: A terrible thunderlizard causes trolley troubles in *The Lost World* (1925). Image courtesy Heritage Auctions.

OPPOSITE BOTTOM: Goofy's feared "dynamitoruses" in Gottfredson's "Land of Long Ago" paralleled the hungry dinos in Disney's recent *Fantasia* (1940).

The most powerful war-related imagery in this book, however, arguably came several stories before "Hidden River." Floyd Gottfredson based "Land of Long Ago" (1940–41) on the silent film *The Lost World* (1925), the first feature to combine stop motion animation with live actors. Willis O'Brien created the special effects for the feature and went on to animate the picture he will always be famous for, *King Kong* (1933).

In Gottfredson's tale, Mickey is visited—seemingly in a dream—by Professor Dustibones, who asks him to journey to an uncharted island where prehistoric beings still live. As in *The Lost World*, Mickey and crew encounter dinosaurs and cavemen coexisting on the island, although the two groups actually lived in entirely different geologic eras.

When Mickey and Goofy encounter the creatures, they are divided into two types, the peaceful and the bloodthirsty: vegetarian brontosauruses versus carnivorous sea serpents, and a domesticated caveman versus other savage cavemen. The division mirrors the dichotomy between Allies and Axis in the emerging conflict.

Cavemen had been marginal figures in *The Lost World*, but "Long Ago" features an entire tribe—who blame Mickey and his cohorts for a gigantic earthquake, thinking the invaders have angered their gods. A fierce fight ensues when the prehistoric men try to kill Mickey and capture Goofy and the Professor. In the end, our heroes escape, but Dustibones is struck by amnesia, destining their adventure to become a faded memory.

"Land of Long Ago" followed on the heels of the "Rite of Spring" sequence in Disney's *Fantasia* (1940), which had also contained graphic scenes of prehistoric violence. The "Rite" plotline featured giant dinosaurs battling to the death amidst erupting volcanoes, and has often been interpreted as symbolizing the coming World War. The fight between the civilized and the savage in "Long Ago," too, seems to portend the imminent conflagration—as does the ring of simmering volcanoes that surrounds Gottfredson's Cave-Man Island. One feels that the coming battle in the real world could not be whisked away as easily as the story suggests.

We'll see Mickey's own part of that battle in our very next volume. ●

1 This and other comics connections to films: Floyd Gottfredson, conversations with the author, 1970s.

2 The singing cowboy Western, admittedly, often had more substance than Gottfredson allowed; dealing—overtly or covertly—with issues engendered by the Great Depression and the New Deal. This made the films especially appealing to working class and rural audiences; see Peter Stanfield, *Horse Opera: The Strange History of the Singing Cowboy* (Urbana: University of Illinois Press, 2002), pp. 139–147.

3 Walt Disney quoted in Richard Holliss and Brian Sibley, *Mickey Mouse: His Life and Times* (New York: Harper and Row, 1986), p. 69.

4 Warren Susman, *Culture as History: The Transformation of American Society in the Twentieth Century* (New York: Pantheon, 1984), pp. 220–221.

5 Pete had featured as a mostly-unseen menace in Barks and Hannah's earlier *Donald's Lucky Day* (1939), but he and Donald shared little screen time together.

6 Floyd Gottfredson to Thomas Andrae, "The Mouse's Other Master: Floyd Gottfredson's 45 Years With Mickey." *Nemo: The Classic Comics Library* 6 (June 1984), p. 10.

7 In interviews, Gottfredson claimed to have used—and disliked—the common alias "Black Pete" for a pegleg-less Pete; in actuality, Pete in the Gottfredson strip was always called Pegleg Pete, even with two realistic feet.

I SAT AT Floyd Gottfredson's DESK!

by STEPHEN DE STEFANO

I first saw Mr. Gottfredson's work in the Smithsonian Collection of Newspaper Comics (1977).

I immediately dismissed it as kid's stuff. I was thirteen years old.

Later in my teen years I was reacquainted with Mr. Gottfredson's "pie-eyed" Mickey in the pages of the Gladstone reprints. This time I was charmed by it.

His stories were lively, intricate and smart. And strangely plausible. The figures he drew had real weight, and occupied defined spaces. His lines curved expressively.

Studying his work, I slowly began to understand true techniques of drawing.

But it was when I saw the 1944 Mickey continuity the WORLD OF TOMORROW (scripted by Bill Walsh) that Mr. Gottfredson became more than just a favorite artist; he became a lifelong influence on my work. His Mickey, by this point, was no longer pie-eyed, but streamlined and modern. Mr. Gottfredson perfected his shapes and structures, and more, PUSHED them. His sense of design went beyond weighty--it was now both musical and muscular.

This was no kid's stuff; to me it was and is humor/adventure comic art at its finest.

In those days, about the most clever idea I had was to draw Mickey wearing what I usually wore myself, for whatever that's worth.

I did get better at drawing Mickey, although I never quite aced it, never quite drew him half as well as I knew he could be drawn. But I never stopped internalizing Mr. Gottfredson's work, either. Even as I grew and worked on Popeye and other classic cartoon stars.

The artwork on LUCKY IN LOVE, the 2010 graphic novel I created along with writer George Chieffet, is an amalgam of my love for several artists, including Milt Gross and Harvey Kurtzman. But chief among those influences is Floyd Gottfredson.
In 2012 I began working as a designer on a new series of Mickey Mouse shorts, produced by Paul Rudish for Disney TV.
Again, my chief influence when working on those shorts is Mr. Gottfredson.

THE BAR-NONE RANCH

APRIL 22, 1940
–
AUGUST 17, 1940

BEST IN THE WEST, BAR-NONE

If you have a comics-loving friend who hasn't yet discovered the joys of Floyd Gottfredson's *Mickey Mouse* comic strip, encourage him or her to read "The Bar-None Ranch." You can safely wager a poke of gold that they'll love it, because it's a thrilling, interesting, and incredibly funny story. More importantly, it serves as an almost-perfect introduction to the Mickey Mouse universe as Gottfredson developed it.

In this one tale, your friend will be introduced to the core cast of the *Mickey* strip and see them not only "performing" in character, but interacting with each other in ways that define their relationships. Gottfredson and scripter Merrill De Maris were clearly well aware that the best way to turn a plot into a story is to let the characters drive it along.

But before we get into said characters and their relationships, it's necessary to point out the omission that puts the "almost" into "almost perfect": Minnie Mouse. She is a nonentity here, her sole purpose being to draw Mickey out to Pete's domain. Still, it's easy enough to find a gutsier Minnie—just turn to "Monarch of Medioka" in Volume 4 of this series.

Moving on to Clarabelle Cow, her role as a "man-crazy" romantic pretty much sums her up. It's interesting to note, though, that until Mickey figures out Clarabelle would make good bait for Pete, he has little to do with her. She's clearly just Minnie's friend.

The real cast surprise is the handling of Goofy. To those of us familiar with years of later Mickey stories—in which he and Goofy were seemingly joined at the hip—it's refreshing to note that Mickey doesn't want Goofy along on this adventure. When Goofy comes anyway, his comic relief sequences are priceless, but have very little to do with helping Mickey or advancing the plot.

I've always had a soft spot for the "Bar-None Ranch" version of Pegleg Pete: an old-school thug, but also much, much more. He's not a criminal genius; but he's crafty as only a seasoned lawbreaker can be, and he knows how to use—and dominate—smarter crooks, like this story's German professor, to give himself a technological edge. Finally, as befits Mickey's nemesis, he recognizes the threat Mickey poses to his schemes, and it wouldn't "bother [Pete's] conscience" if that threat were neutralized.

Which bring us to Mickey himself. Lengthy essays have been written about just why Gottfredson's Mickey is not the boring Mr. Perfect that Mickey is often perceived as; but three points in "The Bar-None Ranch" speak louder than any essay. *Mickey is not infallible*—he fails to catch Pete many times, and only succeeds in the end because he doesn't give up. *Mickey's not a humorless straight man*—not only does he frequently take the "mickey" out of Goofy, but he's quite capable of bearing the brunt of slapstick jokes himself. And *Mickey's definitely "muss-up-able"*—Pete beats the heck out of him in the story's climax.

In conclusion, "The Bar-None Ranch" is the perfect way for your comics-loving friend to test the Gottfredson *Mickey Mouse* waters. And if after dipping their toe in, they don't delightedly dive in for more, well...

...you can always find a new friend with taste!

—Byron Erickson

A LETTER FROM MINNIE? OH, THAT'S RIGHT-- I FORGOT SHE AND CLARABELLE WENT ON A TRIP SOME PLACE!
AN' THEY OUGHTER TAR AN' FEATHER 'EM, I SEZ!
MAIL
RIP
The BUGLE
4-22

WHAT? OH---!
YES, SIR---ANY GUY THET PULLS THIS HERE KINDA BIZZNUSS IS WORSE'N A RAT!
The BUGLE

MAKES MUH BLOOD BILE, IT DOES! LIKE TO GET MUH HANDS ON THUH GOLDURN---!
WHY GET SO EXCITED? JUST A STORY OF A WESTERN BAD MAN WITH A WOODEN LEG, WHO---!
The BUGLE

---WITH A WOODEN---??
GIMME THAT PAPER!

HUMPH! TALK ABOUT GETTIN' EXCITED---GRABBIN' MUH PAPER LIKE THAT!
"DESPERADO TERRORIZES WESTERN DUDE RANCH! KIDNAPS FEMALE GUESTS FOR RANSOM---!"
4-23

DUDE KIDNAPS FOR RANSOM
PRICKLY HEAT, WYOZONA-
Guests at the Bar None Ranch, owned and operated by "Handlebar Hank" Hawkins, have been thrown into a panic by a series of kidnaping raids! The daring bandit has, so far, eluded all attempts at

LISTEN TO THIS---"VICTIMS OF THE KIDNAPER DESCRIBE HIM AS A PICTURESQUE CHARACTER, RATHER HEAVY AND WITH A WOODEN LEG!"
YEAH? WELL, WHAT ABOUT IT?

Y' KNOW WHAT THAT MEANS, GOOFY? PEG-LEG PETE'S ON THE LOOSE AGAIN!
GAWRSH---I BET YOU'RE RIGHT!

MICKEY READS A NEWSPAPER ACCOUNT OF A SERIES OF KIDNAPINGS ON A WESTERN DUDE RANCH. THE DESCRIPTION OF THE VILLAIN CONVINCES HIM THAT IT IS HIS OLD ENEMY, PEG-LEG PETE!
4-24

WELL, AIN'TCHA GOIN' OUT WEST AND HELP KETCH HIM? Y' ALLUS DONE IT BEFORE!
NOTHIN' DOIN'! I'VE HAD TROUBLE ENOUGH WITHOUT GOIN' OUT TO LOOK FOR IT! NO CALL FOR ME TO GET MESSED UP IN THIS!

NO, SIR-- AND I MEAN NO! EXCUSE ME WHILE I READ MINNIE'S LETTER!

BAR NONE
GUEST RANCH
"HANDLEBAR HANK" HAWKINS, PROP.
PRICKLY HEAT, WYOZONA--
April 21, 1940
Dear Mickey:
Clarabelle and I just arrived here today. Had a wonderful trip and the
darling ranch
able! Wish
be with
camp fire and
GOOD GOSH! MINNIE'S STAYIN' AT THE---!!

GOOFY! HELP ME PACK-- I'VE GOTTA CATCH A TRAIN!
WALT DISNEY

WHILE MICKEY GETS THE LOWDOWN FROM THE GIRLS, THE CAUSE OF ALL THE EXCITEMENT GALLOPS INTO A CANYON, PURSUED BY THE RANCH-OWNER AND HIS BOYS!

WHILE MICKEY AND THE GUESTS OF "HANDLEBAR HARRY'S" DUDE RANCH DISCUSS THE LATEST KIDNAPING, THE PROPRIETOR RETURNS FROM A FRUITLESS CHASE OF THE BANDIT!
4-29

YES, SIR---WE HAD 'IM BOTTLED UP IN DEAD-END CANYON, WHEN HE DISAPPEARED CLEAN'S A WHISTLE, HOSS AND ALL!
DOGGONE IT, PETE ALWAYS WAS A TRICKY OLD RASCAL!
Copr 1940, Walt Disney Productions World Rights Reserved

AND THAT MEANS ONE MORE RANSOM I'LL HAVE TO KICK IN! TH' CONFOUNDED RAT'LL HAVE ME BLED DRY IF HE AIN'T CAUGHT SOON!

EASE YORE MIND, HANDLEBAR ---YORE TROUBLES IS OVER! ME AN' MUH LI'L PARDNER'S PLUMB PIZEN TO THET STUMP-FOOTED VARMINT! HIS DAYS IS NUMBERED!
WELL, THEM'S MIGHTY WELCOME WORDS, MISTER --SOUNDS RIGHT ENCOURAGIN'! NOW, JUST HOW Y' PLANNIN' TO DO ALL THIS?

HUH-- HOW?
WHY, UH-- THAT'S WHERE MUH LI'L PARDNER COMES IN!
Distributed by King Features Syndicate, Inc

THE MORNING AFTER HIS ARRIVAL AT THE BAR-NONE RANCH, MICKEY QUESTIONS THE OWNER ABOUT PEG-LEG PETE'S KIDNAP OPERATIONS.

I'D LIKE TO KNOW, MR. HAWKINS, HOW PETE WORKS THIS RACKET --WHO PAYS THE RANSOMS?
WHO PAYS? I DO--DASH-BLANK THE BLINKETY CUSS! AND HE SETS THE AMOUNTS JUST LOW ENOUGH SO I CAN, WITHOUT GOIN' BROKE!
OIL
4-30
Copr 1940, Walt Disney Productions World Rights Reserved

DON'T Y' SEE, SON, WHERE HE'S GOT ME? I'M RUNNIN' A DUDE RANCH, AND IF I DON'T TAKE KEER OF THE CUSTOMERS, HOW'D I GET ANY BUSINESS?

WELL, GOSH--I'M S'PRISED THAT PEOPLE DO COME--- THIS KIDNAPING STUFF'S IN ALL THE PAPERS!
HUMPH! RECKON Y' DON'T KNOW THEM FUDDLE-DUDDY FEMALES F'UM THE EAST! THEY STILL COME, SON--YOU BET THEY DO!
OIL
Distributed by King Features Syndicate, Inc

OH, MR. HAWKINS, I'M SO FRIGHTENED ---DO YOU THINK THAT TERRIBLE BANDIT WILL COME BACK TONIGHT?
HARD TO TELL, MA'AM --ALL Y' CAN DO IS HOPE! I MEAN HOPE THAT HE WON'T, OF COURSE!
WALT DISNEY

THIS LADY THAT PETE KIDNAPED LAST NIGHT, MR. HAWKINS ---HOW DOES HE GO ABOUT GETTIN' THE RANSOM?
TONIGHT I LEAVE THE DOUGH AT A MARKED SPOT IN THE CANYON, AND THEN TOMORROW I GO TO THE SAME PLACE AND PICK UP THE WOMAN!

Y' SEE, HE LEAVES A NOTE EV'RY TIME, TELLIN' THE TIME AN' PLACE-- - AND ALL I CAN DO IS FOLLOW ORDERS, DAD-BURN IT!
5-1

PARDON ME, MR. HAWKINS, I SHUDDER TO MENTION THAT DREADFUL BANDIT, BUT DO YOU THINK I AM IN GREAT DANGER?
NO, MA'AM--I'D SAY YOU WAS PUFFICKLY SAFE- --

? ? ?
---HE NEVER BRINGS MORE'N ONE HOSS!
WALT DISNEY

THE LATEST VICTIM OF OLD PETE'S KIDNAP RACKET HAS JUST BEEN RANSOMED AND IS SAFELY BACK AT THE RANCH!

MIND IF I QUESTION HER, MR. HAWKINS? I MIGHT LEARN SOMEP'N ABOUT PETE'S HIDEAWAY!
HELP YOURSELF, SON! RIGHT NOW SHE'S SPLUTTERIN' TO THE OTHER FEMALES LIKE SHE'D HAD AN OPERATION! WOMEN -- PAH!
5-2

--I WAS NEVER SO ABSOLUTELY PETRIFIED AS WHEN THAT FIEND DREW A HUGE KNIFE! "LISTEN, BABY," HE GROWLED IN A DEEP VOICE ---!
YES, YES --- GO ON--!

EXCUSE ME, MA'AM-- BUT WHILE Y' WERE AT PETE'S, DID Y' LEARN ANYTHING THAT MIGHT HELP US TO NAB THE OLD SCOUNDREL?
!

SCOUNDREL, INDEED! I'LL HAVE YOU UNDERSTAND THAT HE BEHAVED AS A PERFECT GENTLEMAN AT ALL TIMES!

HI-YA, PARDNER, OL' PAL! ANYTHIN' NEW ABOUT PETE?
NO! ALL I'VE LEARNED FROM THE WOMEN IS THAT HE LIVES IN A VALLEY SURROUNDED BY IMPASSABLE MOUNTAINS!
5-3

I CAN'T FIGURE IT! THEY SAY HE LIVES IN HIGH STYLE --- YET HE'S THE ONLY ONE WHO KNOWS HOW TO GET IN OR OUT!

HE BLINDFOLDS THE WOMEN WHEN THEY GET TO THE MOUNTAIN, BUT THEY SAY THEY GET A SENSATION LIKE AN ELEVATOR- ---!
WELL, SAY-- THAT MAKES IT EASY! WE GOT 'IM NOW, MICKEY!

ALL WE DO IS LOOK FER A MOUNTAIN WITH AN ELEVATOR IN IT --- AN' THERE WOULDN'T BE MORE'N ONE!
PLOP!

DARNED IF I'M GONNA SIT AROUND HERE TWIDDLIN' MY THUMBS! I'LL GO SCOUT AROUND PETE'S NEIGHBORHOOD FOR AWHILE!
5-4

SO THIS IS DEAD-END CANYON, WHERE HE DOES HIS MYSTERIOUS DISAPPEARING ACT! HMM-- MUST BE QUITE A TRICK, GOIN' THROUGH THESE WALLS!

THIS PLACE SURE LOOKS INNOCENT AND PEACEFUL ENOUGH---!

HEY! WHAT ---!!?
WALT DISNEY

Conducting a little investigation into Dead-End Canyon, Mickey is suddenly yanked from his horse by a whistling lasso!

RAZZ ME, WILL YUH? I'LL LEARN YUH---!
BRRRRRP!
5-9

---I'LL BLAST YER BLINKIN' EARS OFF!
BANG! BANG!

BANG! BANG!! BANG!!!

SORRY TO LEAVE YUH, PAL, BUT I GOT BIZZNUSS! MEBBE I'LL GIT BACK SOME TIME--IF YUH'RE STILL HANGIN' AROUND!
WALT DISNEY

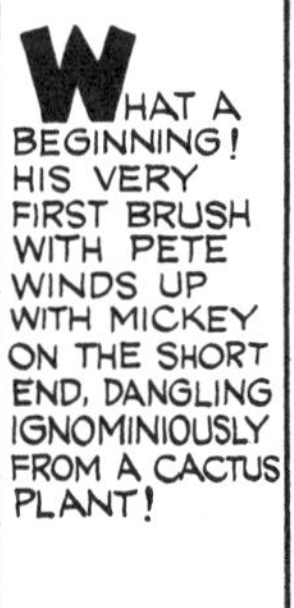
WHAT A BEGINNING! HIS VERY FIRST BRUSH WITH PETE WINDS UP WITH MICKEY ON THE SHORT END, DANGLING IGNOMINIOUSLY FROM A CACTUS PLANT!
5-10

A HORRIBLE FATE LIES IN STORE UNLESS --- WHAT'S THIS? AH-H-- IT'S MICKEY'S FAITHFUL STEED RETURNING!

ALL IS NOT LOST--- THE NOBLE ANIMAL COMES TO HIS MASTER'S RESCUE!
HOT DOG! NICE GOIN', OLD BOY!

STRAIGHT FOR HOME TROTS THE TRUSTY CREATURE, NOT STOPPING FOR EVEN ONE OAT!

WAL, DUST MAH BRITCHES--WHAT'S THIS A-COMIN'?
IT'S OUR LI'L DETECTIVE!
'PEARS TO HEV MET WITH FOUL PLAY SOMEWHAR'!

HAVE YOU SEEN MICKEY, MR. HAWKINS?
HE RID OUT TO DEAD-END CANYON A SHORT SPELL AGO! AIMED TO LOOK OVER THE BANDIT'S COUNTRY, I RECKON!
5-11

BUT A MOMENT LATER OUR HERO RETURNS --- THOUGH NOT UNDER HIS OWN POWER!
JUMPIN' COYOTES!!?
PLOP!

YEH, YOU GUESSED IT--IT WAS PEG-LEG PETE!
AND IT LOOKS LIKE TH' VARMINT TOOK FUST PLACE IN TH' ROPIN' AN' TYIN' EVENT!

HE DID! BUT THERE'S SOME RIDIN' AND SHOOTIN' EVENTS COMIN' UP -- THAT HE MIGHT LOSE!

DAYS GO BY, BUT ALL IS QUIET ON THE WESTERN RANCH! TOO QUIET TO SUIT MICKEY!
5-13

DOGGONE THAT PETE! I WISH HE'D QUIT KEEPIN' US IN SUSPENSE-- THERE'S SOME REASON WHY HE'S LAYIN' LOW!
DURN RIGHT THUR' IS! THET YALLER HOMBRE'S SKEERED TO SHOW HISSELF 'ROUND YERE!
WILD AND WOOLY WESTERN

HOW COME Y' THINK THAT?
'CAUSE THUH VARMINT KNOWS PLUMB WELL IF HE RUNS ACROST ME, HE'S GOTTER BEAT ME TO THUH DRAW!
WOOLY WESTERN WEEKLY

IF HE DON'T, I'LL GIT 'IM JUST LIKE ---JUST LIKE--- LIKE---

---LIKE THAT! WOW!!
BANG!
WALT DISNEY

GOODNESS--WHY DON'T YOU RELAX? FOR ALL WE KNOW, PEG-LEG PETE MAY BE GONE FOR GOOD!
HE'S GOT TOO GOOD A RACKET TO GIVE IT UP! AND WHILE HE'S AT LARGE NOBODY'S SAFE!
5-14

WAL, PICKLE MAH HIDE, EF IT AIN'T BUFFALO BILL!
SHORE 'NUFF! I THOUGHT HE WAS DAID!

LOOKA HERE, YOU-- THEM'S FIGHTIN' WORDS! AN' YUH BETTER RETRACK 'EM, 'LESS YO'RE AIMIN' TO BE PUSHIN' UP DAISIES!

GOSH, MISTER, I DIDN'T MEAN NO OFFENSE--- WOULDN'T THINK O' RIBBIN' YOU, SIR!
ME, NEITHER- --I GOT A WIFE AN' BABY TO THINK OF!
WELL, ALL RIGHT! BUT NEX' TIME BE KEERFUL, THA'S ALL--- MIGHTY KEERFUL!

---ALL EIGHT OF 'EM COME AT ME WITH DRAWED WEEPONS---BUT LIKE A FLASH, MUH GUNS BARKED--!
BOW-WOW -WOW!
TWO GUN TALES
5-15

??
?
??
?
?

LOOK, MISTER-- I AIN'T NEVER PLUGGED A MAN DURIN' THUH PRESENCE OF A LADY, BUT ONE MORE YAP F'M YOU---!
OH, PLEASE, SIR-- I'LL BE GOOD--- HONEST! SPARE MUH LIFE!

UH-HAW! GAWRSH --I NEVER KNOWED I WAS SO TOUGH! GOT 'EM ALL SKEERED SILLY!

YOU DON'T THINK PETE'S QUIT FOR GOOD, DO Y', MR. HAWKINS?
NOPE! NEW BATCH O' FEMALE DUDES PRANCIN' IN T'MORROW! HE'LL BE BACK, DANG IT!
Distributed by King Features Syndicate, Inc.

YES, SIR, IT'S SHORE A LUCKY BREAK FER THUH WIMMERNFOLKS ---HAVIN' A TOUGH BUCKAROO LIKE ME AROUND TO PERTECK 'EM!
5-16

HOLD ON THAR! IS THIS YERE COYOTE ANNOYIN' YUH, MA'AM?
?
WHAT? WHY, NO-- CERTAINLY NOT!

ALL RIGHT, THEN! I'M A-LETTIN' Y' OFF THIS TIME, STRANGER--- BUT DON'T LET IT HAPPEN AG'IN!
!

HOW ABOUT THE SHERIFF, MR. HAWKINS? --WHAT'S HE DONE ABOUT THE KIDNAPINGS?
WHAT'S HE DONE? HUMPH-- THAT STUBBORN COOT DON'T B'LEEVE THEY'RE REAL! THINKS I PLAN 'EM AS LOCAL COLOR FUR TH' DUDES!

THAT 'ERE "GOOFY" DUDE SHO' FIGGERS HE'S BAD MEDICINE!
YEH-- THINKS WE'RE SCARED OF HIS SHADDER!
AN' HE BETTER NOT---!
HE AIN'T MET "GRIZZLY GUS" YET!
5-17

---I AIN'T TAKIN' NONE O' THAT TOMFOOLERY FRUM NO DURN DUDE! I'LL BUST 'IM WIDE OPEN!

OH-OH! HERE HE COMES, NOW, BOYS!
'PEARS TO BE HUNTIN' TROUBLE, TOO!

HEY, MISTAH! IF YO' WANTA SAVE YO' FR'EN', DO SUMPIN' QUICK--HE'S SASSIN' "GRIZZLY GUS"!
WALT DISNEY

WELL, F'R---?? THEY TOLD ME Y' WERE SCRAPPIN' WITH OLD "GRIZZLY GUS", THE TOUGHEST GUY ON THE RANCH!
SCRAP, NUTHIN'! THUH YALLER HOUND COULDN'T TAKE IT! BACKED RIGHT DOWN WHEN I BEAT 'IM TO THUH DRAW!
5-18

WHEN YOU, WHAT??? Y' MEAN Y' GOT YOUR GUN OUT BEFORE HE DID?
'AT'S WHUT I SAID, DIDN' I?

THIS SURE BEATS ME! AN OLDTIMER LIKE "GRIZZLY GUS" BEIN' TOO SLOW IN---!
WELL---'T WASN'T SO MUCH HIS BEIN' SLOW! YUH SEE---
Distributed by King Features Syndicate, Inc.

---WELL, HE DIDN'T HAVE NO GUN--IF YUH GOTTER BE SO GOSH-DARNED TECHNICAL!
WALT DISNEY

Again the kidnap bandit strikes and another victim of Peg-Leg Pete's ransom racket is carried off! "Handlebar" and the boys are in hot pursuit---,

THOUGHT I'D FIND Y' HERE, SON! AND BY YOUR GLUM PAN I RECKON Y' AIN'T LOCATED THE BANDIT'S NEST!
NO, DOGGONE IT! BUT WHEREVER HE WENT IN, HE'S GOTTA COME OUT AGAIN!
5-23

LISTEN, SON--THAT BUZZARD WON'T SHOW HIMSELF 'TIL TH' COAST IS CLEAR! Y' MIGHT'S WELL COME ON BACK TO THE RANCH WITH ME!

LOOK, MR. HAWKINS! TONIGHT Y' LEAVE THE RANSOM MONEY FOR PETE TO PICK UP, DON'T Y'?
YEH, SURE---BUT HE AIN'T PICKIN' IT UP WHILE SOME HOMBRE'S WAITIN' WITH A FORTY-FOUR!

HE WON'T KNOW I'M HERE! I'LL LAY LOW AN' WHEN HE COMES OUT I'LL SU'PRISE HIM!
ALL RIGHT, Y' STUBBORN LITTLE MAVERICK---JEST MAKE SURE HE DON'T SU'PRISE YOU!

NOW, THEN, PETE, OLD BOY--TRY AND COME OUTA THAT WALL WITHOUT ME SEEIN' Y'!
5-24

BUT, AS THE HOURS FLIT BY, AND STILL NO PETE---!

GOSH-DARN THE GUY! I THOUGHT SURE HE'D COME OUT TO COLLECT THAT RANSOM AS USUAL!

?

GOOD GOSH! HE'S BEEN OUT--AND I NEVER EVEN SAW OR HEARD HIM! WHAT IS THIS?
WALT DISNEY

EXPECTING TO TAKE PETE UNAWARES WHEN HE LEAVES HIS HIDEOUT, MICKEY IS FLABBERGASTED TO SEE THE WILY OLD SCOUNDREL RIDE IN FROM THE OPPOSITE WAY!

HOW TH' HECK--? HAS THE GUY TURNED MAGICIAN, OR SOMEP'N---??
5-25

AHH-AH-H--
WELL, BY GOSH, HE WON'T VANISH THIS TIME WITHOUT---
HEY! SHH-H---QUIET---!!

AH-H-H---GLM-B-BAH-H-H---

--CHOOO-O-O!!
SO!

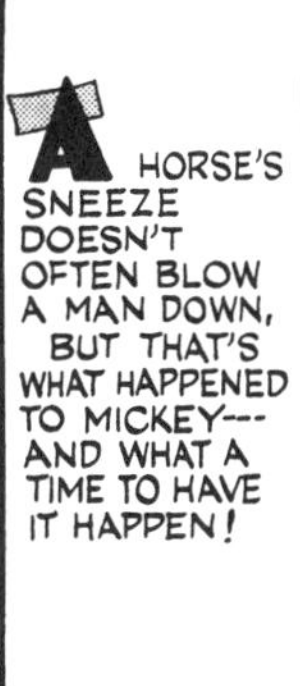
A HORSE'S SNEEZE DOESN'T OFTEN BLOW A MAN DOWN, BUT THAT'S WHAT HAPPENED TO MICKEY--- AND WHAT A TIME TO HAVE IT HAPPEN!
5-27

I'LL LEARN YUH TO SPY ON ME! WHY, YUH BLASTED LI'L SAWED-OFF RAT, I'LL BOIN YUH DOWN!

BANG! BANG! BANG! BANG!
SPAT!
SPAT!
SPAT!

WOT---CAN'T I PLUG THUH BLINKIN' RUNT?
BANG! BANG!

HE DON'T FIGHT FAIR! JEST 'CAUSE HE'S TOO SMALL TO GIT A CLEAN SHOT AT, HE TAKES ADVANTAGE OF ME!
WALT DISNEY

ROUTED BY PETE'S GUNFIRE JUST AS HE IS ABOUT TO LEARN THE VILLAIN'S SECRET MODE OF ESCAPE, MICKEY RETURNS TO THE RANCH AND REORGANIZES FOR A NEW ATTEMPT!

KNOWING THAT THE FOLLOWING NIGHT PETE WOULD RETURN THE RANSOMED LADY, MICKEY IS AGAIN ON HAND!
WELL, S'LONG, BABE! HOPE YUH ENJOYED MUH HORSPITALITY!
BOY--I'M JUST IN TIME! C'MON, TAPIOCA, WE'VE GOTTA BE MOVIN' FAST!
5-28

THIS SHORT CUT'S KINDA ROUGH, BUT WE HAFTA BEAT PETE TO THE END OF THE CANYON!

YOU PARK HERE, TAPIOCA, SO Y' CAN'T GIVE ME AWAY WITH ANY MORE SNEEZES!

AH! Y' DON'T KNOW IT, Y' OLD FOX, BUT THIS IS THE TIME YOUR FAMOUS DISAPPEARIN' ACT'S GONNA BE EXPOSED!

BOY! IF PETE CAN VANISH THROUGH THAT CLIFF, HE'S GOT SOMEP'N!
5-29
Copr. 1940, Walt Disney Productions World Rights Reserved

TWEET PHWEE TWEEDLE-EEE-E

AND DOES HE DO IT? MY GOSH, JUST AS EASY AS PIE!
Distributed by King Features Syndicate, Inc.

SOLID GRANITE---AND ALL HE DID WAS WHISTLE AT IT! HMM---I WONDER IF---??
WALT DISNEY

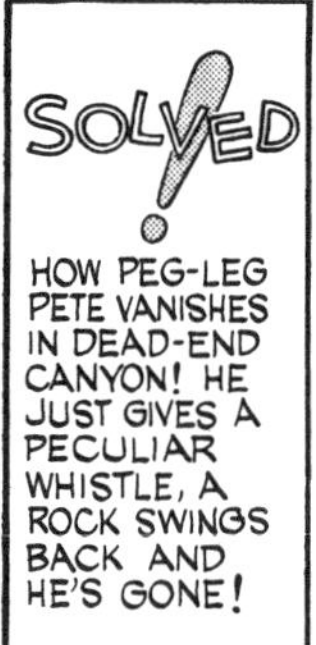

WHEN PETE OPENS A TRICK DOOR IN THE CLIFF BY MERELY A CERTAIN WHISTLE, MICKEY GUESSES THAT IT IS A RADIO-OPERATED DEVICE!

AFTER TRYING EVERY WHISTLE SOUND HE CAN THINK OF, MICKEY STILL DOESN'T HIT THE NOTE THAT WILL OPEN THE RADIO-CONTROLLED DOOR TO PETE'S MOUNTAIN DEN!

MICKEY IS AMAZED WHEN "HANDLEBAR" REVEALS THAT AIRPLANES CAN'T FLY OVER THE ROCKY CLIFFS THAT GUARD PETE'S STRONGHOLD!

I DON'T GET IT, MR. HAWKINS! Y' MEAN THEY'VE BEEN STOPPED TRYIN' TO GET OVER---?
EGGZACTLY, SON--- STOPPED COLDER'N A MOTHER-IN-LAW'S KISS!
G-3
Copr. 1940, Walt Disney Productions World Rights Reserved

BUT WHADDYA MEAN, STOPPED--- WHAT HAPPENED TO 'EM?
WAL, THEY ZOOMED OFF NORMAL ENOUGH, BUT SOON'S THEY HIT TH' AIR ABOVE DEAD-END CANYON--- BAM!

SORTA LIKE BUCKIN' INTO AN INVISIBLE WALL! SKEERED THE DAYLIGHTS OUTA THE PILOTS--- WON'T NONE OF 'EM TRY IT ANY MORE!

CAIN'T SAY AS I BLAME 'EM--- HEY, WHERE Y' BOUND IN SECH A LATHER?
TO THE AIRPORT--GONNA RENT A PLANE!
WALT DISNEY

HERE GOES FOR A LITTLE SIGHTSEEING OVER PETE'S HIDEAWAY! THEY CAN'T MAKE ME BELIEVE IT'S SURROUNDED BY ANY INVISIBLE WALL!
G-4

SHUCKS--WHOEVER HEARD OF SUCH TOMMYROT? WELL, HERE'S DEAD-END CANYON ALREADY---

---SO I'LL SOON EXPOSE THAT CRAZY---!!???
Distributed by King Features Syndicate, Inc.

WOW! WHAT THE HECK??
WHAM!

STOPPED COLD! MICKEY WOULDN'T BELIEVE IT BEFORE, BUT HIS PLANE RAMS INTO PETE'S "INVISIBLE WALL" JUST THE SAME!

GOOD GOSH! FULL SPEED ON--AND NOT MOVIN' AN INCH!
RRR-RRR RRR-R

ZWOOM!!
WOW!!
G-5

PHEW--THAT WAS AWFUL! FELT LIKE THE WHOLE SHIP WAS THROWN BACK BY SOME--- UH---IT'S UNCANNY!

DOGGONIT, I CAN'T QUIT, NOW--- I CAN STILL GET THROUGH FROM THE OTHER SIDE!

AT THE AIRPORT MICKEY LEARNS THAT **ALL** THE FLIERS HAVE MET WITH THE SAME STARTLING DEFEAT, TRYING TO CROSS THE UNSEEN BARRIER THAT GUARDS PETE'S HIDEOUT!

DISCOURAGED BY FUTILE ATTEMPTS AT CRASHING PETE'S LAIR, A VERY FORLORN MICKEY WENDS HIS WAY BACK TO THE RANCH!

GUEST RANCH
WHAT TH'--?
STOP WHAR Y' ARE, STRANGER!

OH-- IT'S MUH LI'L PARDNER! LUCKY I RECKANIZED YUH 'FORE I PULLED THUH TRIGGER!
MY GOSH! ARE YOU STILL BEIN' WILD AN' WOOLY?
6-10

IF Y' WANTA BE THE LONE RANGER, GO OUT AFTER PEG-LEG PETE! HE'S TOO MUCH FOR ME
B'GAWRSH, PARDNER, I'LL DO THET! I'LL SHORE GIT THET ORNERY VARMINT FER YUH!

Y' WILL? REMEMBER --- HE'S PRETTY TOUGH!
YEAH? WELL, SO'M I! AND
LISSEN, PARDNER---I BEEN LAYIN' PLANS --I GOT SOME IDEARS THET ACKCHERALLY SUPPRIZE MUHSELF!

SO YOU'RE GONNA CAPTURE PEG-LEG PETE, EH? HOW DO Y' FIGURE ON GETTIN' PAST THOSE BARRIERS HE'S GOT?
I DON'T FIGGER ON IT! THET'S WHUR I'M SMART--- GONTER MAKE HIM COME OUT!
6-11

YEH? HOW'LL Y' DO THAT?
SHH-H--- CAN'T TELL YUH HERE --- PETE MIGHT HAVE SPIES AROUN'! C'MON OVER BEHIND THUH BARN!

GOSH! MUST BE A MIGHTY SECRET PLAN Y' GOT!
CAN'T BE TOO KEERFUL! IF PETE KNOWED ABOUT IT, 'TWOULDN'T WORK!

I'M GONTER LURE 'IM OUT--- WITH MUSIC!
OWW!

THEN, YOU'RE REALLY SERIOUS? Y' EXPECT TO LURE PETE OUT OF HIDING WITH MUSIC?
DURN RIGHT! ALLA THEM WESTERN BAD MEN ARE SOFTIES FER SAD SONGS! AND KIN I SING 'EM SAD!
6-12

ADIOS, PARD! I'LL BE BRINGIN' THUH VARMINT IN, PRONTO!
WAHOO, "WARPAINT-" --- LE'S GO!
!

BOY, AM I SMART! NOBUDDY ELSE EVER TRIED STRAGEDY ON PETE!
I ALMOST FEEL SORRY FER 'IM!

OH, I'VE RID MUH FINAL H-E-R-D, BOYS--- NO MORE THUH RANGE I'LL R-O-A-M!
SO, SHED JEST A TEAR, FER THUH PAY-OFF IS THEY'RE CALLIN' THE OLD H-E-R-E--- COWHAND H-O-M-E!!
WALT DISNEY
Distributed by King Features Syndicate, Inc.

SO YER PAL WENT OUT TO KETCH TH' BANDIT WITH A GUITAR?
YEH, AND HE WAS SERIOUS! THINKS COWBOY SONGS WILL SOFTEN PETE UP--- OR SOMETHIN'!
6-13

--- SO THEY LAID 'IM OUT IN HIS WRANGLER'S CLO'ES, ALONG WITH HIS FORTY-FOUR! THUH PRAIRIE MOON SHONE DOWN ON HIM, BUT IT HE SAW NO MORE!

OH, IT HE SAW NO MORE---NO MORE--- 'CAUSE HE'D BEEN TOO SLOW WITH HIS FORTY-FOUR! HE'D BEEN TOO---
GIT AWAY, BOYS---YUH BOTHER ME!

AH--WOT A DAY! WARMS A FELLER'S SOUL TO GIT OUT AN' RAMBLE ACROST THUH SMILIN' FACE O' NATUR'!

GOSH--- THINK OF POOR GOOFY TRYIN' TO LURE PETE WITH COWBOY SONGS!
HE MIGHT HAVE SU'THIN' THERE AT THAT! A FEW O' THEM WARBLES OUGHTA SKEER A BANDIT OUTA TH' COUNTRY FUR GOOD!
6-14

THUH WOLVES, THEY HOWL--- BUZZARDS DRAW NIGH! GOOD-BYE, OLE HOSS---OLE PAL, GOOD-BYE! O LAY-EE--LEE O LAY-EE---OOO!

O YAY-OO-EE OOO-EEEEE!
WOZZAT---?? WHOA, VANILLA!

MUH TENDER HEART CAN'T STAND IT! SOME CRITTER'S A-DYIN' IN AGONY---I'LL HAFTER END IT'S SUFFERIN'!

THINKING TO LURE OLD PETE WITH DULCET HARMONY, GOOFY DOES NOT KNOW THAT HIS MOURNFUL REFRAIN HAS BEEN MISTAKEN FOR A DYING CALF!

WHY, IT'S A HOOMAN BEIN'!
---OH, NONE SO FAIR AS CACTUS NELL BEFORE HER HOSS UPON HER FELL!

ALAS, PORE NELL, I KNOWED HER WELL-L-L---!

---UH--KNOWED HER WELL---
Distributed by King Features Syndicate, Inc.

DON'T M-MOVE! STICK 'EM UP---I G-GOTCHUH COVERED!
6-15

I THINK I'LL SADDLE UP AND GO AFTER GOOFY! NO TELLIN' WHAT KINDA TROUBLE HE'LL ---!
SHUCKS, SON --- TAKE IT EASY! HE WOULDN'T TANGLE WITH PEG-LEG --- HE'D RUN LIKE A SKEERED RABBIT!
6-17

BUT OUT ON THE DESERT, OUR TOUGH BUCKAROO IS BOLDLY STANDING HIS GROUND!
S-SS-STICK 'EM UP, I TOLE YUH---!!

EEYOW!!
BANG!

YUH CLUMSY CLOWN--- IF IT'S FIGHTIN' YUH WANT, YUH GOT IT!
BANG!
BANG!
WALT DISNEY

GOSH, I HOPE I GET TO GOOFY IN TIME---I'LL BET MY HAT HE'S IN A JAM!
6-18

AND MICKEY DIDN'T GUESS WRONG!
TANGLE WIT' ME, WILL YUH?
YOW! HEY---!
SNIP!

BANG
?

PLOP!

HERE! NO NEED O' WASTIN' BULLETS--- YUH KIN HAVE MUH CLOTHES!
WALT DISNEY

DOGGONE! I NEVER SHOULD'VE LET GOOFY GO OFF ON HIS HARE-BRAINED SCHEME! GOSH KNOWS WHAT'S HAPPENED!

HAW! HAW! HAW!
STOP! HAVE A HEART, MR. PETE! YUH CAN'T DO THIS---!
BANG!
SNIP!
6-19

JEST STAND QUIET, SISTER, AN' POPPA'LL FIX Y' UP PURTY!
KNOCK! KNOCK!
Distributed by King Features Syndicate, Inc.

NOW, GIT! AN' THUH NEXT MONKEY 'AT FOOLS WIT' ME WON'T BE HANDLED SO GENTLE!
BANG
BANG
SPLAT
SPLAT
SPLAT
SPLAT
SPLAT
SPLAT
SPLAT
WALT DISNEY

Riding out to look for Goofy, Mickey suddenly catches sight of a strange creature wandering across the desert!

Out in the desert, Mickey hears Goofy's sad tale of humiliation by the fancy gunplay of Peg-Leg Pete!

DOGGONE! PETE'S GOT AWAY WITH HIS RACKET LONG ENOUGH! THERE'S SOME WAY TO NAB THE GUY, IF I ONLY USE MY HEAD!
Copr. 1940, Walt Disney Productions World Rights Reserved

NOBODY CAN GET INSIDE HIS HIDEOUT ---! OR--CAN THEY? SAY--- AN IDEA'S RATTLIN' AROUND!

?
LOOK, FOLKS--A RED-HOT SCHEME THAT CAN'T MISS! IT'S GOTTA BE KEPT SECRET, SO COME INSIDE AND I'LL GIVE Y' THE LOWDOWN!
?
6-24

CLARABELLE --- YOU'RE GONNA BE KIDNAPED!
GOOD GRACIOUS!
WHY, MICKEY!

EXPLAIN YERSELF, SON! WHAT'S THIS BRIGHT IDEA THAT BIT YOU?
AND WHAT ABOUT CLARABELLE GOING TO BE KIDNAPED?
SURE---THAT'S THE IDEA! WE JUST LET PETE GRAB HER AND TAKE HER TO HIS HANGOUT---!
Copr. 1940, Walt Disney Productions World Rights Reserved
6-25

---THEN SHE FAKES A SICK SPELL, SO SHE HAS TO STAY A FEW DAYS! SECRETLY, SHE LEARNS THE LAYOUT ---THEN ONE DARK NIGHT---

---SHE OPENS THE TRICK DOOR AND---IN WE GO WITH A POSSE! NEAT, DON'TCHA THINK?
PERFECT, EXCEPT FOR ONE THING---
Distributed by King Features Syndicate, Inc.

---CLARABELLE IS NOT GOING TO DO IT!

MICKEY HAS HATCHED UP A HUMDINGER! HE WANTS CLARABELLE PURPOSELY KIDNAPED, SO SHE CAN OPEN PETE'S SECRET DOOR FROM THE INSIDE! BUT SHE WILL HAVE NONE OF IT!
6-26

YOU'RE RIGHT, CLARABELLE! DON'T YOU DO IT!
I SHOULD SAY NOT! RISK MY LIFE FOR SUCH A--A---!
BUT PETE'S NEVER HARMED TH' LADIES NONE, MISS!
AND THINK OF THE GLORY, CLARABELLE! YOU MAY WIN----
Copr. 1940, Walt Disney Productions World Rights Reserved

---AFTER ALL THE OTHERS HAVE LOST! YOU MAY MAKE HISTORY! AFTER ARMED ASSAULTS HAVE FAILED---THE FORTRESS FALLS THROUGH THE WILES OF A BEE-OOTIFUL SIREN!

THINK OF SAMSON AND DELILAH--- THINK OF CLEOPATRA ---AND HELEN OF TROY! WHAT'D THEY HAVE THAT YOU HAVEN'T GOT? THINK OF --UH-- -THINK OF PEG-LEG PETE---!
WELL-L- -UH---!

ATTA GAL! I KNEW YOU'D COME THROUGH FOR US!
WELL, I WILL--- BUT I'LL ALMOST BET YOU'VE- ---
--BEEN FLATTERING ME, YOU LITTLE IMP!

EXPECTING OLD PETE TO PULL ANOTHER KIDNAP RAID AT ANY TIME, MICKEY HAS CLARABELLE DOLL UP THAT NIGHT FOR HER SIREN ROLE!

MICKEY'S PLOT TO GET CLARABELLE INSIDE PETE'S LAIR IS OFF TO A FLYING START! THE FISH HAS SPIED THE BAIT!

6-28

PETE HAS KIDNAPED CLARABELLE, UNAWARE THAT HE IS FALLING FOR A LITTLE SCHEME OF MICKEY'S TO GET HER INSIDE THE STRONGHOLD AND PRY OUT ITS MYSTERIOUS SECRETS!

7-1

BLINDFOLDING CLARABELLE, PETE GIVES HIS MAGICAL WHISTLE, THE MYSTERIOUS ROCK DOOR OPENS AND IN THEY GO!

YOU SAY YOU'RE ALLOWING CLARABELLE THREE DAYS--- SUPPOSE PETE WON'T KEEP HER THAT LONG?
DON'T Y' REMEMBER? SHE'S GONNA PULL A PHONY SICK SPELL AND CLAIM SHE CAN'T BE MOVED!
Copr. 1940, Walt Disney Productions World Rights Reserved
7-4

COME WIT' ME, BABE --I'LL ESCORCH YUH TO YER ROOM!
LAN' SAKES! ANYBODY'D THINK I WAS A GUEST- ---TEE-HEE!

NEVER LET IT BE SAID I DON'T RUN MUH BIZZNESS STYLISH AN' GENTEEL-LIKE!
YES, IT'S LOVELY! ER--AH--- I FEEL QUEER---!

I---OH, I'M ILL! YES-- YES, I'M SURE I'M ILL!
WOT? HEY! NO, YUH CAN'T--- NOT HERE!

ACCORDING TO MICKEY'S PLAN, CLARABELLE GOES INTO HER BIG SICK ACT!

HERE! YUH CAN'T GET SICK IN MY PLACE!
OHH-H--- I'M TOOK! IT'S ONE OF MY SPELLS! OH-H-H-!
Copr. 1940, Walt Disney Productions World Rights Reserved
7-5

NO WOMAN'S DYIN' ON ME! C'MON---I'LL TAKE YUH BACK!
NO! GOOD GRACIOUS, NO! IT'S MY--MY FLOATING ARTERIES--- I CAN'T BE MOVED!

I MUST HAVE REST FOR AT LEAST THREE DAYS! I MUST NOT TRAVEL--- OH, DEAR, NO!

SOME 24 HOURS LATER MICKEY AND HANDLEBAR ARE AT THE SPOT WHERE PETE USUALLY LEAVES THE RANSOM DEMANDS!
AH, JUST AS WE HOPED--NO NOTE THIS TIME! SHE'S STALLIN' HIM, ALL RIGHT!
HOT DOG! THAT MEANS SHE'S STAYIN' ON, JUST LIKE WE PLANNED! GOOD OLD CLARABELLE!
Distributed by King Features Syndicate, Inc.
WALT DISNEY

SO FAR, CLARABELLE IS A SUCCESS! CARRYING OUT MICKEY'S PLAN, SHE FOOLS PETE WITH A FAKE ILLNESS AND IS ALLOWED TO STAY UNTIL SHE "RECOVERS"!

JUST BECAUSE THERE'S NO RANSOM NOTE FROM CLARABELLE--- DOES THAT PROVE YOUR SCHEME IS WORKING?
SURE! THAT MEANS SHE'S STAYIN' AT PETE'S LONG ENOUGH TO GET THE SECRET OF THAT DOOR!
Copr. 1940, Walt Disney Productions World Rights Reserved
7-6

SO, TOMORROW AT MIDNIGHT SHE OPENS IT UP FOR US, AND IN WE GO WITH A POSSE TO GET PETE AND HIS WHOLE GANG!

MEANWHILE, PETE WISHES THE "SICK WOMAN" WERE OFF HIS HANDS!
HI, BABE---HOWZA GAL? HERE---I BRUNG YUH A BOWKETT!
ME? OH, HOW FOR GUDGEOUS!

LAN' SAKES! IMAGINE A PERSON OF YOUR CALLING BEING SUCH A POLISHED GENTLEMAN! TEE-HEE--- JUST LIKE A MOVIE!
AW, IT'S NUTHIN'--- FERGIT IT!
WHAT'S THIS? IS CLARABELLE HELPING MICKEY OR IS SHE REALLY FALLING FOR PETE? ~~~

THE MIDNIGHT HOUR APPROACHES AND, ACCORDING TO MICKEY'S PLAN, CLARABELLE WILL HAVE PETE'S SECRET DOOR OPEN AT THAT TIME!
7-8

WAL, I HOPE YER RIGHT, SON! I'VE RUN DOWN MANY A BANDIT, BUT THIS IS TH' FUST TIME I EVER DEPENDED ON A FEMALE TO CLEAR TH' WAY!

SO SHE SAID TWELVE O'CLOCK, HUH? IT'S AFTER TWO, AN' THAT CLIFF'S AS SOLID AS TH' WALLS O' JERICHO!
GOSH---UH-- SOMEP'N MUSTA GONE WRONG!

C'MON HOME, BOYS! NO USE SETTIN' HERE ALL NIGHT!

SO! THAT'S YOUR MARVELOUS SCHEME! THREE WHOLE DAYS AND WE DON'T KNOW WHAT'S HAPPENED TO HER!
PLEASE, MINNIE--- I---I'VE GOTTA THINK!
Distributed by King Features Syndicate, Inc
WALT DISNEY

COMES ANOTHER MIDNIGHT... AND STILL ANOTHER! BUT NO RANSOM NOTE. NO WORD FROM CLARABELLE... AND PETE'S ROCKY RETREAT STILL SHUT TIGHT AS EVER!
7-9

I JUST CAN'T FIGURE IT! LOOKS LIKE I'LL HAFTA FIND AN ENTIRELY NEW SCHEME!
YOU AND YOUR SCHEMES! THAT'S WHAT GOT POOR CLARABELLE IN THE FIX SHE'S IN!

I KNOW I'M TO BLAME! AND I'VE JUST GOTTA RESCUE HER.. SOME WAY... SOMEHOW...!

BUT IN SPITE OF ALL THE FRANTIC WORRY ABOUT HER, IT DOESN'T LOOK AS IF SHE WANTS TO BE RESCUED!
MICKEY'LL NEVER FORGIVE ME IF THEY DON'T CAPTURE PETE, BUT... AFTER ALL, WHEN A GIRL MEETS THE MAN...!

HI, BABE... YER LOOKIN' GREAT! TIME WE WERE SENDIN' YUH HOME, EH?
AND LEAVE YOU...?! I MEAN... I'M TOO WEAK TO TRAVEL... JUST UP FROM A SICK BED, AND... OH, DEAR...!
WALT DISNEY

SO YUH'RE STILL TOO SICK TO BE MOVED, EH?
YES, INDEED... I COULDN'T STAND THE STRAIN! STILL SO WEAK, YOU KNOW... I COULDN'T POSSIBLY...!
7-10

PLEASE LET ME STAY ITTY BITTY WHILE LONGER! I'LL GET WELL SO QUICK UNDER YOUR CARE.. ..GREAT BIG MANS!
UH... WELL... IF IT'S LIKE THAT...!

...BUT YUH BETTER NOT BE KIDDIN' ME, OR IT'LL BE TOO BAD, SEE?
MISTER PETE ...HOW COULD YOU?

AFTER LONG HOURS OF HEAVY THINKING, MICKEY SEEMS TO HAVE STRUCK PAYDIRT!
I'VE GOT IT, MINNIE! YIPPEE! I'VE GOT IT!
FOR GOODNESS...!

MICKEY! FOR GOODNESS SAKES...!
I'VE GOT IT! A SCHEME TO RESCUE CLARABELLE, AND NAB PETE, TOO!
7-11

TELL Y' 'BOUT IT LATER, MINNIE! GOTTA FIND GOOFY...!

IT'S YOU.. OR ME, PETE! I'M GIVIN' YUH ONE MORE CHANST... DRAW YER WEEPON!
NEVER MIND THE REHEARSAL! I'VE GOT A JOB FOR Y', PAL... BEND AN EAR!

TONIGHT WE TAKE A MYSTERIOUS... AND SECRET PLANE TRIP! YOU HAVE BEEN SELECTED AS PILOT!
HUH? SEZ WHICH? HEV YOU GONE CUCKOO??

COME, LET'S BE MOVIN', PAL... WE'VE GOT A BUSY NIGHT AHEAD!
WHADDYA MEAN, WE? QUIT SHOVIN'... I AIN'T GOIN' NO PLACE, 'SPESHULLY, I AIN'T FLYIN' NO PLANES!
7-12

WHAT'S ALL TH' RUCKUS, SON? MINNIE SAYS Y' GOT SOME NEW IDEE!
C'MON IN AND I'LL GIVE Y' THE DOPE, WHILE WE GET SOME EQUIPMENT!
EQUIPMENT? I TOLE YUH WE AIN'T GOIN' NOWHERES! WHUT'S YER HURRY?

THAT'S RIGHT... A TWO-SEATER, IF YOU'VE GOT IT!
YES, SIR! FIX YOU RIGHT UP!
NO USE, MICKEY ... I AIN'T LEAVIN' THUH RANCH TONIGHT!

KEEP HER NOSE UP AND HEAD DUE NORTH!
NO SENSE TELLIN' ME... I AIN'T FLYIN' NO.. HUH?? GAWRSH! I AM FLYIN'! WHUT'S BEEN GOIN' ON HERE?

MICKEY'S LATEST BRAINSTORM IS UNDER WAY! WITH GOOFY HIGH-PRESSURED INTO PILOTING THE PLANE, THEY HEAD FOR PETE'S IMPREGNABLE STRONGHOLD!

DAWGUNNIT... WHUT'S THUH SENSE? YUH KNOW WE CAN'T FLY THROUGH THAT INVISIBLE WALL!
NEVER MIND! JUST HOLD HER STEADY AND HEAD FOR IT, ANYWAY!
7-13
Copr. 1940, Walt Disney Productions World Rights Reserved

HOW DO I TELL WHEN WE'RE THERE?
DON'T WORRY.. ..YOU'LL KNOW! NOW, GUN IT A LITTLE MORE!

YOWW!! THAT'S IT!
WHAM!

HOT DOG... SUCCESS! I'M IN AT LAST!
Distributed by King Features Syndicate, Inc.

WITH GOOFY AT THE CONTROLS, MICKEY HAS HIM DRIVE A PLANE AT FULL SPEED INTO PETE'S "INVISIBLE WALL"!
7-15

THE FORCE OF THE SUDDEN STOP CATAPULTS MICKEY THROUGH THE MYSTERIOUS "BARRIER"... WHICH IS JUST AS HE PLANNED IT!
BOY... DID I GUESS RIGHT THIS TIME! THAT WALL IS SOME KINDA MAGNETIC WAVE THAT A METAL PLANE CAN'T CROSS...!
Copr. 1940, Walt Disney Productions World Rights Reserved

...BUT I WENT THROUGH AS EASY AS...
OUCH!

NOW, TO HIDE THIS 'CHUTE AND THEN SEE WHAT KINDA LAYOUT PETE'S GOT DOWN HERE!

WHEW! A SWELL HOUSE, AN AIR-FIELD... AND LOOK AT THAT POWER OUTFIT! WHY, THE GUY'S GOT A WHOLE DARNED ELECTRICAL PLANT IN HIS VALLEY!
Distributed by King Features Syndicate, Inc.

NOW IF I CAN LOCATE CLARABELLE AND FIND OUT WHAT WENT WRONG! MAYBE THAT'S HER WINDOW!
Copr. 1940, Walt Disney Productions World Rights Reserved

OH-OH... SO THAT'S IT! NO WONDER THE TRICK DIDN'T WORK!
7-16

LOOK, BABE... I GOTTER GO! ER.. THINGS TO 'TEND TO.. AND ALL...!
NOW, IS THAT NICE? BIG, BAD MANS LEAVE POOR 'ITTLE DIRL ALL LONESOME-WONESOME!

WOW.. IS SHE SAPPY! GONE GA-GA FOR THE OLD RASCAL! WELL, IT'S A CINCH I'LL GET NO HELP FROM HER, NOW!

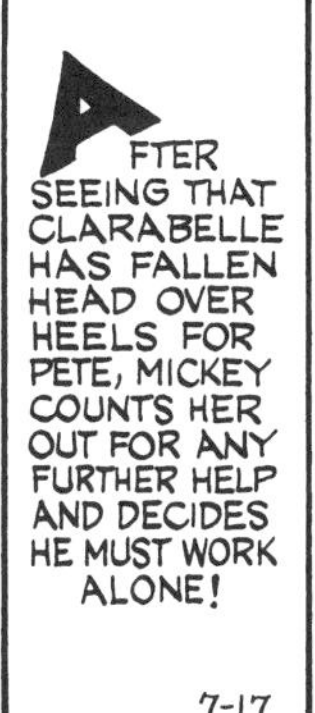
AFTER SEEING THAT CLARABELLE HAS FALLEN HEAD OVER HEELS FOR PETE, MICKEY COUNTS HER OUT FOR ANY FURTHER HELP AND DECIDES HE MUST WORK ALONE!
7-17

HMM... THAT POWER-HOUSE CONTROLS ALL PETE'S TRICK GADGETS! IF I COULD GET INSIDE...!
Copr. 1940, Walt Disney Productions World Rights Reserved

MIGHTY DANGEROUS, THOUGH! GET TRAPPED IN THERE AND IT'S... OH-OH! WOOPS!

HECK! I'M UP TO MY NECK ALREADY... HERE GOES FOR SHOOTIN' THE WORKS!

WALT DISNEY

IN A BOLD GAMBLE TO GET IN PETE'S ELECTRIC CONTROL-ROOM, MICKEY TAILS HIM, TRYING TO STICK CLOSE ENOUGH TO BE UNOBSERVED!

HOPE I GET AWAY WITH THIS... LIKE THEY DO IN THE MOVIES!
7-18

AHA! HERE'S THE BRAINS IN BACK OF THESE INVENTIONS! I KNEW IT COULDN'T BE PETE!
HULLO, PERFESSOR! HOW'S ALL THUH DINGUSES?
THEY ISS ALL WORKINK, PETER! NO TROUBLES!

WELL, I GOT TROUBLES! THAT DOPEY DAME IS DRIVIN' ME DIPPY!
AH... THE ROMANTIC ONE, HEY?

I TELL YUH, SHE'S IN MUH HAIR ALLA TIME! I EVEN THOUGHT I HEARD HER FOLLERIN' ME IN HERE, RIGHT ON MUH HEELS!
WALT DISNEY

YEH, THAT PESKY FEMALE'S FOLLERED ME 'ROUND TILL I'M GROGGY! KEEP FEELIN' SOMEBODY'S BEHIND ME!
HA! HA! THAT ISS FUNNY! AS IF ANYONE WOULD DARE TO ENTER HERE!
7-19

YUH SED A MOUTHFUL THAT TIME, DOC! IF I FOUND A SNOOPER IN THIS PLACE...

...MAN OR WOMAN, I'D FRIZZLE THEIR GIZZARD FER 'EM!

HEY, I HEAR SPARKS CRACKLIN'... SOMETHIN' AROUND HERE MUST BE GITTIN' HOT!
WALT DISNEY

HEAR THEM SPARKS CRACKLIN'? WHAT'S WRONG?
NOTHINK WRONG THAT I CAN SEE!
7-20

YEE-OWTCH!!

LIGHTS! TURN ON THUH BLINKIN' LIGHTS... SOMEBODY'S IN HERE!

SEE WHAT HAPPINGED, PETER? YOU BACKED INTO THIS, CUTTINK OFF LIGHTS AND GETTINK A SHOCK!
YEAH? WELL, I'D 'A SWORN I WUZ STABBED!
WALT DISNEY

DOUSING THE LIGHTS IN THE CONTROL-ROOM, MICKEY DOES A QUICK DIVE OUT OF SIGHT, HOPING THAT THE BLACKOUT WILL APPEAR ACCIDENTAL! PETE, HOWEVER, IS SUSPICIOUS!

7-22

I CAN FIX EF'RYTHINK, PETER! I WILL MAK' ADJUSTMENTS HERE IN THE THERMIC INFREQUENCY CABINET!
YUH MEAN YUH KIN DO IT ALL FROM IN THERE?
7-25

OM'GOSH! AND ME TRAPPED IN HERE!
MUST BE QUITE A DINGUS, PERFESSOR ... OPEN 'ER UP!

AW, THUH BLAZES WITH IT! NUTHIN' IN THERE THAT'D MAKE SENSE TO ME! I'M GONNER HIT THUH HAY!

G'NIGHT, DOC!
GOOT NIGHT, PETER!
GOOD NIGHT!
WALT DISNEY

AH, YES... THE TROUBLE ISS ALL IN HERE!
7-26

HMM... TOO MUCH GAPOSIS IN THE THYMOID...!
WELL, I'LL BE DARNED! HE DIDN'T SEE ME YET!

...EASILY REMEDIED WITH JUS' ONE TURN OF...

...A SCREW-DRIVER! AH... THANK YOU!

NOW A SLIGHT ADJUSTMENT OF THE FREE-WHEELING NIMBUS... AH, THANK YOU!
WHAT A SPOT I'M IN! IF THIS ABSENT-MINDED ZANY EVER WISES UP AND LOOKS MY WAY...!!?
7-27

THAT ISS BETTER ...THE ESCALATOR OSCILLATES VERY GOOT...HMM...!
NOW'S MY CHANCE TO TRY A SNEAKER-OUTER!

CONGRATULATIONS, MICKEY, OLD BOY... YOU'RE MAKIN' IT!

HEY, COM' BACK HERE... I'M NOT FINISH WITH YOU!
WALT DISNEY

WITH PETE AND HIS SCIENTIFIC PAL BOTH SAFELY IN BED, MICKEY IS LEFT IN FULL FREEDOM OF THE BIG POWER PLANT THAT GUARDS THE STRONGHOLD!

FAR INTO THE NIGHT MICKEY PLEADS FOR CLARABELLE'S HELP... BUT NO SOAP! THE GAL THINKS PETE IS "HER MAN" AND SHE'S NOT GOING TO LOSE HIM!

BUT, I TELL Y', IT'S YOUR DUTY... HE'S A CRIMINAL! JUST TELL HIM TO TAKE Y' BACK FOR THE RANSOM MONEY AND...!
I WILL NOT BE A TOOL TO YOUR NEFARIOUS PLOT! AND, BESIDES...
8-1

...HE WOULDN'T LET ME GO FOR MERE MONEY! OUR ATTACHMENT HAS BECOME TOO DEEP!
LOOK, THEN... WILL Y' MAKE THIS TEST? ASK HIM... AND IF HE REFUSES TO LET Y' GO, I'LL GIVE UP! HONEST!

VERY WELL, MR. SMARTY! HIDE IN THE CLOSET AND I'LL GET HIM HERE RIGHT NOW...I'LL PROVE HOW MUCH I MEAN TO HIM!
OKAY... YOU'RE ON!

ALL RIGHT... I'LL BE THERE IN A MINUTE!
WOT THUH BLAZES DOES THAT DUMB DAME WANT AT THIS HOUR??
Distributed by King Features Syndicate, Inc.

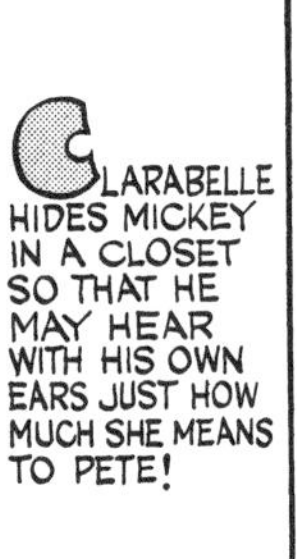
CLARABELLE HIDES MICKEY IN A CLOSET SO THAT HE MAY HEAR WITH HIS OWN EARS JUST HOW MUCH SHE MEANS TO PETE!

YUH WANTED TO SEE ME ABOUT SOMEP'M?
JUST TO TELL YOU THAT I'M NOT SICK ANY MORE! I CAN GO HOME ANY DAY YOU WANT ME TO!
!
8-2

OF COURSE, IF YOU WON'T LET ME GO, PETEY, DE-E-AR... TEE-HEE... IF YOU DON'T WISH TO RANSOM ME, WHY...!

FER YOU, BABE, MONEY MEANS NOTHIN'!
OH-H, PETEY!
SURE, I WON'T RANSOM YUH...
?
?

...I WON'T WAIT THAT LONG! I'M TAKIN' YUH BACK RIGHT NOW... TONIGHT ...'FORE YUH CHANGE YER MIND!
HA-HA-HA!
WALT DISNEY

I'LL GIT SADDLED AN' WE'LL BE ON OUR WAY IN FIVE MINUTES! TO BLAZES WITH ANY RANSOM DOUGH!
WHY...WHY, YOU...!!
8-3

OF ALL THE... DID YOU HEAR THE INSULTS FROM THAT... THAT?? ...OH! HE SCORNED ...ACTUALLY SCORNED ME!
TAKE IT EASY, GAL! YOU'RE IN JUST THE SPOT TO GET VERY EVEN WITH MR. PETE!

AND I WILL, TOO! I'LL DO ANYTHING YOU SAY! I'LL...!
OMIGOSH! YOU'VE GOTTA TAKE A NOTE TO HANDLEBAR AN' I DIDN'T WRITE IT YET! THERE'S ONLY FIVE MINUTES!

GIMME A PENCIL... PAPER, QUICK! ANYTHING! DON'T TELL ME THERE'S NOTHING TO WRITE WITH HERE! THERE HAS TO BE OR THE PLAN WON'T WORK!
WALT DISNEY

EVERYTHING DEPENDS ON CLARABELLE CARRYING A NOTE OF INSTRUCTIONS TO HANDLEBAR, BUT MICKEY CAN'T FIND ANYTHING TO WRITE WITH!

PETE IS THROWN INTO CONSTERNATION WHEN THE INVISIBLE WALL THAT PROTECTS HIS DOMAIN SUDDENLY QUITS WORKING!

LANDING BY PLANE, AFTER MICKEY PUTS THE FAMOUS INVISIBLE WALL OUT OF BUSINESS, THE LAW HAS ROUNDED UP THE ENTIRE KIDNAP GANG ... **EXCEPT** OLD PETE, HIMSELF!

AT PETE'S WHISTLE, THE SOUND-WAVE CONTROLLED GATE TO HIS EMERGENCY EXIT OPENS! BUT BEFORE HE CAN ESCAPE, IT SUDDENLY FALLS SHUT AGAIN!

I JUST REMEMBERED I'VE GOT NO GUN! YOU WOULDN'T PLUG AN UNARMED MAN, WOULD Y', ROLLO?
NO! NOT SOME PEOPLE, I WOULDN'T! I'D BREAK 'EM UP IN LITTLE PIECES, JES' FER THUH FUN OF IT!
Copr. 1940, Walt Disney Productions World Rights Reserved

BAM
GRR..!
OOOF
POW!
UGH!
ARR-R-R!
8-15

SO! TANGLE WIT' ME, WILL YUH?
I'LL LEARN YUH!
Distributed by King Features Syndicate, Inc.

YOWW!!
BANG!
DROP IT, PETE... TH' JIG'S UP!
WALT DISNEY

NICE GOIN', MICKEY! HOW'D Y' FIGGER OUT THAT HE HAD ANOTHER GATE IN THE CLIFF?
A LONG TIME AGO, WHEN I WAS WATCHIN' HIS REGULAR ENTRANCE...
8-16

........I FOUND HE'D GOTTEN OUT WITHOUT ME SEEIN' HIM! LATER, IN THE CONTROL-ROOM I FOUND WHERE THE SECOND GATE WAS LOCATED!

BY THE WAY, DID Y' NAB THE ABSENT-MINDED PROFESSOR?
OH, SURE..HE WAS EASY! HIM AND TH' REST O' THE GANG WENT BACK IN THE EXTRY PLANE WE BROUGHT!

WAL, SON, I SHORE THANK Y' FOR RUNNIN' DOWN THAT BIRD!
MAYBE Y' WON'T! I'M AFRAID THE RANCH HAS LOST IT'S CHIEF ATTRACTION FOR THE WOMENFOLKS!
WALT DISNEY
Distributed by King Features Syndicate, Inc.

PEACE REIGNS ON THE "BAR-NONE" DUDE RANCH ONCE MORE! WITH PEG-LEG PETE IN JAIL, THE ENTIRE AFFAIR FALLS INTO THE DIM, FORGOTTEN PAST!
OH, YEAH?

MR. HAWKINS, ARE WE GIRLS REAHLLY SAFE, NOW?
YES, MA'AM... I'M AFRAID SO!
8-17

"...DEAR DIARY, IT MIGHT HAVE BEEN SO DIFFERENT! I...YES, IT WAS I WHO BETRAYED HIM... BUT HAD HE NOT SCORNED ME...AH! MY HEART FLUTTERS EVEN NOW...!"

"...BUT I FACED 'IM WITH A COLD STARE! 'IT'S YOU OR ME, PETE,' I SEZ BETWEEN CLENCHED TEETH, 'DRAW YER SHOOTIN'-AR'N...!'"

DOESN'T THIS VACATION KINDA BORE Y', MINNIE? THERE'S PRACTIC'LY NOTHING TO DO AROUND HERE!
OH, MICKEY! WILL YOU EVER REST...OR ARE YOU HOPELESS?
WALT DISNEY

AUGUST 19, 1940

–

DECEMBER 21, 1940

BOO WHO?

If the punny title above sounds suitable for a weak *Casper the Friendly Ghost* cartoon short, it should. After an exceptional run of tightly plotted, highly logical *Mickey Mouse* serials, Floyd Gottfredson in 1940 seems to have gotten a bit too comfortable with himself... and with several enduring *Mickey* comic strip clichés. Indulging in a few formulas once too often—less like a Disney man, more like a repetitive Famous Studios spook—Gottfredson churned out two plotlines that didn't quite make sense.

"An Education for Thursday," as seen in our preceding volume, brought back the old theme of Mickey adopting a troublesome charge. Thursday was a young jungle-island aborigine, the brother of "Friday who [Mickey] used to know"; except that Friday, in an earlier serial, had explicitly been an American actor merely *playing* a jungle native. How could his twin be the real thing? Gottfredson never explained it!

If "Thursday" was a flawed comedy, "Bellhop Detective" is a flawed—if fun and lively—mystery. Jump in and see how many Gottfredson tropes we recognize: Minnie insists Mickey find a new job (check), which leads him to a colorful crime (check) with a blustery crime victim (check), eccentric suspects (check), a treasure to be found (check), and ghosts to guard it (checkmate): big, noisy, cartoon-style Lonesome Ghosts, materializing in midair and chasing victims down hallways. Are these ghosts real ghosts? If not—how are they made?

Thus the problem with this endearing, spooky mystery: Gottfredson cannot convincingly explain the ghosts. Alibis become too confusing; clues change in nature. In the end, the case is closed, but only because a basic feature of the ghosts has been noticeably modified along the way.

Did the dysfunction of "Bellhop" raise eyebrows inside Disney? No memos have survived to tell us. But no later Gottfredson serials were quite as goofed up, suggesting that the *Mickey Mouse* strip team got a handle on things.

Upon reading "Bellhop Detective" now, you might find yourself grabbing for a handle, too. For the ghosts *would* seem to have one realistic explanation: one that the plot seems to hint at, then pass over. Alas, that explanation requires technology that—in 1940—was still years in the future.

Enjoy the story; *don't* think *hologram*; and don't let three Lonesome Ghosts scare you.

(Any more than they'd scare Jerry Colonna, that is. It was on Bob Hope's late-1930s radio show that the Italian-American comedian, looking for an absent Yehudi Menuhin, first bellowed "Who's Yehudi?" The question turned into a running gag, then a hit song; the name "Yehudi" became popular slang for an invisible man—and as "Heyudi," it blessed all three of Gottfredson's spooks.) [DG]

BACK IN THE OLD HOME TOWN, MICKEY'S RESTLESSNESS STARTS GNAWING ON HIM AGAIN, BUT WITH STRONG DISAPPROVAL FROM THE GIRL FRIEND!
8-19

FOR GRACIOUS SAKES... RELAX! AND STOP THAT INCESSANT MOONING!
MOONING! SAY... A TRIP TO THE MOON... IF ONLY Y' COULD...!

OH, MY GOODNESS! NOW, THE WHOLE WORLD ISN'T BIG ENOUGH FOR YOU! WHEN WILL YOU EVER SETTLE DOWN AND BEHAVE YOURSELF?

YOU CAN'T GO ADVENTURING ALL YOUR LIFE! IT'S HIGH TIME YOU DID SOME USEFUL WORK... GOT YOURSELF A JOB!
YES, MA'AM! WHAT KINDA JOB?

ANY KIND! SAY! I JUST READ WHERE THE EAGLE THEATRE IS HOLDING A CONTEST.. WITH JOBS TO PRIZE WINNERS! YOU'RE GOING TO ENTER!
UH.. I AM?
WALT DISNEY

YES, YOU'RE GOING TO THE EAGLE THEATRE TONIGHT AND ENTER THAT CONTEST THEY'RE HOLDING! JUST THINK...!
8-20
Copr. 1940, Walt Disney Productions World Rights Reserved

...FOR PRIZES THEY'RE GIVING AWAY GOOD JOBS, AND YOU'RE CERTAIN TO WIN ONE!

ISN'T IT WONDERFUL? NOW YOU CAN REALLY MAKE SOMETHING OF YOURSELF!
SO! ALREADY I'M A WINNER, EH?

ALL RIGHT, FAIR LADY... JUST TO MAKE Y' HAPPY, I'LL REALLY TRY A CRACK AT YOUR OLD CONTEST!

SO, COME TO THE EAGLE THEATRE AND SEE MY STAGE DE-BOOT! TA-TA-TA!
WALT DISNEY

AT MINNIE'S URGING MICKEY FINDS HIMSELF ENTERED IN THE EAGLE THEATRE CONTEST, COMPETING FOR AN UNKNOWN JOB WHICH IS ONE OF THE PRIZES!

OF COURSE, I KNOW THERE'S SOME CATCH TO THIS, BUT MINNIE'D NEVER BE HAPPY IF I DIDN'T TAKE A WHIRL AT IT!
SORRY, MISTER ...YOU GET THE GONG!
BONG!
SHUX!
8-21

NEXT! MR. MICKEY MOUSE!
YES, SIR ...HERE!

WELCOME TO OUR LITTLE CONTEST, MR. MOUSE! MAY I ASK YOUR OCCUPATION?
I DON'T KNOW, YET...

...I'M JUST TRYIN' TO WIN ONE!
HAW! HAW! HA HA HA HA! HA!

ARE YOU PREPARED TO ANSWER THE FIRST QUESTION, MR. MOUSE?
YOU MAY FIRE WHEN READY, SIR!
8-22

IS AN EMU A BIRD, FISH OR A MUSICAL INSTRUMENT?

IT'S A BIRD... SORTA LIKE AN OSTRICH!
QUITE CORRECT! AND WHERE IS IT FOUND?

!
IN CROSS-WORD PUZZLES!
HA! HA!
HAHAHA!
CLAP!
CLAP!
CLAP!
CLAP!
CLAP!
WALT DISNEY

NOW, MR. MOUSE, FOR YOUR NEXT QUESTION! "IN HOW MANY DIFFERENT WAYS...
8-23

..IS WATER USED ON A FARM?"
SEVEN!

WASHING... IRRIGATING...!
THAT'S TWO! CAN YOU NAME FIVE MORE?

...WATERING HORSES, COWS, DOGS, SHEEP AND PIGS!
WALT DISNEY

THE EAGLE THEATRE CONTEST CARRIES ON, AND MICKEY IS STILL IN THE RUNNING!

FOR YOUR FINAL QUESTION, MR. MOUSE, YOU WILL BE BLINDFOLDED! YOU WILL THEN HEAR CERTAIN SOUNDS...
8-24

...AND MUST BE ABLE TO TELL US WHAT IS PRODUCING THESE SOUNDS!

KLANG!
KLINKLETY
PLUNK
KLUNK
PLANG!

SWISS BELL-RINGERS!

THE FINAL RIDDLE ON THE EAGLE THEATRE CONTEST IS A SOUND-EFFECTS TEST WHICH MICKEY HAS TO TAKE BLINDFOLDED!

AWARDED A BELLBOY'S JOB IN A RESORT HOTEL, MICKEY HIES HIMSELF OUT TO THE PLACE WITH DUBIOUS ENTHUSIASM!

CHRISTENING HIS CAREER AS BELLHOP IN THE LIBERTY-BELLE HOTEL, MICKEY ANSWERS HIS FIRST CALL FOR ICE WATER!

EZRA BEEBLE OWNER AND MANAGER.
OF ALL PEOPLE TO SPILL ICE WATER ON, I PICK THE BOSS! HOPE I CAN SQUARE MYSELF!
KNOCK!
KNOCK!
8-29

GOOD MORNING! HMMM... HAVEN'T I MET YOU SOME PLACE BEFORE?
WHY, YES, SIR! A FEW MINUTES AGO... I'M THE BOY WHO RAN INTO YOU AND...!

WHAT! WAS THAT ONE OF OUR EMPLOYEES.. OUR OWN BELLBOY??

HE SHOULD HAVE BEEN REPORTED TO ME! WHAT KIND OF A HOTEL AM I RUNNING HERE?
??
WALT DISNEY

WHATEVER MADE ME HIRE SUCH A DUMB BOY? IN FACT, DID I?
NOT PERSONALLY, SIR... IT WAS ARRANGED THROUGH...!
8-30

AH, THAT EXPLAINS EVERYTHING! IF I DIDN'T HIRE YOU PERSONALLY, YOU CAN'T WORK HERE!
Y' MEAN.. I'M THROUGH?

TRYING TO WIGGLE OUT, EH? WELL, I AM HIRING YOU, RIGHT NOW! REPORT TO THE DESK AND GET BUSY!
YES, SIR!

ALTHOUGH I DON'T KNOW WHY I SHOULD EMPLOY SUCH A STUPID, CLUMSY BOY... DO YOU?
NO, SIR! THANK YOU, SIR!
WALT DISNEY

GETTING ACQUAINTED WITH HIS NEW JOB, MICKEY FINDS THAT BUSINESS IS RATHER QUIET AT THE LIBERTY-BELLE HOTEL!
8-31

AH.. THE FIRST NEW GUEST SINCE I'VE BEEN HERE!
GOOD MORNING, SIR! LET ME...!
JUST A MINUTE! I'M NOT SURE THAT I'M STAYING, YET!

FIRST I WANT TO KNOW ABOUT THE FISHING HERE!
BEST IN THE WORLD, SIR! BARGE, SURF OR PIER... WHATEVER Y' LIKE!

HOW ABOUT FRESH WATER?
YES, SIR! A SWELL LAKE ONLY A STONE'S THROW AWAY!

Y-BELLE
OTEL
SORRY! WON'T DO FOR ME... I HATE ANY KIND OF FISHING!
WALT DISNEY

HAVING A LITTLE SPARE TIME, MICKEY DECIDES TO GET ACQUAINTED WITH SOME OF HIS FELLOW WORKERS!

MAYBE I'LL FIND THE JANITOR A MORE FRIENDLY GUY THAN THE OTHERS I'VE SEEN, SO FAR!
BASEMENT
(JANITOR)
ANDY
9-2

HELLO! I S'POSE YOU'RE ANDY! MY NAME'S MICKEY... I'M THE NEW BELLBOY!
WELL, IF YOU'VE COME TO KICK ABOUT THE HOT WATER, THERE AIN'T ANY! WOT'S MORE...

I DIDN'T COME TO KICK ABOUT ANYTHING! I JUST DROPPED IN TO...!
...THERE WON'T BE ANY, EITHER! NO USE PICKIN' ON ME BECAUSE TH' BOSS WON'T LAY IN ANY COAL!

CAN I HELP IT IF HE'S GONNA WAIT FER TH' FALL CLEARANCE SALES? GO KICK TO HIM ABOUT IT!
OKAY! PARDON ME!
WALT DISNEY

HELLO! I'M MICKEY MOUSE, THE NEW...!
WORK, WORK, WORK! THAT'S ALL I DO! I TELL YOU, I CAN'T STAND IT MUCH LONGER! IT'S ORFUL!
9-3

I STARTED TO SAY...
THE ONLY MAID IN THE HOTEL... AND GUESTS BY THE HUNDERDS! IT AIN'T RIGHT, I SAY!

WHY, NO! THAT DOESN'T SEEM...
AND THE TIPS I GET... PFOOH! IN A WHOLE WEEK IT DON'T AMOUNT TO PINS!
OF COURSE, YOU KNOW WHY...

...THEY AIN'T ENOUGH GUESTS! HARDLY NOBUDDY COMES HERE ANY MORE! IT'S ORFUL!
GEE! 'AT'S PRETTY TOUGH, ALL RIGHT!

YEH, YOU'VE SURE GOT A TOUGH JOB... WHAT WITH NOT ENOUGH GUESTS, AND TOO MANY GUESTS, AND ALL THAT!
OH, IT'S ORFUL! YOU'VE NO IDEAR! IF THEY AIN'T STEALIN' TH' TOWELS THEY'RE COOKIN' IN TH' ROOMS! IT'S JUST ORFUL!
9-4

BOY-OH-BOY! MAYBE I SHOULD QUIT THIS JOB BEFORE I GET LIKE THE OTHERS THAT WORK HERE!

OH, BELLBOY! MY IRON IS OUT OF ORDER... PLEASE HAVE IT FIXED AT ONCE!
I'M SORRY, MADAM, BUT IT'S AGAINST THE RULES TO DO IRONING IN THE HOTEL!

INDEED?? WELL, I'M NOT IRONING! I MERELY INTEND TO FRY AN EGG!

YOU RANG FOR ME, SIR?
YES! LISTEN TO THAT BLANKETY-BLANK NOISY POKER GAME IN THE NEXT ROOM! I'VE ASKED 'EM TWICE TO QUIET DOWN...
9-5

...AND ALL THEY DID WAS TO GIVE ME THE BIRD!
I'LL SEE WHAT I CAN DO, SIR!

FIVE MINUTES PASS!

MARVELOUS, MY BOY... NOT A SOUND! WHAT GOLDEN MAGIC DID YOU USE, ANYHOW?
QUITE SIMPLE, SIR! JUST HINTED THAT IT WASN'T WISE TO ANTAGONIZE YOU...

...AS YOU WERE A TRAP-DRUM SALESMAN AND HAD SAMPLES WITH YOU! THANK Y', SIR!
WALT DISNEY

YOUR COFFEE TOO WEAK, MADAM? SO SORRY! YES, WE'LL BE GLAD TO SEND UP ANOTHER POT!
?
9-6

F'GOSH SAKES! THE FIRST TIME IT WAS TOO STRONG! I NEVER SAW SUCH A COFFEE CRANK!
WELL, SHE'S GOT TO BE SATISFIED! GO DOWN AND TELL THE COOK TO BE EXTRA FUSSY!

MY GOODNESS... I DO HOPE IT'S RIGHT THIS TIME!
SO DO I, MADAM! PARDON ME FOR SAYING WE'VE NEVER HAD ANYONE SO PARTICULAR BEFORE!

AH... THE EXACT SHADE! NOW I CAN DYE MY SLIP TO MATCH MY NEW BEIGE DRESS!
Y-YOUR.. ...?? ULP!
WALT DISNEY

I SAY, BOY... THIS IS THE DULLEST HOLE I EVER SAW! ARE THERE NO AMUSEMENTS IN THIS CRUMBY INN?
CERTAINLY, SIR! WE HAVE BILLIARDS, PING-PONG... LOTS OF THINGS!
9-7

DRIVEL! I'M USED TO LIFE... EXCITEMENT... SOMETHING MOVING!
OH, WE HAVE THAT SORT OF AMUSEMENT, TOO!

YOU DON'T SAY! AND JUST WHEN DOES THIS... ER, EXCITEMENT TAKE PLACE?

JUST AS SOON AS YOU DISCOVER...

...THAT YOUR ROBE'S ON FIRE!

SOME SPECIAL INSTRUCTIONS FOR YOU TODAY... PAY ATTENTION!
YES, MR. SNUVVLY!
9-9
Copr. 1940, Walt Disney Productions World Rights Reserved

ROOM 313 IS GOING FISHING... FROM 9 TO 12 YOU WILL ROW HIM ABOUT THE LAKE! AFTER THAT YOU WILL GUIDE 410-B TO EAGLE CAVE, CARRYING THEIR CAMERA OUTFIT!
?

BUT, MR. SNUVVLY... HOW ABOUT MY REGULAR DUTIES?
YOU HAVE NO DUTIES TODAY...

THIS IS YOUR DAY OFF!
OHH... I SEE...!

SO THIS IS WHAT THEY CALL MY DAY OFF... CADDYING FOR THE VISITING SPORTSMEN!
NOW, REMEMBER, BOY... THE HOTEL ADVERTISES THE FINEST FISHING, SO DON'T SHOW ME ANYTHING INFERIOR!
9-10

WE'VE PASSED SOME LIKELY LOOKING SPOTS, SIR!
I'M AN EXPERT! TAKE ME TO THE DEEP WATER... I CATCH ONLY THE LARGE ONES!

STOP RIGHT HERE! NOW PUT ON THE BEST BASS BAIT... I DON'T CATCH ANY OTHER FISH!
YES, SIR! BEFORE I BAIT, THERE'S JUST ONE THING MORE I HAFTA KNOW!

...DO Y' WISH TO CATCH MALES OR FEMALES?
WALT DISNEY

MICKEY HAS A DAY OFF, WITH NOTHING TO DO BUT ASSIST GUESTS ON THEIR VARIOUS OUTINGS!

WOW! THAT WAS KINDA CLOSE!
GOOD GRACIOUS... BE CAREFUL! YOU'VE GOT $500 WORTH OF EQUIPMENT THERE!
9-11

I'M AFRAID... IT'S A LITTLE TOO MUCH... FOR ME, SIR!
DEAR ME! THIS WON'T DO... I'D BETTER TAKE HALF, MYSELF!

GOSH... THANKS! I CAN HANDLE HALF OF IT ALL RIGHT!

YES, THAT'S BETTER! I'D HATE TO LOSE THIS $250 CAMERA!
UG-GLURGLE!

THANK GOSH, MY "DAY OFF" IS OVER, AFTER I SHOW THESE DAMES THE SUNSET AT VIEW POINT!
DON'T YOU JUST ADORE SUNSETS, ERMYNTRUDE?
THEY POSITIVELY INFATUATE ME, GENEVIEVE!
9-12

ISN'T THIS SUNSET RATHER LATE, YOUNG MAN?
I'M KINDA AFRAID THERE WON'T BE ANY TONIGHT! THE CLOUDS ARE GETTIN' PRETTY THICK!

WELL, OF ALL THINGS! DID YOU HEAR HIM, ERMYNTRUDE?
I DID! GENEVIEVE, IT'S A DELIBERATE SWINDLE!

THE BETTER BUSINESS CLUB SHALL HEAR OF THIS!
I SHALL WRITE MY CONGRESSMAN!
Distributed by King Features Syndicate, Inc.

THE DAY AFTER HIS "HOLIDAY" MICKEY TAKES UP HIS REGULAR DUTIES AT THE LIBERTY-BELLE HOTEL!

NICE LI'L JERNT YUH GOT HERE, SON! HOWZA BOSS... DOES HE TREAT YUH RIGHT?
YES, SIR!
9-13

GOOD! THEN YUH WON'T NEED MY TREAT! HAW-HAW-HAW!

DOGGONE WISE EGG! BOY... Y' MEET SOME WEIRD ONES IN THIS BUSINESS!
WALT DISNEY

OH-OH! WHAT HAPPENS HERE??

NOW, WHO'S THAT BIRD... AND WHAT THE HECK'S HE UP TO?
9-14

BEG PARDON, SIR, ARE YOU LOOKING FOR SOMETHING?

SHHHH...!
BUT.. WHAT...??

SHHH! THERE'S CRIME AFOOT! A REG'LAR HOTBED OF CRIME!
WALT DISNEY

DISCOVERING WHAT APPEARS TO BE A HOUSE DETECTIVE DOING SOME KEYHOLE SNOOPING, MICKEY IS SURPRISED TO LEARN THAT CRIME IS AFOOT!

I BELIEVE I'LL HAVE A LOOK AT THAT ROOM THE GOOFY DETECTIVE WAS EYEING THROUGH THE KEYHOLE!
9-19

OF COURSE, THIS IS SILLY... THE ROOM'S BEEN EMPTY FOR WEEKS!

WELL? WHAT ARE YOU DOING HERE? ARE YOU SUPPOSED TO INSPECT THE ROOMS?
N-NO, SIR!

WELL, I AM! AND EVERYTHING IS IN ORDER HERE! GET ON DUTY!
YES, SIR!
THERE'S SOMETHING GOING ON IN THIS HOTEL... I FEEL IT!
WALT DISNEY

GIVE ME MY BILL! I'M GETTIN' OUT OF THIS BATTY DUMP!
BUT, SIR... IF THERE'S SOME COMPLAINT... PERHAPS ANOTHER ROOM..?
9-20

I'M GETTIN' OUT, I SAID! THE BLASTED HALLS ARE HAUNTED!
AH, DOUBTLESS A GUEST WALKING IN HIS SLEEP! IN THE DARK ... YOU KNOW ...!
!

OH, YEAH? I'M NOT ONE TO OBJECT TO MEETING AN OCCASIONAL SLEEPWALKER...

...BUT WHEN I WALK RIGHT THROUGH ONE, I'VE HAD ENOUGH!
WALT DISNEY

WISH I KNEW IF THERE IS SOME PHONY BUSINESS GOIN' ON HERE! ONE GUEST THINKS HE SAW A GHOST...!
9-21

...THEN THERE'S THAT HOUSE DICK THAT SNOOPS AROUND, BUT DOESN'T WORK HERE... WHAT A CRACKPOT!

AND HOW THE BOSS AND THE CLERK HAVE IT IN FOR HIM! SOME STORY THERE THAT DOESN'T... DOEZN'... DZZ...
Z-Z-Z

EEEE-E-E-YAWK-
OOOWAH-HA-HA-HA-HO-HO-HO-HO...!
GOOD GOSH! WHAT'S THAT??

OOO-WAH-
HA-HA-HO-HO....!
WHAT TH' HECK'S GOIN' ON??
9-23

IT WENT THAT WAY!
...HO-HO-HO-O-O!

WHAT WAS IT, MR. BEEBLE?
OH, HE'S BACK AGAIN...YES, IT'S HIM!
BUT WHO?

"HEYUDI," OUR GHOST!

THIS DOGGONE HOTEL IS GETTIN' MORE MYSTERIOUS EVERY MINUTE! NOW, EVEN THE BOSS THINKS IT'S HAUNTED!
9-24

YOU HEARD THAT WEIRD LAUGHIN' AND SCREAMIN', ANDY... DO YOU BLAME IT ON GHOSTS, TOO?
'COURSE NOT! I GOT MORE SENSE!

THEY CAN'T NOBODY GIT ME TO B'LEEVE IN GHOSTS, 'CAUSE THEY AIN'T NO SECH THING...!

..BUT JEST TH' SAME.. WE GOT 'EM!!
WALT DISNEY

THE MORNING AFTER THE "GHOST" EPISODE MICKEY IS STILL PUZZLED OVER WHAT HAPPENED... AND WHY??

THE BOSS SURE LOOKS WORRIED, TOO!
'MORNING, MR. BEEBLE!
EH? GET AWAY! OH-H, BEG PARDON... MY MIND WAS ON GHOSTS!
9-25

GOSH! Y' DON'T REALLY BELIEVE THAT WAS A GHOST, DO Y'?
WELL-L, NO! BUT WHATEVER IT IS, IT'S HAUNTED THE PLACE FOR WEEKS AND I DON'T KNOW WHAT TO DO ABOUT IT!

SAY, MR. BEEBLE, WILL Y' LET ME SEE WHAT I CAN DO... IN MY SPARE TIME? I'D GET A KICK OUT OF IT!
YOU? WHAT COULD YOU DO? OR..MAYBE YOU COULD ...YES, YOU MIGHT AS WELL TRY!

IF YOU CAN'T GET RID OF IT, MAYBE, AT LEAST YOU CAN MAKE IT KEEP QUIET AFTER TEN O'CLOCK!
YES, SIR... I'LL DO MY BEST!
WALT DISNEY

MICKEY IS DISGUSTED WHEN "HEYUDI," THE GHOST, FAILS TO SHOW UP FOR SEVERAL NIGHTS!
A CHANCE FOR A LITTLE EXCITEMENT AND IT GOES EL FLOPPO! JUST MY... OH-OH! LOOK WHO'S HERE!
9-26

IT'S THAT DOPEY DETECTIVE THE BOSS KICKED OUT! AND UP TO HIS OLD TRICKS, TOO ... WHAT NERVE!

SAY! DON'T YOU REALIZE ...?
SHH-H-H!-SUSPICIOUS FEMALE... PUTTING CHAIR IN FRONT OF DOOR... A CRIMINAL SIGN!

HA! STANDS ON CHAIR! THAT MEANS... UNLESS I'M ALL WET...!

YOW!!
HA-HA-HAHAHA..!

BUT, MADAM ... SURELY, WE CAN ADJUST ANY...!
ADJUST NOTHING! I'LL NOT STAND FOR A PEEPING TOM AT MY KEYHOLE!
9-27

DEAR ME... SHE SEEMS TO HAVE CHECKED OUT! DO YOU KNOW ANYTHING ABOUT THIS PEEPING TOM AFFAIR?
YES, SIR! BUT IN THIS CASE IT'S A PEEPING "DICK"...

...IT'S THAT HOUSE DETECTIVE Y' THREW OUT LAST WEEK!
WHAT?!! HIM?? WHY, I'LL KICK HIM SO FAR...!

OH, NO, YUH WON'T! YOU KICK ME AND I'LL KNOW WHO DONE IT... YOU'LL LEAVE FOOTPRINTS!

I WARNED YUH! YOU'LL LEAVE FOOT-PRINTS!
COME BACK AGAIN AND I'LL LEAVE FINGERPRINTS ...ON YOUR NECK!
MR. BEEBLE ..WAIT!
9-28

I'VE GOT AN IDEA! THE HOTEL THAT HIRES THAT DOPEY DICK NEVER SEES HIM... HE'S ALWAYS SNOOPIN' OVER HERE!
THAT'S RIGHT! BUT...?

WHY DON'T YOU HIRE HIM? THEN HE'LL GO ANNOY SOMEBODY ELSE!
MY BOY, YOU'RE A GENIUS! RUN OUT AND SEE IF YOU CAN FIND THE PEST!

FIND WHO? IF IT'S A MISSING PERSON CASE, BEEBLE, THAT'S MY JOB!
WALT DISNEY

IN THE HOPE THAT THE PESKY HOUSE DETECTIVE WILL DO HIS DETECTING SOMEWHERE ELSE, HE HAS BEEN HIRED BY THE LIBERTY BELLE HOTEL!

HAVING SHOWN THE MYSTERIOUS GENTLEMAN TO HIS THREE ROOMS, MICKEY MEETS THE HOUSE DETECTIVE HEADED THAT WAY!

DESPITE THE LATEST SCARE BY "HEYUDI," THE GHOST, MICKEY FINALLY FALLS ASLEEP...
...THEN COMES MORNING!
10-7

WHAT A NIGHT! I ALMOST WONDER IF I **DREAMED** THAT BUSINESS, IT SEEMS SO FANTASTIC NOW...!
Copr 1940, Walt Disney Productions World Rights Reserved

...HEY!!?

GET OFF, YOU... MMPF...FMM ...LEGGO...!

GOOD GOSH! HOW IN THE WORLD... WHERE DID IT **COME** FROM??
MICKEY MOUSE: KEEP YOUR NOSE OUT OF MY AFFAIRS! THIS CASE IS TOO BIG FOR PEANUTS! LAY OFF! — HEYUDI.
WALT DISNEY
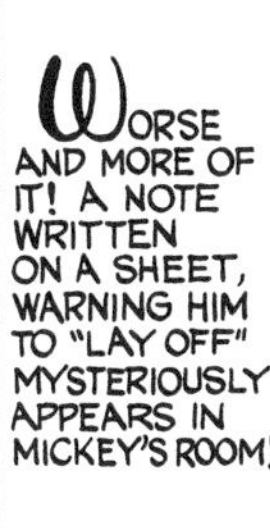
WORSE AND MORE OF IT! A NOTE WRITTEN ON A SHEET, WARNING HIM TO "LAY OFF" MYSTERIOUSLY APPEARS IN MICKEY'S ROOM!
10-8

ONE THING SURE, MR. BEEBLE, IT'S A MIGHTY SOLID GHOST THAT CAN WRITE!
OH, MY! THIS IS THE WORST YET! NO CONSIDERATION AT ALL!

WITH ALL THE WRITING PAPER IN THE HOTEL, **MUST** THEY RUIN MY SHEETS! TSK, TSK, TSK!

BUT, MR. BEEBLE... THE IMPORTANT THING IS...
JUST A MINUTE! ANY FINGERPRINTS?
???

FINGERPRINTS...ON **MY** SHEETS? I'LL HAVE YOU KNOW OUR LINENS ARE SPOTLESS!
WALT DISNEY

'MORNING, MR. SNUVVLY! I'M TAKIN' BREAKFAST TO COL. BOOMASNICKER'S ROOM!
I DO HOPE EVERYTHING PLEASES HIM! I'M WORRIED ABOUT HOW HE WILL TAKE LAST NIGHT'S...ER, LITTLE DISTURBANCE!
10-9

HOPE THE HAUNTED HOUSE BUSINESS DIDN'T KEEP Y' AWAKE, SIR!
TUT, TUT, MY BOY! GHOSTS DON'T SCARE ME ...USED TO BE A PRANKSTER, MYSELF!

HOW... HOW DID HE...?
OH, THE COLONEL'S A GOOD SPORT! **HE'S** NOT RUNNIN' OUT!

AH, **GOOD**! WHAT A RELIEF! I WAS SO AFRAID HE MIGHT ...BUT HE WASN'T SCARED, YOU SAY...AH, THAT'S **FINE**..YES, INDEED!
GOSH! HE'S SURE MIGHTY **ANXIOUS** TO PLEASE THAT GUY!
WALT DISNEY

DOGGONE... THIS LATE SHIFT IS DULL AND DREARY! IT WOULD HAFTA BE A QUIET NIGHT JUST WHEN IT'S MY TURN!
10-10
Copr. 1940, Walt Disney Productions World Rights Reserved

WHAT TH' HECK!
BLURBLE -URBLE -UBBL-

THIS GOOFY PLACE GETS CRAZIER EVERY DAY!
BLURBLE... URBLE...

GOOD GOSH... TWO OF 'EM! AND, SAY... THAT'S COL. BOOMASNICKER'S ROOM!
BLURBLE- URBLE...
UBBL- UBBL- UBL...
19
WALT DISNEY
Distributed by King Features Syndicate, Inc.

YES, IT'S GHOSTS AGAIN... TWO OF THEM THIS TIME! AND IT SEEMS THAT THE OBJECT OF THEIR AFFECTIONS IS COLONEL BOOMASNICKER!

BLURBLE- URBLE...
URBL- UBBL- UBL...!!
10-11
Copr. 1940, Walt Disney Productions World Rights Reserved

HEY, YOU!
WHAM! BLAM!

WELL, I'LL BE...!

DID Y' SEE 'EM? THEY WERE...!
LOOK, MY BOY! ALL I ASK IS GOOD BOARD AND LODGING... PLEASE OMIT THE ENTERTAIN-MENT!
WALT DISNEY

TWO GHOSTS, EH? I'M GLAD IT WAS MY NIGHT OFF... IT'S GETTING ON MY NERVES!
AWAAH-HO-HUM-- IT DOESN'T WORRY THE COLONEL.. HE SEEMS TO THINK WE'RE PUTTIN' ON A FLOOR SHOW FOR HIM!
10-12

BOOMASNICKER? HE, ER.. DOESN'T THREATEN TO LEAVE, OR ANYTHING?
NOPE! AND HE'S THE GUY THAT'S BEIN' HAUNTED, TOO!
Copr. 1940, Walt Disney Productions World Rights Reserved

WELL, I'M GONNA FORGET THE WHOLE THING AND CATCH SOME SHUT-EYE!

OMIGOSH!
MICKEY MOUSE: THIS IS YOUR FINAL WARNING! LAY OFF!!
HEYUDI I.
HEYUDI II.
WALT DISNEY

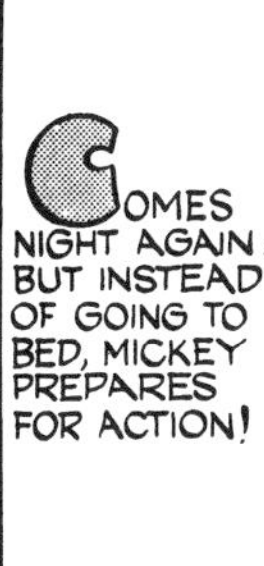
COMES NIGHT AGAIN, BUT INSTEAD OF GOING TO BED, MICKEY PREPARES FOR ACTION!

PHOOEY ON THOSE WARNING NOTES! I'M GONNA HIDE OUTSIDE COL. BOOMASNICKER'S ROOM **BEFORE** ANY MONKEY BUSINESS STARTS!
10-14

WHOEVER TRIES ANY GHOST TRICKS IS DUE FOR A BIG...

GOOD GOSH...!

...**THREE** OF 'EM!
WALT DISNEY

EXPECTING TO FORESTALL ANY NEW GHOST TRICKS, MICKEY IS FLABBERGASTED TO DISCOVER **THREE** "HEYUDIS" HAUNTING COL. BOOMASNICKER'S ROOM!

HEY, YOU...!
10-15

DUMB WAITER
WALT DISNEY

VERY, VERY MAD AT GHOSTS, MICKEY CHASES THEM INTO A DUMBWAITER LEADING TO THE KITCHEN!
10-16

AHA...!
DUMB WAITER

...**GOTCHA**... Y' PHONEY SPOOK!
STOP! HE AIN'T **IT**!

SEE? IT ISS CHUST OUR DETECKATIVE, W'ICH I 'AVE SOCK WIZ A BAG OF FLOUR!
YEH? WELL, WHAT'S THE IDEA? THERE'S SOMEP'N MIGHTY FUNNY ABOUT THIS!

WHAT WERE Y' DOIN' IN THE KITCHEN, ANYWAY?
CHUST A LEEDLE MEESTAKE ...I T'OUGHT HE WAS ZE GHOST!
REASON ENOUGH! I BEAT IT DOWN HERE TO HEAD OFF THEM GHOSTS! THEN HE CROWNS ME WITH A SACK O' FLOUR!
Copr 1940, Walt Disney Productions World Rights Reserved

HOW COME YOU WERE WORKIN' THIS TIME O' NIGHT?
WELL... YOU SEE, IT WASS MY DAY OFF...
10-17

...SO I SAY TO MYSELF, I WILL COOK A LEEDLE TIDBIT FOR MYSELF! CHUST A TEENSY WISP OF SPONGE CAKE, WIZ WHIP' CREAM...!

IF YOU LIKE TO TASTE MY CAKE...?
NO, THANKS! THE BALONEY WAS PLENTY ...I'M GOIN' TO BED!
WALT DISNEY
Distributed by King Features Syndicate, Inc.

NEXT MORNING! MICKEY IS AS PUZZLED AS EVER ABOUT THE SPOOKY EPISODES OF THE NIGHT...AND SUSPICIOUS OF EVERYBODY!

THAT DOPEY HOUSE DICK, AND THE CHEF... WHAT YARNS THEY HANDED ME! THOSE BIRDS WILL BEAR WATCHING!
10-18

MICKEY MOUSE!! THIS IS THE SECOND FINAL WARNING YOU'VE HAD! WHAT ARE YOU, DUMB OR SOMETHING? LAY OFF!!
HEYUDI I
HEYUDI II
HEYUDI III

HERE'S THE LATEST, MR. SNUVVLY! GET A LOAD OF THAT!
GOOD GRIEF! YOU'D BETTER DO WHAT THEY SAY, BEFORE SOMETHING TERRIBLE HAPPENS!

LIKE FUN I'LL... OH-OH! HERE COMES THE COLONEL, AND HE SEEMS TO BE LEAVING!
OH.. DEAR ME ...I WAS AFRAID OF THAT!
WALT DISNEY

I'VE HAD ENOUGH OF THIS HOTEL... I'M CHECKING OUT!
SO SORRY, COL. BOOMASNICKER! OF COURSE, THOSE..ER, GHOSTS MUST HAVE BEEN FRIGHTFULLY ANNOYING!
10-19

ANNOYING? NOT AT ALL... THEY WERE VERY AMUSING! IN FACT...

...I ENJOYED YOUR WHOLE ENTERTAINMENT ...BUT..I HAVE TO SLEEP SOME TIME!
!

JUST A MINUTE, BUD! YOU'RE NOT TAKIN' IT ON THE LAM! YOU'RE COMIN' WITH ME!
WALT DISNEY

FINALLY GETTING ENOUGH OF THE NOCTURNAL HIGH JINKS, COL. BOOMASNICKER CHECKS OUT, ONLY TO BE HALTED BY THE DEMON DETECTIVE!
10-21

WHAT DO YOU MEAN BY STOPPING ME? GET OUT OF MY WAY, YOU DOLT! ONE SIDE!
DON'T GIMME THAT STUFF! I KNOW YUH! PHONY WHISKERS DON'T FOOL JASPER SNOOPBONES!

WHY, YOU...!! OUCH!
COME ON.. ..UNNH... TAKE 'EM OFF..!

THEY'RE REAL... AND SO IS THAT!

WELL... DARNED IF THEY AIN'T!
WALT DISNEY

STRANGE TO SAY, SINCE COL. BOOMASNICKER LEFT THE HOTEL THE GHOSTS HAVEN'T SHOWN UP!

PROB'LY JUST A COINCIDENCE, BUT IT LOOKS LIKE SOMEBODY WANTED HIM TO LEAVE HERE!
BUT, WE'VE HAD GHOSTS BEFORE! PEOPLE ARE ALWAYS LEAVIN' ON ACCOUNT OF THE DURN SPOOKS!

IF IT KEEPS ON, I'LL BE RUINED! NOBODY'LL COME HERE! AND WE'RE NO CLOSER TO SOLVING THE CASE THAN WE EVER WERE!
10-22

IT'S TOUGH ALL RIGHT! ONE THING THAT MAKES IT HARD IS THAT WE CAN'T FIND ANY MOTIVE!
A MOTIVE? GOOD GRAVY...DO WE HAVE TO FIND THAT, TOO?

FIND OUT HOW TO GET RID OF THE GHOSTS, THAT'S ALL I...!
JUST A MINUTE, MR. BEEBLE...I'VE GOT A NEW HUNCH!
WALT DISNEY

WELL, GO AHEAD... WHAT'S THIS NEW BRAINSTORM?
LISTEN, MR. BEEBLE... THESE GHOST SCARES ARE RUINING THE HOTEL'S BUSINESS, AREN'T THEY?

HUMPH! NOTHIN' NEW ABOUT THAT!
BUT WHOEVER'S DOIN' IT MUST STAND TO GAIN SOMETHING BY IT... DON'T Y' SEE?
10-23

NOW, SUPPOSIN' YOUR BUSINESS GOES COMPLETELY BLOOEY... WHAT HAPPENS?
WELL, I'D BE BROKE! THEN I COULDN'T PAY OFF THE MORTGAGE WHEN IT COMES DUE, AND...!

MORTGAGE! NOW WE'RE GETTIN' SOMEWHERE AT LAST!
UH... ARE WE?
WALT DISNEY

THIS MORTGAGE ON THE HOTEL... DO Y' KNOW ANYBODY WHO'D WANTA SEE IT FORECLOSED?
GRACIOUS, NO! NOBODY'D WANT THE OLD PLACE AS A **GIFT**!
10-24

DOGGONE! AND I THOUGHT I WAS ON THE TRACK OF A CLUE THERE!
I GIVE UP! THIS IS ALL TOO MUCH FOR ME!

JUST THE SAME, I'LL KEEP THAT MORTGAGE IN MIND! THERE **MIGHT** BE AN ANGLE!

AHEM... SO **THERE** YOU ARE! WHAT'S THE MEANING OF THIS LOAFING? GET ON DUTY **AT ONCE**!
YES, MR. SNUVVLY!
WALT DISNEY

WHAT WERE YOU DOING IN MR. BEEBLE'S OFFICE, ANYWAY? YOU **KNOW** YOU SHOULDN'T BOTHER HIM!
WELL, HE SENT FOR ME... ABOUT THE GHOST MYSTERY, Y' KNOW!
10-25

YOU'VE GOT NO BUSINESS WITH HIM... YOU JUST TAKE ADVANTAGE BECAUSE HE'S EASY GOING!
THAT'S NOT SO, SIR!

BESIDES, YOU'VE GOT NO TIME! HERE, TAKE THIS TELEGRAM TO ROOM TEN!
YES, SIR!
TELEGRAM

PSSST...!
!

LOOKING FOR ME, MR. BEEBLE?
YES, DON'T PAY ANY ATTENTION TO THAT CLERK! HE'S JUST AN OLD CRAB... ALWAYS FUSSING ABOUT SOME-THING!
10-26

HEY.. WHAT DO Y' SAY YOU AND I GO FISHING?
FISHING, MR. BEEBLE? BUT... UH, MY WORK... DO Y' THINK I SHOULD...?

ALL RIGHT... WE WON'T GO, THEN! THAT'S **ALWAYS** THE WAY! MY EMPLOYEES ARE TOO DURNED BUSY TO DO ANYTHING **I** WANT!

BUT **SOME** DAY YOU'LL WANT **ME** TO GO FISHING WITH **YOU**! AND JUST **SEE** IF I DO IT!
WALT DISNEY

BEEN MIGHTY QUIET AROUND HERE LATELY... SEEMS AS THOUGH THE GHOSTS HAVE GIVEN US UP!
10-28

EE-E-E-- YOWBLE-- --OWBLE- -OWBLE...!
OMIGOSH! THE GHOST SOUNDS!

...AND I THINK I KNOW WHERE THEY'RE COMIN' FROM THIS TIME!

WOO-- WEE-YAWW...!
WELL, OF ALL THE.. ..IT'S ANDY!

HEARING SPOOKY SOUNDS COMING FROM A HEAT REGISTER, MICKEY RACES TO THE CELLAR IN TIME TO CATCH THE JANITOR YELLING INTO THE PIPE!

WAH! WAH! WOW!
SO! THIS IS HOW THE GHOST NOISES ARE MADE, IS IT, ANDY?
10-29

HUH? GHOST NOISES! DON'T BE SILLY... I'M, ER.. JUST TESTING THE PIPES!
JUST TESTING, EH? BY WARBLING INTO 'EM?

CERT'NLY! IF TH' SOUND COMES OUT TH' OTHER END, I KNOW TH' PIPE'S CLEAR...!

...IF IT DON'T, TH' PIPE'S CLOGGED! SIMPLE ENOUGH, AIN'T IT?
OH, YEH... VERY SIMPLE!
WALT DISNEY

YOU'RE TRYIN' TO TELL ME THAT YELLIN' THROUGH THE FURNACE PIPES WILL TEST IF THEY'RE CLEAN?
THAT'S WHAT I SAID! IF THE NOISE DON'T COME OUT UPSTAIRS, IT SHOWS THE PIPE'S CLOGGED!

AND JUST HOW DO Y' KNOW IF THE NOISE IS HEARD UPSTAIRS?
10-30

THAT'S EASY! SOME IDIOT ALWAYS COMES DOWN TO COMPLAIN... LIKE YOU JUST DID!
OH-H...!

DOGGONE! FIRST ONE SUSPECT, THEN ANOTHER! HIS ALIBI IS AS PHONY AS THE REST...BUT HOW CAN I PROVE IT?
WALT DISNEY

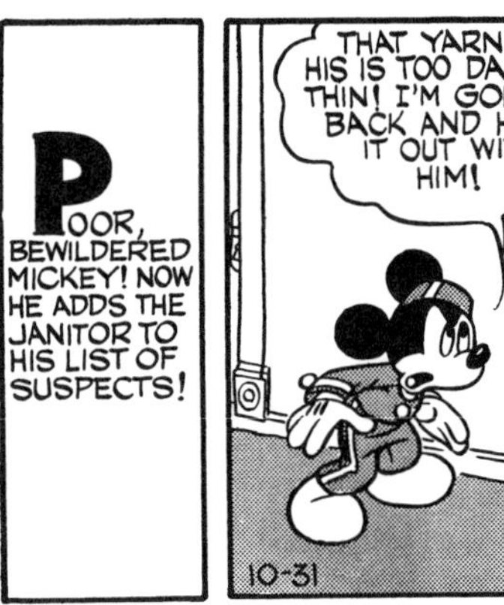
POOR, BEWILDERED MICKEY! NOW HE ADDS THE JANITOR TO HIS LIST OF SUSPECTS!
THAT YARN OF HIS IS TOO DARN THIN! I'M GOIN' BACK AND HAVE IT OUT WITH HIM!
10-31

OHO...!!

WHAT? UH..OH, IT'S YOU AGAIN!
A GHOST DISGUISE, EH? GIVE IT HERE!

NOW, TRY AND EXPLAIN THIS ONE, BROTHER!
WHY, CERT'NLY ...IT'S...IT'S ...SURE I KIN EXPLAIN!

TRYIN' TO BURN A GHOST DISGUISE... BUT, OF COURSE, YOU CAN EXPLAIN IT!
WEL-L... I CAN, TOO!
11-1

Y' SEE, IT'S... WELL, IT'S A MASQUERADE COSTUME MY WIFE GOT FOR ME...!

...SHE WANTS ME TO GO TO A PARTY...AND I HATE PARTIES, SO...
"...SO I SAYS TO MY-SELF, IF SOMETHIN' HAPPENED TO MY COSTUME I COULDN'T GO! SUDDENLY I THOUGHT OF THE FURNACE!"

YEH...THAT'S IT! THAT'S JUST TH' WAY I FIGGERED! YOU UNDERSTAND!
WALT DISNEY

BURNIN' A GHOST OUTFIT SO YOUR WIFE CAN'T MAKE Y' GO TO A PARTY! AM I SUPPOSED TO SWALLOW THAT ONE?
WELL... THAT'S THE WAY IT IS!

BEFORE THAT HE WAS YOWLING SPOOK NOISES INTO A FURNACE PIPE! PHOOEY!
11-2

YORBLE-ORBLE ...AH-WAH...!
WHAT TH'...!!? GHOST NOISES AGAIN?

...WHEE-E-E...!
IT'S COMIN' FROM ROOM 30, AND THAT'S VACANT!

...WHEE-AH.. LULU-LU-LU...!
OMIGOSH! NOW IT'S THE CHAMBERMAID!
WALT DISNEY

AGAIN HEARING WEIRD WAILS, MICKEY BURSTS INTO A SUPPOSEDLY VACANT ROOM AND CATCHES THE MAID AT IT THIS TIME!

YORBLE-- ORB...!! GLUG... ???
COME CLEAN, SISTER... THE JIG'S UP!
11-4

OH, DEAR! I'VE BEEN DISCOVERED!
YOU SAID IT! NOW, JUST WHAT'S BEHIND THIS GHOST RACKET, HORTENSE?

GHOST?? SAKES ALIVE... I AIN'T NO GHOST! I WAS ONLY PRACTISIN' MY SINGIN' LESSONS!
OH, SURE! Y' ALWAYS SING UNDER A BUCKET, I S'POSE!

YEH! YOU SEE, MY VOICE AIN'T SO GOOD YET... AND I DIDN'T WANT NOBODY TO HEAR ME!

I S'POSE Y' KNOW THAT SINGING YARN OF YOURS SOUNDS PRETTY FISHY, HORTENSE!
MAYBE SO.. ..TO THEM AS HAS LOW, SUSPICIOUS MINDS!
11-5

OKAY, OKAY! BUT JUST THE SAME...!

...JUST THE... AHA! WHAT'S THIS... WHAT'S THIS??

WELL, MISS MUFFET, DOES THIS SPOOK DISGUISE GO WITH YOUR SINGIN' LESSONS?
OH, FUDGE! SAKES ALIVE ...IF YOU MUST SNOOP, THAT'S ONLY... JUST A MASQUERADE COSTUME!

OWOO! WHERE HAVE I HEARD THAT ONE BEFORE?!!

ALL RIGHT, LITTLE BO-PEEP, IF THIS GHOST COSTUME IS FOR A PARTY, WHY WERE Y' HIDING IT?
SO'S MY HUSBAND WON'T FIND IT... IT'S FOR HIM, THAT'S WHY!
11-6

YOU SEE, I ALREADY MADE HIM ONE AND HE CLAIMS HE LOST IT! HE JUST NATCHER'LY HATES PARTIES!
!

HE... YOUR HUSBAND... LOOK, HORTENSE, ARE YOU MARRIED TO ANDY, THE JANITOR?
WELL... WE'RE TRYIN' TO KEEP IT SECRET, BUT... YES, I AM!
WALT DISNEY

GOOD NIGHT! WHERE AM I GETTIN'? THIS MEANS BOTH THEIR COCK-EYED ALIBIS COULD BE TRUE!

BEWILDERED FROM CHASING UP TOO MANY BLIND ALLEYS, MICKEY GOES BACK TO HIS ROOM FOR SOME HEAVY THINKING!

DOGGONE IT... EVERYTHING SUSPICIOUS AROUND HERE ALWAYS TURNS OUT TO HAVE SOME GOOFY REASON FOR IT!
11-7

-THOUGHT SURE I HAD SOMEP'N ON THE JANITOR ...AN' THEN THE MAID! BUT ALL THAT'S GONE BLOOEY!

THEN THERE'S THE CHEF.. ..THE CLERK..THAT DOPEY DETECTIVE... BUT, GOSH..THERE'S NO **MOTIVE!** IF ONLY...

...IF ONLY...
SAY..!!

ONE SIDE, GLOOM! LITTLE ROLLO HAS A **PLAN!**
WALT DISNEY

THIS IS MY NIGHT FOR DESK DUTY, ISN'T IT, MR. SNUVVLY?
YES, BUT NOT FOR TWO HOURS YET!
11-8

OH, THAT'S ALL RIGHT! YOU CAN LEAVE NOW IF Y' WANT TO!
HMMM! THIS AMBITION IS RATHER SUDDEN!

I DON'T FATHOM YOUR BURNING INTEREST IN WORK, BUT IT'S ALL RIGHT WITH ME!

NOW! HERE'S WHERE I **REALLY** GET BUSY!

ON HIS NIGHT FOR DESK DUTY, MICKEY OPENS A NEW LINE OF INVESTIGATION BY SEARCHING THROUGH SOME OLD REGISTERS OF THE HOTEL!

MARCH 13TH... AH! A NEW GUEST TOOK THREE ROOMS!
11-9

NOW LET'S LOOK AT MR. BEEBLE'S RECORD OF GHOST APPEARANCES! MARCH...!

HOT DOG! GHOSTS ON MARCH **14TH** AND THE GUEST LEFT THE NEXT DAY!

NOW TO MAKE SURE THAT'S NO FLUKE, THERE OUGHTA BE **MORE** CASES! BOY-OH-BOY, THIS IS REALLY GETTIN' WARM!

MICKEY IS HOT ON A NEW TRAIL, CHECKING THE GHOST SCARES AGAINST DATES IN AN OLD REGISTER!

HERE'S ANOTHER ONE...AND THIS GUY HAD THE SAME ROOMS AS BOOMASNICKER! JULY THIRD...!
11-11

...JULY THIRD... YEP, HERE IT IS! SPOOKS THAT NIGHT AND THE NEXT...AND THE GUY WAS SCARED OUT ON THE FIFTH!

THAT SETTLES IT! THEY CHECK EVERY TIME! THE GHOSTS ONLY SHOW UP WHEN THERE'S SOMETHIN' UNUSUAL ABOUT THE GUESTS!

IZZAT SO?
OH-OH! NOW, WHAT'S GOIN' ON?
YOU HEARD ME! GET OUT!
WALT DISNEY

HEARING SOUNDS OF A HEATED ALTERCATION, MICKEY RUNS OUT AND CATCHES THE BOSS AND THE HOUSE DETECTIVE AT IT AGAIN!
IS IT MY FAULT THE DAME LEFT BECAUSE I ASKED HER A ROUTINE QUESTION?
ROUTINE!! ASKIN' HER IF SHE WORE HER OWN TEETH!
11-12

WHY DID I EVER HIRE YOU IN THE FIRST PLACE?
OH, YEAH? IF YUH'D HIRED ME THREE YEARS AGO, YUH WOULDN'T BE IN TH' JAM Y' ARE NOW!

GET OUT...BEFORE I LOSE MY TEMPER!
YOU'LL BE SORRY!
JAM...?

..WONDER WHAT THAT GUY MEANT BY THE "JAM" BEEBLE IS IN NOW?
WALT DISNEY

I'D SURE LIKE TO KNOW WHAT TROUBLE BEEBLE IS IN! I COULD ASK HIM...BUT I'M DARNED IF I TRUST EVEN HIM ANY MORE!
11-13

SAY! I'VE GOT A HUNCH THIS OLD RECORD BOOK WILL SPILL THE BEANS!

ACCORDIN' TO THE DETECTIVE, IT WAS THREE YEARS AGO! LET'S SEE...THIS SHOWS THAT...!

...YIPPEE!!
HERE IT IS!

HIT IT RIGHT ON THE NOSE! I'VE GOT THE MOTIVE!

Tickled pink by discovering the motive behind the ghost scares, Mickey scurries down to the police station on his day off!

FROM THE LOCAL POLICE CHIEF, MICKEY GETS THE PRISON RECORD OF A CERTAIN "SLIPPERY SAM"! THE INFORMATION FITS MICKEY'S OTHER DEDUCTIONS TO A "T"!

AND DO Y' KNOW ANYTHING ABOUT HIM SINCE HE LEFT PRISON?
OH, SURE! HE'S WORKIN' AS A TRAVELIN' SALESMAN ... SEEMS TO BE GOIN' STRAIGHT!
11-18

THAT'S ALL I NEED TO KNOW! THANKS A LOT, SIR!
OKAY, SON ... GLAD TO HELP!

ELATED, MICKEY REPORTS BACK TO THE HOTEL!

I WANT THE THREE BEST ROOMS IN THE HOUSE ..AND ABSOLUTE QUIET! UNDERSTAND?
YESSIR... YESSIR! IT WILL BE A PLEASURE, SIR!
OH-OH! HERE'S WHERE THINGS START POPPIN' AGAIN!
WALT DISNEY

BOY TAKE MR. KLUMPH TO ROOMS 17 19 AND 23. AND SEE THAT HE RECEIVES OUR MOST ELITE SERVICE!
YES SIR! THIS WAY MR. KLUMPH!
11-19

JUDGING BY WHAT I'VE UNCOVERED, THIS BIRD IS DUE FOR A MERRY NIGHT!

HERE Y' ARE SIR! THE FINEST ROOMS THE HOTEL OFFERS!
WELL...I GUESS THEY'LL DO! BUT REMEMBER...I DEMAND ABSOLUTE QUIET!

HMMM...THIS IS VITAL! FOOTSTEPS TWENTY-SEVEN AND A HALF INCHES APART... AHH...!
MY GOSH... ARE YOU AT IT AGAIN?
WALT DISNEY

THAT NIGHT AS MICKEY PREPARES TO GO OFF DUTY !

SURE SEEMS FUNNY HAVIN ANOTHER GUEST TAKE THE SAME THREE ROOMS THAT COL. BOOMASNICKER HAD!
YES, A MOST STRANGE COINCIDENCE.. BUT OF NO IMPORTANCE!
11-20

I DO HOPE OUR SERVICE PLEASES HIM. HE'S SO VERY FINICKY!
YEH...HE'S ALWAYS HARPIN' ON THE QUIET HE EXPECTS! WELL, G'NIGHT, MR. SNUVVLY!

ONLY I'M NOT GOIN' TO BED YET! THESE BACK STAIRS COME OUT RIGHT CLOSE TO MR. KLUMPH'S ROOMS!

AND IF MY DEDUCTIONS WORK OUT ..!
BRR-R-R-RAT-A-TAT-TAT-TA-TAT
OH-OH! IT COMMENCES!
WALT DISNEY

HISTORY REPEATS ITSELF! A NEW AND UNUSUAL GUEST ON THE FIRST NIGHT OF HIS ARRIVAL, IS HAUNTED BY THE HOTEL SPOOK!

NEXT MORNING!

THE SECOND NIGHT OF MR KLUMPH'S STAY FINDS MICKEY STAKED OUT NEAR HIS DOOR ALL SET FOR CHAPTER TWO OF THE BIG HAUNTING ACT!

BOY-OH-BOY ...HOW DO THEY THINK 'EM UP?
WEEDLE-OODLE-EEDLE-OOO--!
BRR-R-RUM-DUM-DUM!

LOOK HERE, WHAT'S...??
OWWW!!!
11-25

WHEE-EE-E-E-E...! BLUBBLE-UBBLE-UBBLE..!
HALP! HALP!!

COME COME, MR. KLUMPH, YOU'RE TAKING YOUR SPOOKS TOO SERIOUSLY!
WALT DISNEY

THE SECOND SPOOK SCARE FINISHES MR. KLUMPH ...HE CAN'T TAKE IT!

NOW, DON'T BE HASTY, MR. KLUMPH...!
OUT OF MY WAY, SIR! DO YOU EXPECT ME TO SLEEP, HAUNTED BY A FIFE AND DRUM CORPS?
11-26

GRACIOUS! SOMETHING WRONG...?
MR. KLUMPH... BE REASONABLE!
BAH! THIS IS NO HOTEL... IT'S A FREAK SHOW! GOOD-BYE!

GOOD RIDDANCE! A DANGEROUS UNDERWORLD CHARACTER, IF YUH ASK ME!
?!

WHO ASKED YOU...?
AND NOW.. ..BEFORE I GO TO BED THERE'S ONE THING MORE, AND MY CASE'LL BE CINCHED!
WALT DISNEY

6-A
JUST ONE THING MORE I NEED TO KNOW, AND THE ANSWER'S PROB'LY IN THIS ROOM!
11-27

HOT DOG! THAT'S HOW THE GHOSTS ARE DONE! AND ALSO WHO DOES IT! YIPPEE!

6-A
HEY! YOU CAN'T GO IN THERE! ANY INVESTIGATING AROUND HERE IS MY JOB!

OKAY, JASPER, OLD BOY...THEN, I WON'T GO IN!
WALT DISNEY

THE MORNING AFTER THE LATEST GHOST COMMOTION, MICKEY SEEKS A PRIVATE INTERVIEW WITH THE BOSS!

I CAN'T SEE THE SENSE OF TALKIN'... IT DON'T STOP THOSE DURN SPOOKS!
MR. BEEBLE... I THINK YOU'VE SEEN YOUR LAST GHOST!
11-28

EH!? WHAT'S THAT? YOU MEAN YOU'VE REALLY FOUND OUT...?
YES, SIR! I KNOW WHO'S BEEN DOIN' IT... AND WHY!

WELL, GOOD GRAVY! WHY AREN'T THE SCOUNDRELS UNDER ARREST? WHAT'S THE...?
WHOA, MR. BEEBLE! KNOWIN' WHO THEY ARE IS ONE THING... PROVIN' IT IS SOMETHING ELSE!

TO DO THAT, I NEED A SPECIAL PIECE OF FURNITURE BUILT! THIS IS THE PLAN FOR IT!
EH? WHAT'S THAT...?
WALT DISNEY

YOU WANT A SPECIAL DESK BUILT? WHAT'S THAT GOT TO DO WITH THESE SPOOK SCOUNDRELS?
A WHOLE LOT! THAT'S THE WAY I'M GONNA GET THE GOODS ON 'EM!
11-29

I KNOW WHO THE VILLAINS ARE.. BUT TO ARREST 'EM, WE'VE GOTTA HAVE PROOF!
WELL, OKAY! IT'S TOO DEEP FOR ME, BUT YOU SEEM TO KNOW WHAT YOU'RE DOIN'!

I'VE GOT IT ALL WORKED OUT! WHEN THE DESK'S READY, HAVE IT PUT IN A BIG ROOM THAT CAN BE LOCKED!
AND THEN WHAT?

THEN COMES THE PAY-OFF! LISTEN...PSST..SST... SST...!
WELL, I DECLARE! HOW'D Y' EVER THINK OF THAT?
WALT DISNEY

CONFIDENT THAT HE KNOWS WHO THE GHOST-MAKERS ARE, BUT LACKING PROOF, MICKEY HAS CONCOCTED A SCHEME TO TRAP THEM!

LET'S SEE...THE 'PHONE GOES HERE ...WIRING'S ALL SET, ACCORDIN' TO PLAN...!
11-30

THE COPS KNOW THEIR PART... THEY'LL BE READY! MR. BEEBLE WILL TAKE CARE OF GETTIN' THE SUSPECTS IN HERE...!

...OH, YES...THE VERY SPECIAL DESK... THAT'S MOST IMPORTANT OF ALL! SET IT OVER THERE, BOYS!

I EXPECT EVERY EMPLOYEE AT THE MEETING... SO THAT EVEN INCLUDES YOU, I'M SORRY TO SAY!
AHA! GETTIN' SOME SENSE, EH?
WALT DISNEY

BEEBLE ORDERS A SPECIAL MEETING OF THE HOTEL EMPLOYEES, THE PURPOSE OF WHICH IS UNKNOWN TO ALL BUT MICKEY, WHO CONCOCTED THE SCHEME!

TO EXPLAIN LATER DISCLOSURES, MICKEY STARTS OUT BY TELLING OF A $10,000 ROBBERY IN THE HOTEL THREE YEARS BEFORE!

ALL RIGHT! BUT WHAT'S A ROBBERY THREE YEARS OLD GOTTA DO WITH SPOOKS NOW?
I'M COMIN' TO THAT!
12-5

Y' SEE, THE ONLY SUSPECT IN THE CASE HAPPENED TO BE A GUEST HERE! HE WAS HELD, BUT THEY COULDN'T FIND THE MONEY ON HIM!

AW, THEM SMALL-TIME COPS! SHOULD 'A HAD ME ON TH' CASE!

ANYWAY.. THE IMPORTANT POINT IS THIS... THE SUSPECT OCCUPIED THESE SAME THREE ROOMS...
THE HAUNTED ONES!
OH, MY STARS!
WALT DISNEY

MICKEY REVEALS THAT THE SUSPECT IN THE OLD ROBBERY WAS LIVING IN THE NOW FAMOUS THREE HAUNTED ROOMS!

WOT FINALLY BECAME O' THIS YEGG THEY COULDN'T GET TH' GOODS ON?
HE WAS SENT UP AND SERVED A TERM FOR ANOTHER CRIME! AND HERE'S A VERY IMPORTANT POINT...
12-6

...WHILE IN PRISON, HE STUDIED THEATRICALS! HE BECAME AN EXPERT ON MAKE-UP AND WAS ESPECIALLY GOOD...

...AT CLEVER DISGUISES!
OHH! I MUS' GO! I CHUST NOW T'INK OF MY KANOODLE ZOUP!

OH, YEAH? SIDDOWN, YOU! NOBODY'S TAKIN' A POWDER ON ME!
BUT... MY KANOODLE ZOUP! IT ISS RUIN'!

YOU'RE SO DANGED SMART... WHAT'S THIS BIRD WITH HIS DISGUISES GOTTA DO WITH US?
YES.. I DON'T SEE...!
I'LL TELL YOU, MR. BEEBLE...!
12-7

...AT LEAST ONE OF THE EMPLOYEES HERE HAS BEEN EXPECTIN' THIS GUY TO RETURN IN SOME UNRECOGNIZABLE DISGUISE!

THE REASON BEING THAT THIS EMPLOYEE KNOWS THAT THE $10,000 IS STILL HIDDEN IN ONE OF THE THREE ROOMS WHERE THE CROOK DITCHED IT!

SO.. WHEN ANYONE UNUSUAL TAKES THOSE ROOMS, WHAT HAPPENS? A LITTLE SPOOK SHOW, CAREFULLY PLANNED TO SCARE HIM OUT!
HUMPH! WHO'S GOIN' TO B'LIEVE THAT TOMMYROT?

MICKEY REVEALS THAT ONE OF THE HOTEL'S EMPLOYEES KNOWS THAT THE MISSING $10,000 IS STILL CONCEALED WHERE THE FIRST ROBBER HID IT THREE YEARS BEFORE!

Mickey's demonstration settles beyond all doubt how the ghosts have been produced, by means of two movie projectors!

WELL, BEEBLE, THESE FINE ROGUES WON'T BE TROUBLIN' Y' NO MORE!
THANKS TO HIM, THE PESKY LITTLE SNOOPER!
YEAH... WE WUZ DOUBLE-CROSSED!
12-16

JUST A MINUTE, CHIEF! BEFORE Y' TAKE AWAY THAT PHONY DICK, I'VE GOT ONE MORE PIECE OF BUSINESS!

YOU'LL REGRET THIS, BEEBLE!

THERE! THAT TAKES CARE OF EVERYTHING!
NOT QUITE! MR. BEEBLE... THIS IS NOT THE $10,000! THAT MONEY IS STILL MISSING!

YOU MEAN, THAT... THAT PACKAGE... IS NOT THE MISSING CASH?
NO! IT'S JUST A DUMMY I PLANTED TO TRAP THE CROOKS!

THEN... IN SPITE OF ALL YOU'VE DONE, I'M LOST! I'LL STILL HAVE TO MAKE GOOD THE TEN THOUSAND!
12-17

UNLESS WE CAN FIND THE REAL PACKET, WHEREVER IT WAS HIDDEN BY THAT "SLIPPERY SAM" WHAT'S-HIS-NAME...

...OH, YEH... SNICKLEFRITZ!
SNICKLEFRITZ? SAY! I REMEMBER, NOW... IT'S ALL COMIN' BACK TO ME!
WALT DISNEY

THIS SAM SNICKLEFRITZ ..WHAT DO Y' KNOW ABOUT HIM, HORTENSE?
LET ME THINK... IT WAS THREE YEARS AGO HE STAYED HERE WASN'T IT?
12-18

YES, BUT WHAT...?
I RECALL HIM... HE WAS HAN'SOME ... WORE FINE CLOTHES...!
NEVER MIND THAT, WOMAN! WHAT HAPPENED?

WELL... THE DAY HE LEFT, HE SAID HE'D COME BACK SOMETIME, AND HE GAVE ME A PACKAGE TO KEEP FOR...!
A PACKAGE!!

...I'VE BEEN DUSTIN' IT OFF EVERY DAY, EXPECTIN' HIM TO...!
GET IT, WOMAN... GO GET IT!
QUICK, HORTENSE! WHERE IS IT?
WALT DISNEY

THE CHAMBERMAID HAS JUST RECALLED THAT THE MYSTERIOUS SAM SNICKLEFRITZ LEFT A PACKAGE IN HER CARE THREE YEARS AGO!

LAND OF LONG AGO

DECEMBER 23, 1940
–
APRIL 12, 1941

LAST OF THE (STONE AGE) GOLDEN AGE

A nightmare after overeating sounds like a mundane experience. Things get more interesting, however, when a character in the nightmare challenges you to an astounding adventure—and promises you an airplane by morning if you dare to accept his invitation. But your jaw truly *drops* when you wake up and find there's *really* an airplane in your backyard as promised, with sealed orders attached!

You open the envelope; the orders say that you must fly blindfolded to a secret destination—and of course, at this point you just respond "forget it," as most people would. The challenge is just too weird, too dangerous now. But there's one person who instead jumps for joy at the assignment and is ready to depart immediately: Mickey Mouse, of course, once again showing that adventure is part of his DNA.

"Land of Long Ago" is perhaps the last great Golden Age adventure of our Mouse: the last story plotted by Gottfredson that perfectly meshes realism and thrills—even if some quasi-magical plot elements require a stronger suspension of disbelief than before. Professor Dustibones can enter Mickey's dream; his plane can take off almost vertically; an island hosts live dinosaurs, and so forth. We have moved from the logical weirdness of "Blaggard Castle" (1932) to an adventure that is slightly less rational—but at the same time more humorous, as in a sequence where Dustibones' plane dodges midair obstacles by itself.

The core plot idea owes much, of course, to Arthur Conan Doyle's influential 1912 novel, *The Lost World*—likely mediated through the 1925 movie of the same name that Gottfredson, as a former projectionist, was certainly familiar with. Conan Doyle's powerful and evocative tale inspired many sequels and remakes, from the 1960 and 2001 *Lost World* movies to—more loosely speaking—*King Kong* (1933), *Godzilla* (1954), and even Crichton's *The Lost World: Jurassic Park* (1997).

Of course, Gottfredson and De Maris put their own original spin on the theme. Mickey is the resourceful hero who can get out of major trouble with a combination of endurance, wits, and time-honored agility (the February 28, 1941, strip directly recalls an earlier scene in 1937's "Island in the Sky"). Mickey even manages to repair a damaged airplane and build a bomb from raw chemical elements, defying danger and death in order to rescue Dustibones. Despite all of Mickey's successes, however, his intellectual curiosity leaves him unsatisfied in the end—at the thought that Cave-Man Island will remain unknown to the larger world. Having escaped alive wasn't enough. That's our Mickey.

"Land of Long Ago" dates from 1941, when World War II was already raging but the United States was not yet involved. Roosevelt was still fighting the isolationism of those who preferred not to get involved with international politics. "Long Ago" is perhaps the Mickey strip's last "innocent" adventure, untainted by echoes of war;[1] it is thus quite appropriate that it should be set in a forgotten, prehistoric place.

—Leonardo Gori and Francesco Stajano

1 For an alternate reading that perceives some wartime imagery in "Long Ago," see Thomas Andrae's foreword in this volume.

BOY...THAT WAS SURE A SWELL FEED CLARABELLE DISHED UP FOR MINNIE AND ME! ONLY I WISH I HADN'T EATEN **QUITE** SO MUCH!
12-23

I HOPE I'M NOT GONNA HAVE NIGHTMARES! SURE MADE A PIG OF MYSELF...!

...CLARABELLE'S FAULT FOR BEIN' SUCH A GOOD COOK... ROAST HAM... APPLE SAUCE...CREAM PIE...AND CREAM PIE...CREAM-M-M ...MM-M--Z-Z-Z-Z...

GOOD EVENING!
UH... WH.. WHAT..?
WALT DISNEY

Z-Z-Z...DID..MM-M ...DID SOMEONE SPEAK?
I JUST SAID, GOOD EVENING!
12-24

MM-M...OH! PARDON ME ...GOOD EVENING!
PERMIT ME TO INTRODUCE MYSELF...PROFESSOR DUSTIBONES, CHAIR OF SCIENCE, DRYUPP UNI-VERSITY!

GLAD TO...KNOW YOU, PROFESSOR! WHAT CAN I DO FOR...

GOOD GOSH! ARE YOU REAL?
QUITE REAL, YOUNG SIR, I ASSURE YOU! BUT DO NOT BE ALARMED...MY VISIT IS A FRIENDLY ONE!

JUST A MINUTE! YOU CLAIM I'M NOT DREAMIN'...BUT IF NOT, HOW DID **YOU** GET IN MY ROOM?
MY MISSION CALLS FOR EXTREME SE-CRECY...YOU MUST PARDON MY UNCONVENTIONAL... ER, APPROACH!
12-25

HMM...DID Y' SAY WHO Y' WERE...?
DEEPING DUSTIBONES, DOCTOR OF SCIENCE! ALLOW ME TO SAY THAT **YOUR** REPUTATION IS WELL-KNOWN TO ME!

MY REPUTATION??
...AS A YOUNG MAN WHO REVELS IN THE UNUSUAL ...ONE TO WHOM DANGER IS A CHALLENGE... ADVENTURE AN INVITATION...!

AHEM...THANKS! BUT, MAYBE YOU'D BETTER...SORTA GET DOWN TO BUSINESS!
AH...QUITE SO! LISTEN CLOSELY, FOR WHAT I HAVE TO SAY WILL ASTOUND YOU!
WALT DISNEY

THE STRANGE SCIENTIST OFFERS MICKEY A CHANCE TO JOIN AN EXPEDITION IN AN UNKNOWN LAND OF MYSTERY!

THE FOLLOWING MORNING!

FEELING SURE HIS EXPERIENCE THE NIGHT BEFORE WAS JUST A DREAM, MICKEY IS KNOCKED FOR A LOOP BY THE DISCOVERY OF AN AIRPLANE IN HIS BACK YARD!

WH-WHY...IT'S **EXACTLY** LIKE THE PROFESSOR SAID...! COULD IT BE I **WASN'T** DREAMING..?
12-30

...OR MAYBE I'M **STILL** ASLEEP ...**OUCH!** NO, I'M AWAKE, ALL RIGHT!

NOPE, IT'S NOT AN ILLUSION, EITHER!
TAP TAP

AND...WELL, I'LL BE DARNED! HERE'S EVEN THE SEALED INSTRUCTIONS HE WARNED ME ABOUT!
Sealed Orders, to be opened only by Mr Mickey Mouse, in person!
WALT DISNEY

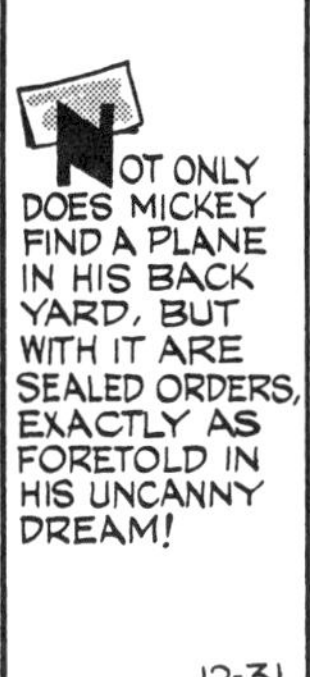
NOT ONLY DOES MICKEY FIND A PLANE IN HIS BACK YARD, BUT WITH IT ARE SEALED ORDERS, EXACTLY AS FORETOLD IN HIS UNCANNY DREAM!
12-31

SURE ENOUGH...SIGNED BY PROFESSOR DUSTIBONES! "TAKE ONE ASSISTANT WITH YOU AND PILOT THIS PLANE AS INSTRUCTED I AM FLYING A SECOND PLANE AND WILL MEET YOU..."

When you gain enough altitude you must both be blindfolded.
F' GOSH SAKES! **BLINDFOLDED???**

don't be alarmed, this is a most unusual ship and will guide itself safely by radio beam. Follow all instructions to the letter. Do not delay

DELAY? DOC, OLD BOY, I'M PRACTIC'LY IN THE AIR **RIGHT NOW!**
WALT DISNEY

ELATED OVER THE PROSPECTIVE ADVENTURE, MICKEY HOTFOOTS IT TO GOOFY'S HOUSE WITH THE BIG NEWS!

I MIGHT AS WELL TAKE HIM! NOBODY ELSE WOULD BELIEVE MY STORY AND IT WOULD TAKE TOO LONG TO CONVINCE 'EM!
1-1

...AND THEN THIS QUEER OLD PROFESSOR SAID HE'D PICKED **ME** TO GO TO THIS MYSTERIOUS LAND! ALL THIS IN THE DREAM, GOOFY!
PURTY GOOD, ALL RIGHT... BUT I'VE DREAMED BETTER ONES!

BUT WAIT! THIS MORNING THE PLANE WAS **THERE** ...JUST AS HE SAID IT WOULD BE!
IN YER BACK YARD, HUH?

WELL, THAT'S MIGHTY DUMB DREAMIN'...THERE'S NO ROOM TO TAKE **OFF** THERE!
!

IS THAT ALL YUH COME OVER FER...
JEST TO TELL 'BOUT YER DREAM?! AN' ME SO BUSY LIKE I AM!
DON'T Y' SEE, GOOFY ...THIS DREAM WAS LIKE IT WAS REAL!
AND I'M ACTUALLY GOING ON THE TRIP!

AW, YOU'RE GOIN' DAFFY, THAT'S WHUT! YUH CAN'T GO TO THEM PLACES YUH DREAM ABOUT, 'CAUSE WHEN YOU'RE AWAKE THEY AIN'T NO SECH PLACE!
1-2

I'M GLAD I'M NOT SO DOPEY AS TO B'LEEVE...!
ALL RIGHT... OKAY! WHAT I CAME OVER FOR... DO YOU WANTA GO ALONG, OR DON'T YOU?

HUH? WHY, SURE, MICKEY... I'LL BE GLAD TO! WHEN DO WE START?
RIGHT AWAY! I JUST GOTTA SAY G'BYE TO MINNIE!
WALT DISNEY

...THIS PROF DUSTIBONES WOULDN'T TELL ANY MORE... SAID IT WAS VERY SECRET, BUT...!
ALL THIS IN THE DREAM, OF COURSE!
1-3
Copr. 1941, Walt Disney Productions
World Rights Reserved

YES! AND THEN THIS MORNING...!
I KNOW...LO AND BEHOLD, THERE WAS THE AIRPLANE, ALL FITTED OUT AND READY TO GO! JUST LIKE A MIRACLE!

THAT'S RIGHT! HOW'D Y'...??
MICKEY MOUSE, THAT'S THE MOST OUTRAGEOUS, FLIMSIEST EXCUSE TO GET AWAY YOU'VE EVER STUFFED ME WITH! GO AHEAD

... SEE IF I CARE!
BUT...!
NOT ANOTHER WORD!
Distributed by King Features Syndicate, Inc.
WALT DISNEY

AFTER HIS HASTY FAREWELL TO MINNIE, MICKEY IS BACK HOME READY TO TAKE THE AIR! CO-PILOT GOOFY IS ALSO ON DECK, RARIN' TO GO!

MIGHTY SLICK-LOOKIN' JOB, MICKEY! MUST BE A DE-LOOX '41!
IT'S GOT SOME UNUSUAL FEATURES ...BUT ALL I ASK IS THAT IT FLIES!
1-4

DARNED IF I SEE HOW WE CAN TAKE OFF IN THIS SPACE, BUT SOMEBODY LANDED IT HERE!
LOOKS TO ME LIKE WE'RE GONNA DO SOME FENCE BUSTIN'!

UH... GAWRSH...!!
YIPPEE!! CLEAN AS A WHISTLE!

GAWRSH! DURNED IF WE DIDN'T TAKE OFF RIGHT INTO TH' AIR!
AND HOW! OLD DOC DUSTIBONES WASN'T FOOLIN' WHEN HE SAID WHAT THIS CRATE COULD DO!
1-6

WHUT'RE WE DOIN' NOW, MICKEY?
JUST GAININ' ALTITUDE! ACCORDING TO INSTRUCTIONS, AFTER WE REACH A CERTAIN HEIGHT, THE PLANE PICKS UP A RADIO BEAM!

YEAH? AN' WHUT HAPPENS THEN?
THEN WE BLINDFOLD OURSELVES... AND LET THE SHIP FLY ITSELF!
IT'S TO KEEP IT SECRET WHERE WE'RE HEADED FOR!

YEAH, WELL, NOBUDDY'S BLINDFOLDIN' **ME**... HEY!?? SUMPIN'S WRONG!
WE'RE **STOPPED**... IN THE AIR... LIKE SOMEBODY THREW ON THE **BRAKES**!

WHUT'S WRONG, MICKEY? WHY'D SHE STOP?
I DON'T KNOW! THE MOTOR'S STILL RUNNIN', ONLY...

...ONLY THE SHIP'S OUTA **CONTROL!** CAN'T SEEM TO STEER...!!
1-7

WHEE-EE! WE'RE GOIN' **NOW** ...LIKE A BLUE STREAK!
IT'S THE RADIO BEAM! THE SHIP'S ON IT, FLYIN' **ITSELF**! AND **WHAT** A BEAM... IT PLAYS TUNES!
SCRUB ME, MAMA, WITH A BOOGIE BEAT...

WITH THE PLANE AT THE RIGHT ALTITUDE AND ZOOMING ALONG BY THE MUSICAL RADIO BEAM, MICKEY PREPARES THE BLINDFOLDS, AS PER THE SEALED ORDERS!
1-8

NO, SIREE! Y'AIN'T GITTIN' **ME** TO FLY LIKE A BAT! IF I GIT KILT, I WANNA KNOW WHUT DONE IT!
BUT WE'RE UNDER ORDERS, GOOFY.. WE **HAFTA**...!
HOT PATOOTIE, WITH A JIM JAM JIVE!
Copr. 1941, Walt Disney Productions World Rights Reserved

OH, YEAH? WELL, **I** AIN'T AGREED! ANYWAY, HOW'LL THUH DOC EVER **KNOW**?

FOLLOW INSTRUCTIONS **EXACTLY**, PLEASE, OR RISK SERIOUS DISASTER!
THE **PROFESSOR'S** VOICE!
WOZZAT?

YESSIR, YESSIR! I WUZ ONLY FOOLIN', SIR!
Distributed by King Features Syndicate, Inc.

HOURS PASS, AND THE LITTLE AIRPLANE DRONES ON, GUIDED ONLY BY A RADIO BEAM THAT SPECIALIZES IN SWING MUSIC!

1-10

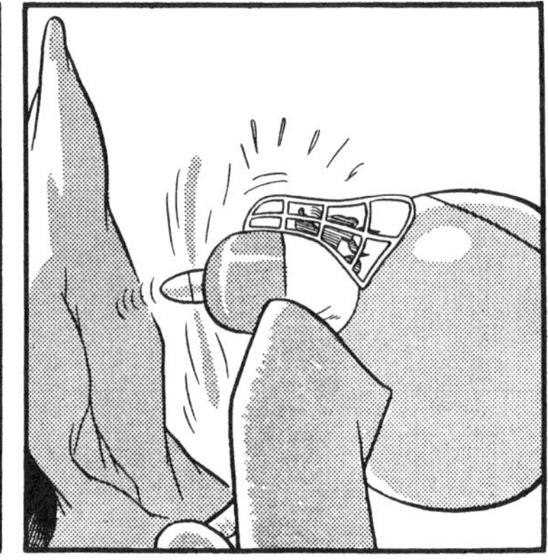

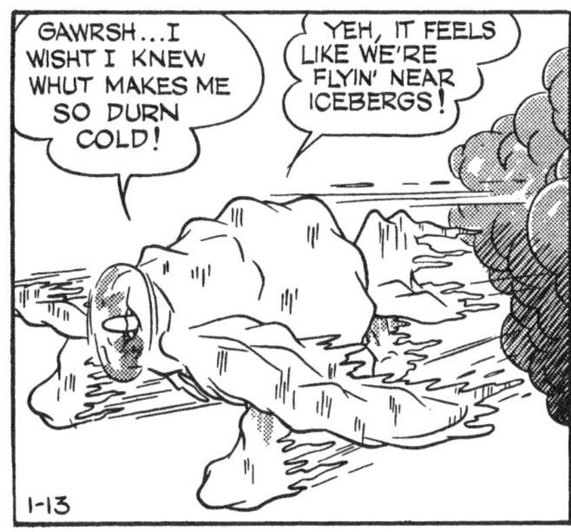

COMING TO AN AREA OF TROPICAL HEAT, THE VOYAGERS ARE OVERJOYED TO HEAR THE PROFESSOR'S VOICE OVER THE RADIO, TELLING THEM TO REMOVE THE BLINDFOLDS!

1-14

FOLLOWING THE PROFESSOR'S ORDERS, MICKEY HEADS THE PLANE FOR A VOLCANIC ISLAND RISING FROM AN UNKNOWN TROPICAL SEA!

1-15

WITH THE LITTLE PLANE POISED ABOVE A VOLCANIC ISLAND, AS DAYLIGHT FADES, MICKEY GETS FINAL INSTRUCTIONS FROM THE PROFESSOR!
1-16

...YOUR POSITION IS FINE! NOW, PUT THE SHIP INTO A POWER DIVE... IT'S THE ONLY WAY TO LAND IT!
HUH... WOZZAT??
OUCH! WELL, HERE GOES... HANG ONTO YOUR HAT!
Copr. 1941, Walt Disney Productions World Rights Reserved

HEY... DOES HE TELL US WHEN TO COME OUT OF IT?
THAT'S ONE ORDER I WON'T WAIT FOR!

BRAVO! WELCOME, MY FRIENDS, TO DUSTIBONES MANOR!
WHEW...!
MADE IT, B'GAWRSH!
WALT DISNEY

SUCCESS! LANDING THE PLANE IN THE CRATER OF AN EXTINCT VOLCANO, MICKEY AND GOOFY ARE GREETED BY PROFESSOR DUSTIBONES!
1-17

Y' WEREN'T FOOLIN' WHEN Y' SAID YOU'D FOUND SOMETHING UNUSUAL!
AH! YOU HAVE SEEN NOTHING, YET!
Copr. 1941, Walt Disney Productions World Rights Reserved

I WON'T GO INTO DETAILS, NOW! YOU'LL FIRST NEED A NIGHT OF REPOSE!
SLEEP'S ALL I NEED, THANKS!

MY RETAINER WILL PREPARE YOUR BEDS!
OOMPA! GLUG IB-BOO-BOO!

DON'T BE ALARMED! A CAVE MAN... BUT EXCELLENTLY TRAINED!
UH... A CAVE MAN!!?
ULP...!

Y' MEAN HE'S A REAL CAVE MAN... LIKE IN THE STONE AGE?
YES, BUT QUITE HARMLESS! I'LL EXPLAIN IN THE MORNING, BUT YOU MUST WANT TO GET SOME REST NOW!

JUST FOLLOW MY MAN... HE'LL FIX YOUR BEDS!
UH.. DON'T BOTHER... I AIN'T TIRED NO MORE!
1-18

AW, C'MON, GOOFY... GO TO SLEEP, WILL Y'?
ALL RIGHT... I WILL GO TO SLEEP...

!
...BUT I'M KEEPIN' MUH EYES OPEN, JEST THUH SAME!

REFRESHED FROM A NIGHT'S SLEEP IN THE CAVE BEDROOM, MICKEY WAKES NEXT MORNING. GREETED BY THE AFFABLE PROF. DUSTIBONES!
1-20

I'M GLAD YOU SLEPT WELL, MY FRIEND! AND WHERE IS YOUR PARTNER?
HE MUST'VE GONE OUT! PROB'LY PROWLIN' AROUND TO SEE WHAT SORTA COUNTRY IT IS!

DEAR DEAR...HE REALLY SHOULDN'T HAVE! THERE ARE CERTAIN PERILS ABOUT THAT...!
HALP!!

HALP, MICKEY! HALP! WAKE ME UP...!
?
Distributed by King Features Syndicate, Inc.

...I'M HAVIN' A NIGHTMARE!
WALT DISNEY

WAKE ME UP, QUICK! I'M HAVIN' A NAWFUL NIGHTMARE!
HELP, PROFESSOR!
1-21

DOWN, BRONTO! DROP THAT!

FORTUNATE THAT HE ENCOUNTERED ONE OF OUR YOUNG AND GENTLE SPECIMENS... ALSO A VEGETARIAN!

G-GAWRSH... IT WUZ REAL!
FOR PETE'S SAKE! WHAT KINDA WORLD IS THIS?
COME INSIDE... I'LL EXPLAIN, WHILE WE HAVE BREAKFAST!
Distributed by King Features Syndicate, Inc.

BEFORE Y' EXPLAIN THIS PLACE, PROFESSOR, TELL ME WHY I THOUGHT I WAS DREAMING THAT FIRST NIGHT!
A LITTLE SECRET INVENTION OF MINE... A HARMLESS DRUG I GAVE YOU IN YOUR SLEEP!

IT TEMPORARILY WOKE YOU UP, BUT GAVE THE ILLUSION THAT YOU WERE DREAMING!
BUT WHY? WHAT WAS THE OBJECT?

SECRECY! IN CASE YOU WERE NOT INTERESTED IN MY PLAN, THE NEXT MORNING THERE WOULD HAVE BEEN NO AIRPLANE...!
OH, I GET IT! I'D JUST THINK THE WHOLE BUSINESS WAS A DREAM!
1-22

'SCUSE ME, DOC, BUT HOW 'BOUT EXPLAININ' THAT! IT'S GIVIN' ME NERVOUS FRUSTRATION!

OH, DON'T BE AFRAID OF OOMPA! HE IS MERELY A PLEISTOCENE PRIMITIVE!
OH, YEAH? WELL, I NEVER KNOWED **ONE** O' THEM GUYS YUH COULD TRUST!
Copr. 1941, Walt Disney Productions World Rights Reserved
1-23

YOU MEAN, PROFESSOR, THAT THIS COUNTRY HAS **ACTUAL** STONE-AGE MEN?
EXACTLY! AND THIS SPECIMEN I HAVE EVEN TAUGHT SOME OF OUR LANGUAGE! **OOMPA!**

UG-GLUG...MASTER... TALKY.. ME..? UG!
SO! HE TALKS ENGLISH, HUH? THA'S DIFFRUNT!

LOOK... YUH SAWED-OFF, TURNIP-EARED BABOON...I KIN LICK **YOU** AND YER HULL **FAMBLY**... BLIND-FOLDED!
WALT DISNEY

WHY, IT SEEMS **IMPOSSIBLE!** CAVE MEN HAVE BEEN EXTINCT FOR... FOR GOSH KNOWS **HOW** LONG!
IN ALL **KNOWN** PARTS OF THE WORLD... YES!
1-24
Copr 1941, Walt Disney Productions World Rights Reserved

AND THAT **HUGE** ANIMAL, THE... THE WHATCHAMACALLIT ...ARE THERE ANY **MORE** LIKE HIM?
YOU MEAN THE BRONTOSAURUS? COME... FOLLOW ME!

THAT SCENE, MICKEY, AS SCIENCE KNOWS IT, IS **200,000,000 YEARS AGO!** BUT THERE IT IS...**TODAY!**

WELL, CAN Y' TIE THAT!!? A WHOLE HERD OF **REAL** DINOSAURS ...**ALIVE!**
YES, MICKEY... ALIVE, AND IN THEIR NATURAL STATE!
1-25
Copr. 1941, Walt Disney Productions World Rights Reserved

INCREDIBLE ...BUT THAT'S THE SECRET OF THIS LAND! **EVERYTHING** HERE IS IN THE CONDITION OF THE WORLD **MILLIONS OF YEARS AGO!**

NOW THAT YOU KNOW THE SITUATION, CAN YOU GUESS THE PURPOSE OF MY EXPEDITION?
UH..NO, SIR...NOT EXACTLY!
Distributed by King Features Syndicate, Inc.

WE'RE GOING TO TAKE A LIVE DINOSAUR BACK TO CIVILIZATION!
YIPPEE!!! THAT'S A **WOW** OF A STUNT!
WALT DISNEY

WHAT I DON'T SEE, PROFESSOR, IS **HOW** Y'CAN TRANSPORT A DINOSAUR!
IT **IS** A BIG UNDERTAKING ...BUT WAIT TILL YOU SEE WHAT I'M WORKING ON!
1-27

OF COURSE, YOU KNOW THAT THE ONLY WAY OUT OF HERE IS BY AIR!

I'M STILL PUZZLED! NO PLANE COULD CARRY ONE OF **THOSE** BABIES!
NO, NOT A PLANE...!

BUT HERE YOU ARE... THE DINOSAUR AIR EXPRESS!
OH, BOY! A BLIMP!

AN AIRSHIP TO CARRY A DINOSAUR ...THAT'S A **SWELL** IDEA!
YOU MAY WONDER WHY I DIDN'T FLY A SHIP FROM HOME INSTEAD OF BUILDING IT HERE!
1-28
Copr 1940, Walt Disney Productions World Rights Reserved

THERE'S A REASON... TROPICAL WINDS IMPOSSIBLE TO GET THROUGH WITH A BULKY AIRSHIP! THESE CURRENTS BLOW **AWAY** FROM THE ISLAND...!

THAT'S WHY I COULDN'T BRING A SHIP **HERE**, BUT **CAN** FLY IT BACK THE OTHER WAY!
I SEE! THEN IT LOOKS LIKE OUR **BIG** JOB IS TO CATCH A DINOSAUR AND GET HIM ABOARD!
OH, YEAH? YUH THINK **THAT'S** A BIG JOB...?

...GITTIN' **ME** ON THUH SAME SHIP WITH THUH CRITTER IS **REALLY** DOIN' SUMPIN'!
WALT DISNEY

DO Y' WANT US TO GO TO WORK NOW, PROFESSOR?
I'M NOT QUITE READY! OOMPA AND I FIRST HAVE TO SET UP SOME INSTRUMENTS FROM THE SUPPLIES YOU BROUGHT!

OH, THAT EXPLAINS THE BIG ROUND FUSELAGE...IT WAS STORAGE SPACE!
YES... CONSTRUCTED TO CARRY AS MUCH AS POSSIBLE!
1-29

WHILE WE'RE NOT NEEDED, COULD WE... SORTA EXPLORE AROUND A LITTLE?
ALL RIGHT! BE CAREFUL, THOUGH... AVOID THE **VICIOUS** BEASTS!

UH... AVOID THUH... ULP! UH.. DON'T KNOW IF I KIN GO, MICKEY... M' ARCHES JEST FELL!
WALT DISNEY

EAGER TO SEE MORE OF THE UNBELIEVABLE ISLAND, MICKEY UTILIZES HIS SPARE TIME IN EXPLORING THE NEARBY COUNTRY!
1-30

JUST THINK OF IT, GOOFY ...EVERY PLANT AND ANIMAL HERE IS JUST AS THEY WERE MILLIONS OF YEARS AGO!
I DON'T MIND PLANTS THAT OLD, BUT I'D FEEL SAFER IF TH' ANIMALS WUZ YOUNGER!
JUST WATCH OUT FOR DINOSAURS THAT MIGHT BE DANGEROUS!
DINERSORES... THAT'S THEM GUYS AS BIG AS A BARN AND THEY GOT LEATHERY HIDES?

YEH, THAT'S RIGHT!
OH... THEN I FEEL BETTER! THIS FELLER THET'S BEEN TRAILIN' US...

...HE'S PURTY SMALL, AN' GOT FUR ON 'IM!
GOOD GOSH! A SABER-TOOTHED TIGER!
WALT DISNEY

RUN, GOOFY! IT'S A SABER-TOOTHED TIGER!
KIN THEY CLIMB TREES?
1-31

I DON'T... KNOW... YET!

NO, THEY CAN'T!! WHEW... WE'RE SAFE!

MICKEY! L-LOOK WHUT'S...!!
OMIGOSH!!
WALT DISNEY

G-GAWRSH... A FLYIN' CROCODILE!
IT'S A D-DEROTAC... A PTERODACTYL!
2-1

GOOD NIGHT ... WE'RE DONE FOR!

WELL, FOR...!!?
ARRR.. PHTTT!!
YIPE!

I'LL BE GAWRSH-DURNED! IT WUZ THUH TIGER HE WUZ SORE AT!
WHAT A BREAK! LET'S US BE GETTIN' OUTA HERE!
WALT DISNEY

LET'S GIT BACK TO CAMP, 'FORE WE MEET ANY MORE TIGER-TOOTHED SABERS!
OH, WHY WORRY? I'M GETTIN' TOO BIG A KICK OUT OF BEING IN A PREHISTORIC LAND!
2-3

JUST THINK... ANYTHING CAN HAPPEN HERE! THIS COUNTRY IS BACK IN THE AGE OF VOLCANOS ...GEYSERS... EARTHQUAKES...

...UH..UH ...EARTHQUAKES...!
G-GAWRSH!

WELL, F'R... IT'S JUST DINOSAURS PLAYIN'!
WALT DISNEY

DAWGGONE! THEM WHATCHAMASAURUSES GIVE ME THUH WILLIES! LET'S GIT BACK TO CAMP!
THEY'RE NOT SO DANGEROUS! PROF. DUSTIBONES TOLD ME THEY'RE MOSTLY VEGETARIANS!
2-4

YEAH? WELL, THAT'S DIFF'RUNT ...I AIN'T SKEERED OF 'EM, THEN! SHUCKS ...I'M NO HEAD O' LETTUCE!

?
UH.. ULP...!

!

I THOUGHT Y' WEREN'T SCARED OF 'EM ANY MORE!
I AIN'T! ONLY...THUH WAY THAT ONE LOOKED AT ME, I COULD TELL HE ET MEAT WITH HIS VEG'TABLES!
WALT DISNEY

BOY! ISN'T HE A WHOPPER? THAT'S THE KIND WE OUGHTA CAPTURE TO TAKE HOME!
I STILL SAY IT AIN'T POSSIBLE TO KETCH ONE O' THEM BRUTES!
2-5

HEY! WHERE YUH GOIN'?

OOOPH!

DAWGGONE...YUH GOT 'IM, MICKEY! I DIDN' THINK YUH COULD DO IT!
WALT DISNEY

SLIPPING FROM THE EDGE OF A CLIFF, MICKEY TUMBLES ONTO THE BACK OF A HUGE BRONTOSAURUS PASSING BY! GOOFY MISUNDERSTANDS THE SITUATION ...SLIGHTLY!
2-6

NICE GOIN', MICKEY! YUH CAUGHT 'IM SINGLE-HANDED!

WOW! IF I FALL... IT'S JUST... TOO... BAD!

END OF THE LINE! HERE'S WHERE I GET OFF!

G-GOSH! NOW IT'S SEA SERPENTS!
WALT DISNEY

MICKEY CONGRATULATES HIMSELF TOO SOON! DIVING FROM THE BRONTOSAUR'S BACK, HE IS MENACED BY PREHISTORIC SEA MONSTERS!
2-7

SOMEPN'S GOTTA BE DONE IN A HUR...BLE-UBBLE-UBBLE...!
SNAP!
SNAP!
SNAP!

YIPPEE! IT WORKED!
SNAP! SNAP! SNAP!

THAT WAS A CLOSE CALL! BUT HOW AM I GONNA GET **AWAY** FROM THOSE BRUTES ?

LOOK, BRONTY! NICE CABBAGE... YUM-YUM!
2-8

SO LONG, BOYS! SEE Y' NEVER!

NICE GOIN', OLD FELLOW! TAKE YOUR SALAD...AND WELCOME!
Distributed by King Features Syndicate, Inc.

HEY, WHAT'S THE IDEA...COMIN' BACK TO CAMP WITHOUT ME?
WELL, THERE WUZ WORK TO BE DID! I CAN'T BE FOOLIN' AROUND WITH THEM OVERSTUFFED WOMBATS!
2-10
Copr. 1941, Walt Disney Productions World Rights Reserved

YOUR FRIEND DOESN'T SEEM TO APPRECIATE OUR ANIMAL LIFE, MICKEY!

I LIKE ANIMULES! BUT THUH TROUBLE WITH THIS COUNTRY... THERE'S TOO MANY DYNAMITORUSES...

...AN' NOT ENUFF RABBITS!

THOSE SEA SERPENT THINGS THAT ATTACKED ME... WHAT WERE THEY, PROFESSOR?
PROBABLY PLESIOSAURS... A VERY BLOODTHIRSTY MARINE LIZARD!
2-11

IN THIS LAND IT IS WELL TO KNOW THE DANGEROUS BEASTS FROM THE MILDER ONES! FOR INSTANCE... THE BRONTOSAURUS, STEGOSAURUS AND TRICERATOPS...

...THEY ARE RELATIVELY HARMLESS... AS ARE THE DIPLODOCUS AND THE PROTOCERATOPS, DO YOU SEE?
THE DIP... THE PROTO... OH, SURE!

BUT WATCH OUT FOR MOSASAURUS, AND ABOVE ALL, IF YOU ENCOUNTER TYRANNOSAURUS REX, BE VERY CAREFUL!
YES, SIR! THANKS... I WILL!

AS TIME FLITS BY, CONSTRUCTION OF THE DINOSAUR TRANSPORT SHIP ROLLS SMOOTHLY ALONG!

WHENEVER WORK IS SLACK, MICKEY ROAMS THE ISLAND, MAKING NEW DISCOVERIES ALL THE TIME!
WONDER WHAT I CAN SEE FROM THE TOP OF THESE CLIFFS!
2-12

WELL, I'LL BE DARNED! CAVE-MEN... JUST LIKE OOMPA!

I DON'T SUPPOSE THEY CAN TALK, BUT MAYBE BY SIGN LANGUAGE I CAN...
WOOPS! OH-OH!

SOMETHING TELLS ME THEY DON'T WANTA MAKE FRIENDS!
Distributed by King Features Syndicate, Inc.

WOW! THERE'S MORE DIFFERENT WAYS TO GET KILLED IN THIS COUNTRY!
2-13

MAYBE I SHOULD'VE STAYED AT HOME WITH A GOOD BOOK!

LATER... BACK AT THE BASE!

OH... THE CAVE-MEN! I FORGOT TO WARN YOU THEY MIGHT BE DANGEROUS! YES, THEY COULD BE!
AND **HOW** THEY COULD!

BUT THEY'RE AFRAID OF ME... SEEM TO REGARD ME AS SOME SORT OF GOD!
I COME A LITTLE LOWER IN THE SCALE! THEY REGARD **ME** AS SOME SORT OF SOUP MEAT!

?
HOW COME, PROFESSOR, THAT THE WILD MEN ON THIS ISLAND THINK YOU'RE SOME SORT OF A GOD?
WELL... THE AIRPLANE MYSTIFIED THEM TO BEGIN WITH...
2-14

...THEN, OF COURSE, ALL THIS MACHINERY AND CONSTRUCTION SEEMS SUPERNATURAL TO THE PRIMITIVE MIND! AND LUCKY FOR ME, TOO!

IF THOSE SAVAGES WERE **ENEMIES**, I'D BE... BEG PARDON?
'SCUSE ME, DOC, BUT THAT HEATHEN OF YOURN ...I DON'T LIKE THUH WAY HE'S ACTIN'!

BOOLA-MA-GOOBER BEEG COME MUCH BAD WUK-WUK!
SKOOB **MUCH BAD!**
HE'S TRYING TO SAY HE FEELS BIG TROUBLE COMING! SOME KIND OF DISASTER IN THE AIR!
Distributed by King Features Syndicate, Inc.

BOOLA-MA-GOOBER...MUCH BAD!
I DON'T LIKE OOMPA'S FOREBODING OF DISASTER! SAVAGES ARE LIKE ANIMALS...THEY **FEEL** THINGS!
OH, I WOULDN'T WORRY! HE MAY JUST FEEL A THUNDERSTORM COMING!
2-15

ANYHOW, A FEW DAYS MORE AND OUR AIRSHIP WILL BE COMPLETE! THEN WE'LL LEAVE HERE... WITH THE STRANGEST CARGO EVER CARRIED!

BR-R-RUMBLE...
BOOM!
OH-OH! IS THAT THUNDER?

R-R-ROAR...
BOOM...
KA-RASH!
GREAT CAESAR! A PALEOZOIC EARTHQUAKE!!
WALT DISNEY

AS MICKEY AND HIS PARTY ARE ON THE WAY BACK TO THEIR CAMP IN THE CLIFFS, THEY ARE THROWN INTO A PANIC BY A TERRIFIC EARTHQUAKE!

BOOM!
KA-RASH!
GET OUT IN THE OPEN TILL IT PASSES!
RUN, GOOFY! GET AWAY FROM THE WALL!
2-17
Copr. 1941, Walt Disney Productions
World Rights Reserved

IS IT... DO Y' THINK IT'S OVER WITH?
PERHAPS... UNLESS THERE IS A SECOND SHOCK!

BOOM-A-R-RRIP...
BAM!
BLAM!
HALP, MICKEY! THINK UP SUMPIN', QUICK!
WALT DISNEY
Distributed by King Features Syndicate, Inc.

HALP! WHERE KIN WE GO?
WE CAN'T GO ANYWHERE! THE QUAKE'S ALL AROUND US!
Copr. 1941, Walt Disney Productions
World Rights Reserved

LOOK!
STAMPEDING DINOSAURS... THEY'RE HEADED RIGHT FOR US!
2-18

PROFESSOR!

WALT DISNEY

IN THE NICK OF TIME MICKEY HAS SAVED PROF. DUSTIBONES FROM BEING TRAMPLED BENEATH STAMPEDING DINOSAURS, FRIGHTENED BY THE 'QUAKE!

I DON'T KNOW HOW TO THANK YOU, MICKEY! THAT WAS A MIGHTY CLOSE SHAVE!
PHEW! CLOSE IS RIGHT!
2-19
Copr. 1941, Walt Disney Productions
World Rights Reserved

WELL, THANK GOODNESS, THE 'QUAKE SEEMS TO BE OVER... SAY! OUR AIRSHIP...!!
JUST WHAT I WAS GOING TO ...AND OUR MACHINERY!

C'MON! LET'S KNOW THE WORST!

OMIGOSH! LOOK WHAT IT DID TO OUR BIG GATE!
OH-H... THIS IS AWFUL!
WALT DISNEY
Distributed by King Features Syndicate, Inc.

I TREMBLE TO THINK WHAT THAT EARTHQUAKE MAY HAVE DONE TO OUR EQUIPMENT!
MAYBE IT WASN'T SO BAD INSIDE!
Copr. 1941, Walt Disney Productions World Rights Reserved

PERHAPS THE CLIFFS PROTECTED...
OWOOO!!
2-20

OF ALL THE TERRIBLE LUCK... JUST WHEN OUR BLIMP WAS NEARLY FINISHED!
THIS... THIS IS HOPELESS! WE'RE RUINED!
GAWRSH!
Distributed by King Features Syndicate, Inc.
WALT DISNEY

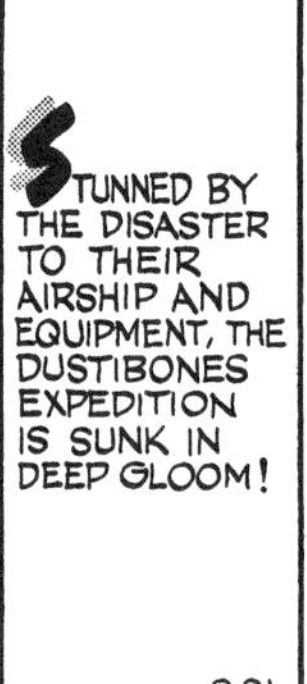
STUNNED BY THE DISASTER TO THEIR AIRSHIP AND EQUIPMENT, THE DUSTIBONES EXPEDITION IS SUNK IN DEEP GLOOM!
2-21

I CAN HARDLY BELIEVE IT! MY WHOLE EXPEDITION A TOTAL LOSS!
JUST WHEN EVERYTHING WAS GOING SO SWELL, TOO!

EEE-E-E... YAKKLE... OWW!!
GOOD GOSH! WHAT...??

EEE-E-E... YARR-R... AWP!!!
CAVE-MEN!
AND BLOODTHIRSTY, TOO... THAT'S THEIR HUNTING CRY!
Distributed by King Features Syndicate, Inc.
WALT DISNEY

EEE-E-E... YARR-R... AWP!
LET'S GET OUT OF HERE... THOSE SAVAGES MEAN BUSINESS!
Copr. 1941, Walt Disney Productions World Rights Reserved

WAIT! HERE'S OOMPA!
UG, MASTER, GO LAM JIBBER WOO GLUB-BLOOD, MUCH BAD MOOLA WUP...!
2-22

...JIBBER-UG YAKKLE POW-POW...!
HE SAYS THE CAVE-MEN BLAME US FOR THE EARTHQUAKE AND INTEND TO KILL EVERY ONE OF US!

TO OUR CAVE! WE CAN DEFEND OURSELVES THERE!
Distributed by King Features Syndicate, Inc.
WALT DISNEY

NOT BAD ENOUGH THAT AN EARTHQUAKE HAS DESTROYED THEIR NEARLY COMPLETED AIRSHIP, MICKEY'S PARTY IS BLAMED BY THE SAVAGES AS THE **CAUSE** OF THE QUAKE!
2-24

WOW! THOSE GUYS ARE REALLY MAD AT US!
IF WE CAN REACH OUR CAVE... WE MAY BE ABLE TO FIGHT THEM OFF THERE!
Copr. 1941, Walt Disney Productions World Rights Reserved

PROFESSOR! WE HAVEN'T **GOT** A CAVE... THE EARTHQUAKE WRECKED IT, TOO!

SCATTER... IT'S OUR ONLY CHANCE! EVERY MAN FOR HIMSELF!
WALT DISNEY

IN A DESPERATE EFFORT TO ESCAPE THE ATTACKING CAVEMEN, MICKEY, GOOFY AND THE PROFESSOR SCATTER IN THREE DIFFERENT DIRECTIONS!

DOGGONE! THESE MONKEYS ARE GONNA BE TOUGH TO SHAKE!
2-25
Copr. 1941, Walt Disney Productions World Rights Reserved

OWW! THEY GOT MUH!

EEE-E-E... YAKKLE...!

THE GOSH DARN APES HAVE A ONE-TRACK MIND... AND I'M STILL ON THE TRACK!
WALT DISNEY
Distributed by King Features Syndicate, Inc.

DOGGONE IT! CAN'T I EVER SHAKE THESE BLOODTHIRSTY MUGGS?
Copr. 1941, Walt Disney Productions World Rights Reserved
2-26

MAYBE THEY CAN BE DISCOURAGED A LITTLE!

Distributed by King Features Syndicate, Inc.

KNOCKED **ONE** OF 'EM COLD... BUT THE OTHER TWO ARE STILL COMIN', MEAN AS EVER!
WALT DISNEY

OMIGOSH! I'M CORNERED!
2-27

BOY! WAS THAT CLOSE!.. BUT THEY HAVEN'T GOT ME... YET!
WALT DISNEY

GOODNIGHT! I'M A GONER... UNLESS...!!?
2-28

THAT BABY'LL GO HOME WITH A HEADACHE! BUT... GOLLY! STILL ONE LEFT... AND I'M ...ABOUT... ALL IN!
WALT DISNEY
Distributed by King Features Syndicate, Inc.

GOSH! I'M ALL IN... AND THAT APE... NEVER TIRES!
3-1

IF HE DOESN'T GIVE UP SOON... I'LL HAVE TO...!

...CAN'T GO ...ANOTHER ...STEP!

EEE-E-E... YAKKLE ...YAKKLE! YOW-W-OOO!
IT... LOOKS LIKE... CURTAINS!
WALT DISNEY

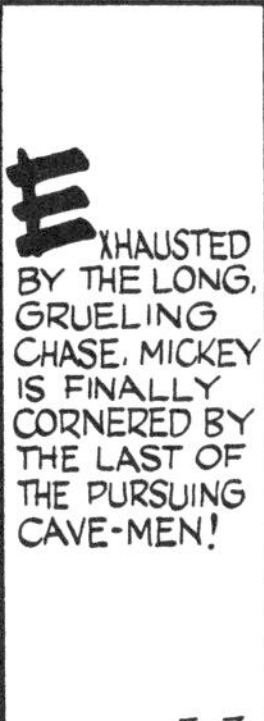
EXHAUSTED BY THE LONG, GRUELING CHASE, MICKEY IS FINALLY CORNERED BY THE LAST OF THE PURSUING CAVE-MEN!
3-3

EEE-E-E... YAKKLE ...YAKKLE! YOWW-OOO!
JUST KEEP ON CROWIN' AND MAYBE I'VE GOT A CHANCE!

?!
!?

?!?
Distributed by King Features Syndicate, Inc.

WALT DISNEY

OH, BOY...HE'S GOIN' RIGHT ON PAST!
3-4
Copr. 1941, Walt Disney Productions World Rights Reserved

...AND NOT COMIN' BACK, IF I CAN HELP IT!

THAT'S THAT!
YEEE-E-OWWW

AT LAST! REST ...AND... PEACCCE....
Distributed by King Features Syndicate, Inc.

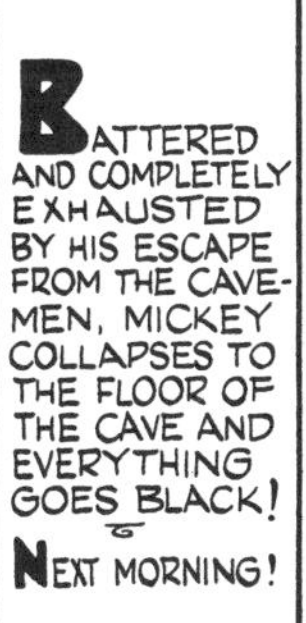
BATTERED AND COMPLETELY EXHAUSTED BY HIS ESCAPE FROM THE CAVE-MEN, MICKEY COLLAPSES TO THE FLOOR OF THE CAVE AND EVERYTHING GOES BLACK!
NEXT MORNING!

OWOOOO... MY HEAD...DID ANYONE GET THE NUMBER OF THAT TRUCK? WHERE... WHERE AM I...??

G-G-GOSH, I...I'M NOT DREAMING... IT ALL MUST BE REAL!...THE EARTHQUAKE...THE CAVEMEN ATTACKING US... ...US??
Copr. 1941, Walt Disney Productions World Rights Reserved

...US! MY GOSH, I'M ALONE! THE CAVEMEN GOT GOOFY AND PROFESSOR DUSTIBONES!
3-5

I DON'T KNOW HOW, BUT SOMEHOW I'VE GOT TO FIND OUT WHAT HAPPENED TO 'EM ...M-MAYBE IT'S STILL NOT TOO LATE...!
WALT DISNEY

I'VE GOT TO FIND OUT WHAT HAPPENED TO GOOFY AND THE PROFESSOR! MAYBE IT'S NOT TOO LATE... OH-OH!... THE CAVEMEN! I'LL HAVE TO HIDE OUT 'TIL NIGHT!

I WON'T BE MUCH HELP TO THEM IF I GET CAU...
OUCH!
3-6

THAT SETTLES IT! I'VE GOT TO HAVE SHOES! BUT WHERE CAN I GET SHOES IN THIS COUNTRY? HAVEN'T GOT A KNIFE TO SKIN AN ANIMAL EVEN, IF I DID...

...TRAP ONE, AND I DON'T KNOW OF ANY THAT COME WITH ZIPPERS AND...
OH-OH!

AH HAH-H-H!

THIS ISN'T AS SIMPLE AS SHOPPING FOR A SPRING OUTFIT BACK HOME, BUT I'LL BET IT GETS RESULTS! NOW FOR A LITTLE WINDOW SHOPPING!
3-7

DOES MADAME RECOMMEND THE GOWN THE PLUMP MANNEQUIN IS MODELING? AH, SHE DOES!

NOW, I'LL NOT ONLY HAVE SHOES, BUT A SUIT...UH...TAILORED BY MICKEY MOUSE IN PERSON!

POOR GOOFY AND PROFESSOR DUSTIBONES! I HOPE IT'S NOT TOO LATE TO HELP THEM ... IF THE CAVEMEN GOT THEM ... BRRR... I'D BETTER NOT THINK ABOUT THAT!
© Copr. 1941, Walt Disney Productions World Rights Reserved
3-8

DOGGONE EARTHQUAKE CAUSED ALL THE TROUBLE...SMASHED OUR DIRIGIBLE ...RUINED OUR EQUIPMENT ...AND TURNED THE CAVEMEN AGAINST US!

THERE'S NOTHING LEFT BUT TO TRY TO ESCAPE ALIVE... BUT FIRST I'VE GOT TO FIND OUT FOR SURE WHAT HAPPENED TO GOOFY AND...
OH-OH!
Distributed by King Features Syndicate, Inc.

THE CAVEMEN CAPTURED THEM ALL RIGHT, BUT... BUT DID THEY CAPTURE THEM...... ALIVE?!!
WALT DISNEY

BACK AT THE SCENE OF THE ORIGINAL FRACAS, MICKEY FINDS GLOOMY EVIDENCE THAT HIS FRIENDS WERE EITHER KILLED OR CAPTURED!

REALIZING IT IS GOING TO REQUIRE A PLANNED CAMPAIGN, IF IT IS POSSIBLE AT ALL TO RESCUE HIS PALS, MICKEY HAS HAD TO FIND A SAFE HOME TO WORK FROM!

HAVING FOUND A SAFE CAVE TO HIDE AWAY IN, MICKEY'S NEXT URGENT PROBLEM IS FOOD! THAT NIGHT HE SALLIES FORTH!

MICKEY SPENDS A BUSY NIGHT, COMBING THE ISLAND FOR PROSPECTS OF FOOD! NEXT MORNING...

NOTHING WRONG WITH THIS... GRILLED TROUT A LA PRIMEVAL!
3-17

FRIED EGG AU GIGANTICUS! 'COURSE, I **SHOULD** BE FOUR GUYS TO EAT THIS... BUT I'M KINDA HUNGRY!

BOY... WAS I SURPRISED TO FIND THESE OVERSTUFFED STRAWBERRIES! I DIDN'T THINK THERE WAS ANY FRUIT ON THE WHOLE ISLAND!
Distributed by King Features Syndicate, Inc.

...NO DANGER OF STARVIN', ANYWAY! NOW, A LI'L SLEEP 'TIL NIGHT, THEN I'LL GET BUSY... B-U-S-Y... BZZ-Z-Z-Z-Z
...N-N-N
WALT DISNEY

PEPPED UP AGAIN BY FOOD AND SLEEP, MICKEY SALLIES FORTH AT NIGHTFALL, EAGER TO FIND A MEANS OF RESCUING HIS PALS!

HAFTA BE SURE AND LEAVE THE LATCH STRING OUT, SO I CAN GET BACK!
3-18
Copr. 1941, Walt Disney Productions World Rights Reserved

THE FIRST THING TO FIND OUT IS WHETHER OUR AIRPLANES HAVE BEEN RUINED BEYOND ALL REPAIR!

DOGGONE IT! NOT A CHANCE OF **THAT** CRATE EVER TAKIN' THE AIR AGAIN!

BUT THIS ONE'S NOT SO BAD! BY GOLLY... WITH A LITTLE WORK AND SOME PARTS OFF THE OTHER MACHINE, THIS BABY CAN **FLY!**
WALT DISNEY

YES, SIR... JUST GIVE ME TIME AND I CAN PUT THIS CRATE IN FLYIN' CONDITION!
Copr. 1941, Walt Disney Productions World Rights Reserved
3-19

...BUT WHAT ABOUT **GAS?** PROBABLY OUR WHOLE SUPPLY WAS LOST IN THE 'QUAKE!

NO, BY GOLLY! EXCEPT FOR A FEW DENTS, THESE DRUMS ARE AS GOOD AS NEW! BOY! NOW I CAN GET TO WORK!

FIRST THING IS TO STRAIGHTEN OUT THIS... GOOD NIGHT, I **CAN'T!** ONE "KLUNK" AND THERE'D BE FIVE HUNDRED CAVE MEN ON MY NECK!
Distributed by King Features Syndicate, Inc.
WALT DISNEY

HIDING OUT DURING THE DAY AND WORKING NIGHTS, MICKEY IS GRADUALLY GETTING THE WRECKED PLANE INTO SHAPE WHERE HE HOPES IT WILL FLY!

3-21

TELL ME, GOOFY... WHAT HAPPENED? HOW'D Y' GET AWAY FROM THE CAVE MEN... AND WHERE'S PROFESSOR DUSTIBONES?
HIM? OH, HE'S STILL A PRISONER, I GUESS!
Copr 1941, Walt Disney Productions World Rights Reserved

BUT HOW DID **YOU**...?
AW, I GOT TIRED O' THUH PLACE THUH FOOD WUZ TURRIBLE!

BUT...??
WELL, THEY GOT KINDER KEERLESS IN WATCHIN' ME LAS NIGHT SO I JEST LIT OUT!
I NEVER DID **LIKE** THEM PEOPLE, ANYWAYS!
3-24
Distributed by King Features Syndicate, Inc.

GOOFY! HOW'D Y' GET **IN** HERE? IT'S IMPOSSIBLE! THE VINE WAS ON THE OTHER SIDE OF THE CLIFF AND **NOBODY** COULD GET IN!
COULDN'T THEY? OH...I DIDN'T KNOW ABOUT THAT!
WALT DISNEY

HERE'S WHY I CAN'T UNDERSTAND HOW Y' GOT IN! SEE THIS VINE?
UH-HUH!
Copr 1941, Walt Disney Productions World Rights Reserved

WHEN I CAME BACK IT WAS FASTENED ON THE **OTHER SIDE** ...YOU **COULDN'T** HAVE USED IT!
NO, I DIDN'T! SHOULD I?
3-25

SHOULD YOU? IT'S THE **ONLY** WAY TO GET IN!
OH! WELL, I COME UP THUH FIRE-ESCAPE!

SEE WHUT I MEAN?
GOOD GOSH! HAS THAT LADDER BEEN THERE ALL THE TIME?
WALT DISNEY
Distributed by King Features Syndicate, Inc.

ALL THE TIME I THOUGHT I WAS SO SAFE. **ANYBODY** COULD'VE COME UP THAT LADDER! WHEW!
Copr 1941, Walt Disney Productions World Rights Reserved
3-26

NOW, WHAT WE'VE GOTTA DO IS GET THAT PLANE READY AS QUICK AS WE CAN, AND RESCUE THE PROFESSOR!
MAYBE HE DON'T WANTER BE RESCUED 'TIL AFTER THUH PARTY!

PARTY? WHAT DO Y' MEAN, GOOFY?
SURE! THE CAVE MEN ARE PLANNIN' ONE FOR US! THAT'S ONE REASON I LEFT...I **HATE** PARTIES!
Distributed by King Features Syndicate, Inc.

QUICK, GOOFY...TELL ME ALL YOU KNOW! THERE'S SOMETHIN' BEHIND THIS!

C'MON, GOOFY...EXPLAIN YOURSELF! WHAT'S THIS ABOUT THE CAVE MEN PLANNIN' A PARTY FOR YOU AND THE PROFESSOR?
SURE, THEY WERE ... A REG'LAR JAMBOREE!
3-27

BUT HOW DID Y' KNOW? YOU DON'T UNDERSTAND THEIR LINGO!
WELL, YUH SEE, THIS HERE HUT WHERE THEY WUZ KEEPIN' US, HAD A LOTTA PITCHERS PAINTED ON THUH WALLS...!

PICTURES... YES, GO ON!
...AND THESE MONKEYS WOULD POINT TO THUH PITCHERS AN' JABBER ... THEN
THEY'D POINT TO US, SEE?

GOOFY...CAN YOU DESCRIBE EXACTLY WHAT WAS IN THESE PICTURES?
OH, SURE... LEMME THINK A MINUTE ...!
WALT DISNEY
Distributed by King Features Syndicate, Inc.

LE'S SEE...YUH WANTER KNOW WHAT WUZ PAINTED ON THEM WALLS WHERE THUH CAVE MEN HAD US!
YES! WHAT MADE Y' THINK THEY WERE PLANNIN' A PARTY FOR YOU AND THE PROFESSOR?
3-28

WELL, THEY WUZ ALL PITCHERS OF FOLKS CELEBRATIN' WITH FEASTS AN' ALL THAT! SINGIN' AN' DANCIN'... YOU KNOW!

IN ONE SCENE, A COUPLA BIG BRUISERS WERE AMUSIN' THUH GUESTS BY TOSSIN' A GUY INTO A VOLCANO, IT LOOKED LIKE! AND EVER'BODY CHEERIN'!
OWOO! JUST WHAT I WAS AFRAID OF!

PERSON'LY, I WOULDN'T BE A GUEST AT THAT KINDA PARTY... IT AIN'T HUMANE!
GOOFY...CAN'T Y' SEE? YOU WEREN'T MEANT TO BE A GUEST!
WALT DISNEY
Distributed by King Features Syndicate, Inc.

OF COURSE, THUH CAVE MEN WERE FIXIN' THUH PARTY FER US! AIN'T I TOLE YUH HOW THEY'D POINT AT THUH PITCHERS, THEN AT DOC AN' ME?
SURE... BUT DON'T Y' UNDERSTAND ...?
3-29

...THOSE SAVAGES BLAME US FOR THE EARTHQUAKE... THEY THINK WE MADE THEIR GODS ANGRY! THAT PAINTING YOU SAW OF THE MAN BEING THROWN INTO A VOLCANO.. ...!

...THAT WAS A PICTURE OF A SACRIFICE TO APPEASE THE GODS! NOW, DO Y' SEE?
ULP... YUH MEAN...??
Distributed by King Features Syndicate, Inc.

EXACTLY! YOU WERE LUCKY ENOUGH TO ESCAPE...BUT THE POOR PROFESSOR...!
G-GAWRSH! SUMPIN'S GOTTA BE DID!
WALT DISNEY

REALIZING FROM GOOFY'S STORY THE URGENCY OF THE PROFESSOR'S PLIGHT, MICKEY RACKS HIS BRAINS FOR A WAY TO SAVE HIM!
3-31

EVEN NOW IT MAY BE TOO LATE! THOSE APES MAY HAVE SACRIFICED HIM ALREADY!

GOOFY, WAS THERE ANY WAY YOU COULD TELL FROM THOSE CAVE-MEN WHEN THEY INTENDED TO...?
TO BUMP US OFF? NO, I DON'T B'LEEVE...!

HOLD ON! THAT EXECUTION PITCHER I TOLE YUH 'BOUT HAD A FULL MOON IN IT THET THUH MONKEYS KEPT POINTIN' AT!
THAT EXPLAINS IT, GOOFY... THAT'S WHAT THEY'RE WAITIN' FOR!

AND IT GIVES US ABOUT THREE MORE NIGHTS TO GET OUR PLANE IN SHAPE! LET'S GET SOME REST, FOR WE'RE GONNA BE MIGHTY BUSY!
WALT DISNEY

WITH ONLY THREE NIGHTS BEFORE THE FULL MOON, MICKEY AND GOOFY WORK FEVERISHLY TO GET THEIR WRECKED PLANE IN FLYING CONDITION.
4-1

B'GAWRSH... I THINK SHE'S FITTIN', MICKEY!
I THINK SO, TOO! I ONLY WISH WE COULD TEST THE MOTOR, BUT THE NOISE WOULD BE TOO RISKY!

NOW SHOW ME WHERE THE CAVE-MEN'S VILLAGE IS!
KEEP GOIN'...BUT BEAR OVER TO THUH STEEPEST CLIFFS! THAT'S WHERE THUH SENTRIES AIN'T!
Copr. 1941, Walt Disney Productions World Rights Reserved

SO THAT'S THE LAYOUT! WHERE HAVE THEY GOT THE PROFESSOR?
IN THUH LONG THATCHED HUT THERE IN THUH CENTER!

GOT ANY IDEAR HOW WE KIN RESCUE THUH POOR DUFFER?
I THINK I HAVE! FOLLOW ME ...WE'RE GOIN' DOWN TO THE SULPHUR PITS!
WALT DISNEY
Distributed by King Features Syndicate, Inc.

HERE'S THUH SULPHUR YUH WANTED! WHAT'S THAT WHITE STUFF YUH GOT THERE?
THIS IS POTASH!
Copr. 1941, Walt Disney Productions World Rights Reserved
4-2

NOW WE MIX THEM TOGETHER ...VERY CAREFULLY!

...THEN ADD A FEW ROCKS!
BUT HOW IN THUNDER IS THIS GONTER RESCUE DOC DUSTIBONES?

THIS, OLD BOY, DROPPED IN THE RIGHT PLACE, MAY DO WONDERS! IT'S A BOMB!
THAT...A BOMB? WELL... KIN Y' IMAGINE ...?!
WALT DISNEY
Distributed by King Features Syndicate, Inc.

Working like beavers, Mickey and Goofy manage to get their plane ready the night before the full moon!

SCATTERING THE CAVE MEN BY THE EXPLOSION OF HIS HOME-MADE BOMB, MICKEY CIRCLES BACK TOWARD THE HUT WHERE THE PROFESSOR IS A PRISONER!

G-GAWRSH, MICKEY... YUH CAN'T LAND AT THIS SPEED!
BRACE YOURSELF, GOOFY... I'M NOT GOING TO LAND!
4-7

YIPPEE! WE GOT HIM!
WALT DISNEY CO.

IN YUH COME, DOC!
4-8

YOU PERFORMED A MIRACLE, MY BOY! I DIDN'T THINK IT POSSIBLE TO ESCAPE FROM THOSE DREADFUL SAVAGES!
A MIGHTY CLOSE CALL FOR ALL OF US, SIR!

DOGGONE IT, I'D STILL LIKE TO HAVE ANOTHER TRY AT BRINGING HOME A DINOSAUR! WOULDN'T YOU, PROFESSOR?
PERHAPS... SOME DAY! RIGHT NOW, I'VE HAD ENOUGH!
AS FER ME, THE FARTHEST I KIN GIT FRUM THET ISLAND IS TOO DURN CLOST!
WALT DISNEY CO.

AND NOW FOR HOME! WHICH WAY, PROFESSOR?
I'LL SET THE COURSE FOR YOU, THEN ALL YOU'LL HAVE TO DO IS STAY ON IT!
4-9

NOW, SINCE I'M NOT NEEDED, I'LL TAKE A LITTLE NAP! VERY...TIRED...!
YES, SIR... GO RIGHT AHEAD!

POOR OLD DUFFER...HE SURE CORKED OFF IN A JIFFY!
YEH! MUSTA BEEN ALL TUCKERED OUT!
Z-Z-Z Z-Z..

A DAY AND NIGHT PASS AND STILL THE PROFESSOR SLEEPS ON! THEN, SUDDENLY...

WHERE AM I? WHAT AM I DOING ON A PLANE... AND WHO ARE YOU?
W-WHA-WHAT??
Distributed by King Features Syndicate, Inc.
WALT DISNEY

WHAT IS THE MEANING OF THIS? WHY AM I ON A PLANE ...AND WEARING THESE RAGS?
PROFESSOR! DON'T Y' REMEMBER...?
4-10

OF COURSE, I REMEMBER! I'M DUSTIBONES... CHAIR OF SCIENCE... DRYUPP UNIVERSITY! AND I'M DUE IN CLASS THIS VERY MINUTE!

GAWRSH... MAGNESIA!
THIS IS AN OUTRAGE! I'LL HAVE YOU ARRESTED FOR KIDNAPING!
BUT, PROFESSOR! THIS IS YOUR PLANE! HAVE YOU FORGOTTEN THE ISLAND... THE CAVE MEN...?

MY PLANE... ISLAND... CAVE MEN... FIDDLE FADDLE! TAKE ME TO THE UNIVERSITY... AT ONCE!
Y-YES, SIR!
WALT DISNEY

WITH PROFESSOR DUSTIBONES A VICTIM OF AMNESIA AND REMEMBERING NOTHING OF THE EXPEDITION, MICKEY LANDS THE PLANE AND TELLS HIS STORY TO THE DEAN OF DRYUPP UNIVERSITY!

YES, HE HAS HAD THESE LAPSES BEFORE, BUT USUALLY HIS MEMORY RETURNS!
I DIDN'T KNOW, SIR! AFTER ALL THIS TERRIBLE EXPERIENCE HE STILL THINKS HE NEVER WENT AWAY!
GOODNESS ME! ALL THIS NONSENSE WHEN MY CLASS IS WAITING FOR ME!
4-11

WELL, IT IS NOT TOO SERIOUS...WE CAN STILL SEND ANOTHER EXPEDITION, WITH FULLER EQUIPMENT!
BUT...WITHOUT PROF. DUSTIBONES, WHO KNOWS THE WAY?

WHY, AH... DON'T YOU?
NO, SIR! BUT I SUPPOSE THE UNIVERSITY HAS A CHART OR SOMETHING THAT THE PROFESSOR MADE!
Distributed by King Features Syndicate, Inc

EH? WELL...AH...WE SHOULD HAVE, BUT...I'M AFRAID THAT'S A LITTLE OVERSIGHT WE, AH...!
OH! THAT'S TOO BAD!
WALT DISNEY

DEAR, DEAR ME! THE RAREST SPOT ON THE FACE OF THE EARTH ...AND NO ONE KNOWS HOW TO GET THERE!
UNLESS THE PROFESSOR RECOVERS HIS MEMORY!
FIDDLE FADDLE! ALL THIS TALK...
4-12

...DINOSAURS...CAVE MEN... NONSENSE! YOUNG MAN, YOU SEEM TO MEAN WELL, BUT I'M TOO BUSY TO BE BOTHERED WITH THIS FICTION!

ALL RIGHT, SIR, I'LL BE GOING! BUT I'M GLAD TO HAVE KNOWN YOU...AND WISH IT COULD HAVE TURNED OUT BETTER!
THANK YOU! YOUR TALE IS INTERESTING... IF I HAD MORE TIME!

SO HE NEVER COME TO, HUH? WELL, WHAT DO WE DO NOW?
I GUESS WE TAKE THE TRAIN FOR HOME! BUT, GOSH... IF WE COULD ONLY HAVE GONE BACK TO THE ISLAND AGAIN... OH, WELL!
?
WALT DISNEY

APRIL 14, 1941
–
JULY 5, 1941

MINNIE'S REVOLT

If any narrative during Floyd Gottfredson's "Golden Age" deserves the label of a guilty pleasure, then "Love Trouble" is it. A drawing-room comedy of manners on the order of the contemporary film *The Philadelphia Story* (1940), "Love Trouble" at first seems to fly in the face of all that made the *Mickey* strip great during the 1930s. Faraway vistas and lost treasures are set aside in favor of social "one-upmouse-ship" and catty verbal fencing.

But seen from another perspective, Minnie's rebellion against her established role in Mickey's life hands Mickey a challenge every bit as significant as those he has faced in foreign climes. For this dauntless he-Mouse, a social challenge is a different breed of cat—or rodent.

The impetus for a story like "Love Trouble" had been simmering for quite a while. As early as 1937, Minnie's characterization had regularly evinced an amplified concern with image and social status. In 1941, Gottfredson and scripter Merrill De Maris cleverly lit a long-burning fuse at the start of "Land of Long Ago," with a splenetic Minnie attacking Mickey for going off on yet another far-ranging adventure. It is not too surprising that she should consider a new boyfriend in his absence.

The caddish Montmorency Rodent, a far better realized character than the comparatively crude Mortimer of *Mickey's Rival* (1936), is a "social antagonist" without peer. Rather than use Mickey as a butt of clumsy jokes, Monty displays a distinct talent for putting Mickey in awkward social situations. This line of attack initially flusters Mickey before he decides to fight back in kind, with new girl "Millicent Van Gilt-Mouse" at his side.

Though Minnie can't be faulted for using the available tools—jealousy and social humiliation—to assert her own identity, there's no question that the depiction of female wiles and whims in "Love Trouble" has not aged particularly well. A good number of strips mid-story are taken up with a string of relentlessly bitchy gags in which the two mouse-gals butt heads. Minnie comes off the worse in these exchanges, but Millicent's tart tongue is also far from attractive. Though repetitive, however, the gags do serve a useful purpose. We can see the tide gradually turning against Minnie in each back-and-forth, culminating in "humiliation"—when Minnie's invitation to the Van Astorocks' party comes about entirely thanks to Millicent's social status.

At the party, Monty's pseudo-sophistication runs aground on the shores of the real thing; but we'll leave the exact details for you to discover as you read.

Of course, the conclusion of "Love Trouble" is foreordained; we know that Mickey and Minnie are fated to get back together, just as Dexter and Tracy wound up remarried at the end of *The Philadelphia Story*. Given the nature of Mickey's and Minnie's conflict, it would be a little misleading to state that getting to that conclusion is "half the fun." But it's the next best thing.

—Christopher E. Barat

ALMOST HOME, B'GAWRSH! WONDER IF ANYBUDDY KNOWS WE'RE A'COMIN'?
MINNIE DOES! I WIRED HER WHEN WE STARTED!

SHE'S ALWAYS SO TICKLED TO SEE ME BACK, I KNEW SHE'D WANTA MEET THE TRAIN!
4-14

I ONLY HOPE SHE DOESN'T GET MUSHY! KINDA EMBARRASSING IN FRONT OF...!
HEY... WE'RE PULLIN' IN!

THAT'S FUNNY... SHE DOESN'T SEEM TO BE HERE! I DON'T UNDERSTAND...!
WELL, FER A GAL THET'S SO GLAD TO SEE YUH, I'LL SAY SHE AIN'T TOO MUSHY!
BURBAN
WALT DISNEY

WELL, S'LONG, SPORT! DON'T TAKE IT TOO HARD, 'CAUSE YER GAL DIDN'T MEET THUH TRAIN! THEY'RE ALL FICKLE, YUH KNOW!
OH, NOT MINNIE! UH...PROB'LY HAD A SICK RELATIVE. OR...MAYBE DIDN'T GET MY WIRE... YEH, THAT'S IT!
4-15

I KNOW! SHE THOUGHT IT WOULD BE MORE COZY GREETING ME AT HOME! GOOD OLD MINNIE!

OH, IT'S... GOOD AFTERNOON, MICKEY!
HELLO! I CAME STRAIGHT HERE... JUST GOT BACK IN TOWN, Y'KNOW...!

OH! HAVE YOU BEEN AWAY?
HAVE I B...?? UH-ULP...!

Y'MEAN...ULP...Y' FORGOT I'D BEEN AWAY? I GUESS Y' DIDN'T GET MY WIRE EITHER?
HMM...YES, I DO RECALL A TELEGRAM! BUT REALLY, MY TIME IS SO TAKEN UP...!
4-16

UH...WON'T YOU COME IN...FOR A WHILE?
WHY, SURE, MINNIE! I KNOW YOU'RE DYIN' TO HEAR ALL ABOUT MY ADVENTURE!

IT ALMOST SEEMS LIKE A DREAM TO ME NOW, IT'S SO...!
PLEASE, MICKEY... SOME OTHER TIME! I HAVE A DATE THIS AFTERNOON!

LA-DE-DA... PAH...
BOOP-BEEP-BEEP!
OH! THERE'S THE DEAR BOY, NOW!
THE... THE WHO!??
WALT DISNEY

LA-DE-DA...PAH...
BOOP-BEEP-BEEP!
OH, THAT'S MONTY'S CAR!
W-WHO'S MONTY?
4-17

LAHDY-Y-DOOP-BEEP-BEEP!!

C-O-M-E-IN!!

AH, MY BEAUTEOUS BABE!
SMACK!
SMACK!
SMACK!
SMACK!
OH, MONTY... YOU SAY THE CUTEST THINGS!
WALT DISNEY

OKAY, TOOTS...LET'S TODDLE!
BRRHMPH...AHEM!
OH... EXCUSE ME!
4-18

I'D LIKE TO PRESENT MONTMORENCY RODAWN! THIS IS MICKEY MOUSE!
HOW D' DO!
AH...THE EX-BOY FRIEND! HOW WERE YOU? HA-HA-HA!

PARDON ME... I DIDN'T CATCH YOUR LAST NAME! HOW DO Y' SPELL IT?

R-O-D-E-N-T... RODAWN, STUPID!
I THOUGHT SO!

YOU'RE SURE IN THE GROOVE, BABY... LOOK LIKE A MILLION!
OH, MONTY ...YOU'RE SO CUTE!
UH...HOW ABOUT TONIGHT, MINNIE?
4-19

OF COURSE, WE'LL GO OUT TONIGHT AND CELEBRATE... UH.. MY JUST GETTIN' HOME ..AN' ALL...!
YOU SEEM TO FORGET THAT I MIGHT HAVE OTHER OBLIGATIONS OF A SOCIAL NATURE!

BUT, MINNIE... I THOUGHT...!
GOOD-BYE!
R-RRRRRR-ROARR

NOT TAKING MINNIE'S NEW "CRUSH" TOO SERIOUSLY, MICKEY BOUNCES BACK NEXT AFTERNOON WITH ALL HIS OLD-TIME PERKINESS!
AFTER ALL, WHAT'S THAT BOZO GOT THAT I HAVEN'T?
...EXCEPT A SPORTY CAR, AND...GOSH-DARN, HE'S HERE AGAIN! OH, WELL...!
4-21

H'LO, MINNIE... I BROUGHT YA LITTLE...!
OH, YES...THANK YOU!
HI YA, JASPER! BEEN ROBBIN' ASH-CANS AGAIN? HA-HA-HA!

MONTY, YOU SAY THE **CLEVEREST** THINGS!
WALT DISNEY

IF YOU'D LIKE TO DANCE, MONTY, I HAVE SOME **LOVELY** NEW RECORDS!
DELIGHTED! I'LL CLEAR THE FLOOR!
!
4-22

HERE'S A PERFECTLY **THRILLING** RHUMBA!
THE HOTTER, THE BETTER, BABE!

OH, MONTY, YOU DANCE **DIVINELY!**
SO THEY TELL ME! MUST BE FROM MY TRAVELS IN SOUTH AMERICA!

YOU CUT A WICKED RUG YOURSELF, TOOTS!
WALT DISNEY

OOOO-O-O... AREN'T YOU **STRONG!** I ADORE **MASTERFUL** MEN!
4-23

CLICKETY CLACK CLICK!

WHAT AM I DOIN', LETTING THAT CLOWN BEAT MY TIME, ANYHOW?

C'MON, MINNIE, LET'S SHOW 'IM SOME **REAL** FANCY STEPPIN'!
OUCH! YOU DON'T HAVE TO BE SO **BRUTAL** ABOUT IT!
WALT DISNEY

WELL, WELL ... NICE GOIN', WILBUR! I'VE ALWAYS WONDERED WHAT THE TURKEY TROT LOOKED LIKE!
4-24

WOOPS! PARDON ME!
OH, FOR GOODNESS SAKES ... YOU CLUMSY OX!

HE'S GOOD, MINNIE! I BET HE EVEN LEARNS TO CHARLESTON SOME DAY!
OH-OH... TOO MANY LEFT FEET, JASPER!
EEK!!
KA-PLUNK!

SORRY, MINNIE ... I MUSTA SLIPPED
ALLOW ME!
YOU...YOU BLUNDERBUSS! HEREAFTER, WHEN I DANCE IT WILL BE WITH A GENTLEMAN!
WALT DISNEY

SORRY I DIDN'T DANCE SO WELL, MINNIE! GUESS I'M A LITTLE OUTA PRACTICE!
THE VERY IDEA! HUMILIATING ME IN MY OWN HOME! COME, MONTY... TAKE ME OUT SOMEWHERE!
RIGHT-O!
4-25

AH ... JUST A MINUTE! HULA-BOOLA KADOOLA...

...PRESTO! HA-HA-HA!
SNAP!

SO! A CHEAP MAGICIAN, TOO!
CHEAP MAGICIAN! THAT'S NOT VERY POLITE, MICKEY MOUSE!

HI Y', MICKEY, OLD SOCKS! I DIDN'T KNOW Y' WERE BACK IN CIVILIZATION!
OH, HELLO, HORACE! YEH, I'VE BEEN HOME A COUPLA DAYS!
4-26

GUESS YOU'D NEVER A' LEFT IF YOU'D KNOWN A CITY SLICKER WAS GONNA STEAL YOUR GAL! OR HAVEN'T Y' HEARD?
AWW...THAT'S NOT SERIOUS! MINNIE'S GOT A RIGHT TO GO OUT WITH SOMEBODY ELSE OCCASIONALLY!

OCCASIONALLY! HAW-HAW! SAY, THIS BIRD'S A REAL LADY-KILLER...HE'S GOT HER GROGGY ON THE ROPES! TOUGH LUCK, SON!

HORACE THINKS HE'S GOT ME WORRIED! I GUESS I KNOW WHAT I'M DO...
OOPS!
PARDON ME, LADY!
WALT DISNEY

SORRY FOR BUMPIN' INTO Y', CLARABELLE! DIDN'T EVEN KNOW IT WAS YOU... GUESS MY MIND WAS SORTA WANDERIN'!
NATURALLY! AND I DON'T BLAME YOU AT ALL! WHAT WITH MINNIE GA-GA OVER THAT NEW BOY FRIEND AND...!
4-28

AW, I'M NOT WORRIED OVER THAT PARLOR PARASITE... MINNIE WOULDN'T GET SERIOUS WITH HIM!
NO, OF COURSE NOT! SHE'S ONLY BEEN GOING OUT WITH HIM BECAUSE YOU WERE AWAY SO MUCH!

PERSONALLY, I CAN'T ABIDE THE WRETCH! THE WAY HE'S BEEN RUSHING MINNIE... MORNING, NOON AND NIGHT... SHE.. SHE CAN'T STIR WITHOUT HIM...!

...OF COURSE, HE IS.. ...FASCINATING!
CLARABELLE! YOU, TOO?
WALT DISNEY

GOSH... ACCORDING TO HORACE AND CLABABELLE, MINNIE SURE SEES A LOT OF THAT NEW GUY! MAYBE, THOUGH, THEY WERE JUST KIDDIN' WITH ME!
4-29

AFTER ALL, JUST 'CAUSE HE CAN DANCE AND DO PARLOR TRICKS IS NO...
WHY, MICKEY! WHAT A SURPRISE! I HAVEN'T SEEN YOU IN AGES!
OH, GOOD MORNING, PATRICIA!
PERCY PIGG

NO, I'VE BEEN AWAY QUITE A BIT!
I SEE A LOT OF
MINNIE! SHE'S EVERYWHERE IN THE SOCIAL WHIRL, SINCE SHE'S BEEN GOING WITH MONTY!

HE'S SUCH A CHARMING GENTLEMAN, I DON'T BLAME HER FOR...
OH, DEAR ME... HAVE I SAID SOMETHING WRONG?
WALT DISNEY

DEAR ME...I'M ALWAYS PUTTING MY FOOT IN IT! I SHOULDN'T HAVE PRAISED MINNIE'S NEW FLAME TO YOU!
THAT'S ALL RIGHT PATRICIA... MAYBE THE GUY IS OKAY...
4-30

...BUT A TWERP THAT JUST GOES DANCING AND PARTYING ALL THE TIME... WELL, THAT'S NOT MY LINE!
THAT REMINDS ME...I'M GIVING A LITTLE PARTY TOMORROW NIGHT! IF YOU'D CARE TO COME...?
PIGG

SAY... THANKS, PATRICIA! I'LL BE THERE!

HOT DOG! I'VE GOT THE JUMP ON MONTY THIS TIME!
MINNIE MOUSE
WALT DISNEY

SLAM!
GOODNESS, MICKEY... YOU'RE ALL IN A DITHER!
I KINDA ...HURRIED ...WANTA ASK Y' SOMETHING ...
5-1

...WILL Y' GO TO PATRICIA PIGG'S PARTY WITH ME TOMORROW NIGHT?
OH, UH... LOOK... ISN'T THIS GOING TO BE PRETTY? IT'S FOR AUNT ABBIE!

YEH, IT'S NICE ... BUT Y' HAVEN'T ANSWERED MY...!
GOOD GRACIOUS... LOOK AT THE TIME! AND I HAVE TO GO TO THE HAIR-DRESSER'S, TOO!

MINNIE! WILL YOU PLEASE PAY ATTENTION TO WHAT I...?
OH, PARDON ME! YOU SAID YOU WANTED TO ASK ME SOMETHING, DIDN'T YOU?
WALT DISNEY

I ASKED YOU IF YOU'D GO TO PATRICIA PIGG'S PAR...!
OH, EXCUSE ME JUST A MINUTE... THERE'S SOMEONE AT THE DOOR!
5-2

WHY, MONTY! WHAT A PLEASANT SURPRISE!
HI Y', CUDDLE-CAT? WHAT SAY TO HELPING ME PUT SOME LIFE IN THE PIGG PARTY TOMORROW NIGHT?

I'D BE DELIGHTED, MONTY! I ADORE PARTIES!

MINNIE! I ASKED Y', THREE TIMES!
OH, IS THAT WHAT YOU WERE SAYING? I'M SO SORRY... BUT, NOW I'VE PROMISED MONTY...!

A FINE TRICK! STALLIN' ME OFF SO'S Y' COULD GO TO THE PARTY WITH HIM!
I'M AWFULLY SORRY! BUT, YOU SEE, I'VE PROMISED...
?!
5-3

...AND YOU WOULDN'T WANT ME TO BREAK A PROMISE... WOULD YOU, MICKEY?

MICKEY MOUSE! YOU... YOU...!
IF I'VE BROKEN ANYTHING, I'LL PAY FOR IT!
WALT DISNEY

I'LL SHOW MINNIE! I'LL GO TO THAT PARTY, ANYWAY, AND LET HER SEE SHE HASN'T GOT ME DOWN!
5-5

IF MONTY THINKS HE'S CUT ME OUT, HE'S CUCKOO! I CAN DRESS UP...AND MAKE FANCY SPEECHES, TOO!

WAIT 'TIL MINNIE GETS A LOAD OF MY ENTRANCE!
Distributed by King Features Syndicate, Inc.

WHY, MICKEY! HOW THOUGHTFUL! IT WASN'T NECESSARY...!
ALLOW ME, PATRICIA! PRAY, DO ME THE HONOR TO ACCEPT THIS SLIGHT TOKEN OF MY FRIENDLY ESTEEM!
SHUCKS! WASTED... SHE'S NOT HERE YET!
WALT DISNEY

SO GLAD YOU COULD COME, MICKEY! I DON'T KNOW WHAT'S KEEPING MINNIE AND...
HERE THEY ARE, NOW!
5-6

HOW CHARMING!
...DELIGHTFUL COUPLE!
AREN'T THEY TOO CUTE?
THEY WOULD STAGE A LATE ARRIVAL TO GET ATTENTION! AND LISTEN TO THOSE GALS RAVE!

HELLO, EVERYBODY!
LET THE FESTIVITIES COMMENCE! HA-HA-HA!
!

SORRY JASPER, OLD CHAP! DIDN'T RECOGNIZE YOU IN COSTUME... TERRIBLY EMBARRASSED HA-HA-HA!
THINK NOTHING OF IT... HEH-HEH-HEH!
WALT DISNEY

PATRICIA PIGG'S PARTY IS IN FULL SWING WITH MINNIE'S NEW BOY FRIEND THE CENTER OF ATTRACTION!

ISN'T THAT GRACEFUL?
SHUCKS, PATRICIA... THAT'S AN EASY ROUTINE!
5-7
Copr. 1941, Walt Disney Productions World Rights Reserved

I'LL TOP ANY STEP HE'S GOT!
HOT-CHA...!

!

AFTER ALL...THERE'S NOTHING LIKE THE CLASSIC STYLE I ALWAYS SAY!
WALT DISNEY

FAIR DAMSEL, PERMIT ME TO LAY AT THY FEET A CUP OF AMBROSIA!
WHY, MONTY ... HOW SWEET!
BOY, WHAT A CORNY LINE THAT SAP'S GOT!
5-8

AND THE WOMEN THINK IT'S CUTE! IT'S ABOUT TIME SOMEBODY SHOWED HIM UP!

OH, FAIREST CLARABELLE...

...PERMIT ME TO LAY AT THY FEET...!!
EEEK!
HA HA-HA!
HAW-HAW!!
HA
HA-HA
HA
WALT DISNEY

GOSH, CLARABELLE, THAT WAS AWFULLY CLUMSY OF ME! I'M TERRIBLY SORRY...!
OH, DON'T WORRY ABOUT IT... IT WAS JUST AN ACCIDENT!
PERMIT ME, FAIR LADY...
5-9

...TO OFFER YOU ANOTHER...WOOPS! A LITTLE SLIP!
EEK!!

HA-HA-HA--
CLAP
CLAP-CLAP
CLAP CLAP
CLAP!
CLAP!!
NEVER A DULL MOMENT! HA-HA-HA!!

LADIES AND SO FORTH... FOR YOUR EDIFICATION, A LITTLE SLEIGHT-OF-HAND! AS YOU SEE, NOTHING HERE...
PRESTO!
5-10

NOW, CHAUNCEY, WILL YOU KINDLY SHOW THE AUDIENCE THE CHICKENS YOU HAVE CONCEALED ON YOUR PERSON?
BUT I HAVEN'T ANY CHICKENS!

CAN YOU PROVE THAT?
SURE I CAN PROVE IT! MY POCKETS ARE EMP...!!??

TSK! TSK! FOR SHAME, WILBUR! SUCH YOUNG CHICKENS, TOO!
HA-HA HA!!
CLAP!
CLAP-
CLAP!
CLAP CLAP!
CLAP!

G'NIGHT, PATRICIA... IT WAS A **SWELL** PARTY! I HAD A ..UH.. WONDERFUL TIME!
I'M SO GLAD, MICKEY! GOOD NIGHT!
5-12

DELIGHTED YOU CAME... YOU WERE THE LIFE OF THE PARTY, MONTY!
THANKS! GLAD YOU **MET** ME! TOODLE-OO!
OH, AREN'T YOU **AWFUL**... TEE-HEE!

SORRY YOU WERE OUTA YOUR CLASS TONIGHT, CHARLIE! SEE Y' AT SOME OTHER PARTY I **DOUBT**!
YOU WILL BROTHER!

I DON'T KNOW **WHAT** BUT SOMETHING'S GOTTA BE DONE ABOUT THAT WISE GUY!
WALT DISNEY

G'MORNIN, MICKEY.. WELL GUESS YUH HAD A SWELL TIME AT THE PARTY LAST NIGHT HUH?
YEAH YEAH A SWELL TIME!
5-13

BOY, I'LL BET Y' SHOWED THAT SLICKER, MONTY, UP! HEARD YUH PLAYED SOME KINDA EGG TRICK ON 'IM!
WELL.. UH ..I SORTA HELPED OUT ON A TRICK!

YUP, YUH SHORE MUSTA MADE A MONKEY OUTA THET DON JAWN!
WELL.. ER ..IT DEPENDS ON HOW UH.. THAT IS.. !
OH, YEH?

THAT AIN'T THE WAY I JEST HEERED IT!
?
WALT DISNEY

OH, YEAH? WUZ **YOU** AT THUH PARTY?
YAA YAA! LOST YER GIRL, DIDN'T YUH?
5-14

YAA! CITY SLICKER STOLE YER GIRL! CAN'T KID ME, MY UNCLE JOE WAS THERE!
DOES MINNIE LIKE MONTY BETTER'N YOU MR. MOUSE?
ARE Y' GONNA FIGHT?

AWW, YOU'RE SCAIRT TO FIGHT, I BET!
CAN MONTY LICK Y', MR. MOUSE?
Cheri'
DRESS SHOP

WONDER WHAT HE DID THAT FOR?
MAYBE HE WAS TRYIN' IT ON!
YOU CAN COME OUT NOW, MR. MOUSE!
Cheri'
DRESS SHOP
WALT DISNEY

YAA... YAA! SOMEBODY STOLE YER GIRL FRIEND! YAAA!
5-15

WHEW! GUESS I'VE SHAKEN THOSE PESTS! GOSH, HAS EVERYBODY IN TOWN HEARD ABOUT ME?

HOME AT LAST! AND IF I'VE GOT ANY SENSE I'LL STAY HERE, WHERE I CAN'T BE PESTERED WITH FOOL QUESTIONS!

IS IT TRUE, UNCA MICKEY... WHAT THEY SAY?
IS AUNTIE MINNIE GOING WITH A NEW BOY FRIEND?
OWW! YOU, TOO?
Distributed by King Features Syndicate, Inc

IS AUNTIE MINNIE IN LOVE WITH MONTY, UNCA MICKEY?
ARE Y' GONNA FIGHT WITH HIM. ARE Y', HUH?
PIPE DOWN QUIET! STOP PESTERIN' ME!
5-16

I DON'T B'LIEVE UNCA MICKEY LIKES MR. MONTY, DO YOU?
NO! P'RAPS HE'S KINDA JEALOUS! SHOULD WE ASK HIM?

MAYBE IT'S AUNTIE MINNIE THAT'S JEALOUS, HUH?
COULD BE!
SNAP!

TRANS-UNI
TELEGRAPH CO.
WALT DISNEY

TRANS-UNIO
TELEGRAPH CO.
5-17

H'LO, FOLKS! SWELL DAY, ISN'T IT?
HI Y', JASPER! HERE... HAVE A TREAT ON ME!
YE CANDY SHOP

THANKS, BUT I'VE JUST GRADUATED FROM THE "ALL-DAY SUCKER" CLASS!

WELL! WHAT'S COME OVER LITTLE BOY BLUE?

HI DIDDLE DEE DEE...
OH, HELLO, MINNIE!
GOOD MORNING! UH... HAVE YOU BEEN SHOPPING ... SO EARLY?
5-19

YEH... JUST BLEW MYSELF TO SOME NEW DUDS!
OH! ARE YOU GOING TO SOME ...UH...SPECIAL EVENT?

NO..NOTHING SPECIAL! WELL, SO LONG, MINNIE SEE Y' AROUND!

WELL! IF HE ISN'T ACTING VERY SUSPICIOUSLY, ALL OF A SUDDEN!

WELL, WELL! HERE'S LITTLE ROLLO COME OVER TO PLAY!
I JUST STOPPED BY FOR A MINUTE...!
5-20

...I'VE GOT TWO PASSES FOR THAT NEW SHOW, MINNIE, AND I THOUGHT...!
OH! THAT'S VERY KIND... BUT I'M AFRAID, REALLY, I CAN'T GO! AH... YOU SEE...!

WHAT I MEANT WAS I WON'T BE ABLE TO USE 'EM... SO I THOUGHT THERE WAS NO USE HAVIN' 'EM GO TO WASTE!

WELL, BUTTER MY SHOE STRINGS!
I'D JUST LIKE TO KNOW WHAT HE'S UP TO LATELY!
WALT DISNEY

"PURPLE SOUL-MATES," MY... THIS LOOKS THRILLING! I WONDER...
Ye OLDE BOOKE NOOKE
POPULAR NOVELS REDUCED ONE-HALF
5-21

WHY, MICKEY MOUSE... HOW DELIGHTFUL! I HAVEN'T SEEN YOU IN AGES!
HOW D' DO, MRS. UPPACRUST! YES, IT'S BEEN QUITE A TIME!

YOU'VE HEARD ME SPEAK OF MICKEY, DEAR! THIS IS MY NIECE, MISS MILLICENT VAN GILT-MOUSE!
HOW DO YOU DO!
DELIGHTED TO MEET YOU, MISS VAN GILT-MOUSE!

MY FRIENDS CALL ME MILLICENT!
OH! UH, GOSH... THANKS, MISS... I MEAN... MILLICENT!
WALT DISNEY

YES, I'M STAYING WITH AUNT AGATHA, WHILE MY FOLKS ARE OPENING UP THEIR SUMMER HOME!
THAT'S SWELL! MAYBE YOU'LL LET ME... WELL, SORTA SHOW Y' AROUND A LITTLE!
5-22

OH, HOW PERFECTLY DELIGHTFUL! IT'S SWEET OF YOU TO WANT TO GO TO ALL THAT TROUBLE!

SHUCKS, MILLICENT... THAT'D BE FUN!
MM-HMM! IS HE FALLING!
PURPLE SOUL-MATES

CAN I HELP YOU, LADY?
OH! WHY, AH... NO, THANK YOU! THAT IS... I'M JUST LOOKING!
POPULAR NOVELS REDUCED ONE-HALF

AREN'T I LUCKY, AUNTIE, TO MEET SUCH A NICE BOY ON MY VERY FIRST VISIT?
YES, INDEED, MILLICENT! I'M SURE YOU TWO WILL GET ALONG FAMOUSLY!
5-23

THEN, IT'S A DATE! I'LL CALL FOR Y' TOMORROW AND WE'LL "DO" THE TOWN!
OH, THAT WILL BE LOVELY!
PURPLE SOUL-MATES

YES... THIS IS VERY GOOD, BUT... UH, NOT WHAT I'M LOOKING FOR!
POPULAR NOVELS

HAVE I GOT SOMETHING TO TELL... BUT, OF COURSE, I WOULDN'T BREATHE IT TO A SOUL!

GUESS WHAT, PATRICIA! MICKEY MOUSE JUST MET THE CUTEST LITTLE BLONDE... HAS SHE GOT GLAMOUR...!
5-24

...SHE'S MRS. UPPACRUST'S NIECE... AND DID HE FALL FOR HER! MY DEAR, YOU'D NEVER BELIEVE...!
SHHH-H-H..!

...YOU COULD TELL HOW GA-GA HE WAS BY... WHAT ARE YOU SHUSHING ME FOR?

I PUT AWAY YOUR SEWING-MACHINE, PATRICIA! THANKS FOR LETTING ME USE IT!

WALT DISNEY
Distributed by King Features Syndicate, Inc

WHAT A GORGEOUS NIGHT! WHERE ARE WE GOING?
YOU'D BE SURPRISED, TOOTS! HAVE I DISCOVERED THE LAST WORD IN NIGHT CLUBS!
5-26

IT'S STRICTLY CREME-DE-LA-CREME! THE DOORMAN STICKS A PIN IN YOU TO SEE IF YOUR BLOOD'S BLUE ENOUGH!
OH, HOW CUTE!

HOW DO Y' LIKE IT, BABY? STRICTLY UPPERCRUST, EH?
YES, IT'S LOV...!!

!
WELL, LOOK WHO'S HERE! C'MON OVER AND JOIN US!
OH... FRIENDS OF YOURS? HOW NICE!

MINNIE, I'D LIKE YOU TO MEET MILLICENT VAN GILT-MOUSE! SHE'S VISITING MRS. UPPACRUST, HER AUNT!
INDEED? I'M HIGHLY HONORED, I'M SURE!
THANK YOU! THE PLEASURE IS MINE!
5-27

AND THIS IS MONTY RODENT... PARDON, RODAWN!
DEE-LIGHTED!
HOW DO YOU DO!

HI, GARSONG! TWO MORE CHAIRS AND A LITTLE SERVICE OVER HERE!
SNAP!

SORRY, WE DIDN'T HAPPEN IN SOONER...MUST'VE BEEN PRETTY BORING...
NOT AT ALL! WE ..!
SURE, I KNOW! JASPER MEANS WELL... BUT IN A PLACE LIKE THIS Y' NEED CLASS!
WALT DISNEY

WHAT...LEAVING SO SOON? YOU SHOULDN'T LET WILBUR TEACH YOU HIS SMALL TIME HABITS, MILLICENT!
THANK YOU...IT'S MY OWN IDEA! I DON'T LIKE LATE HOURS!
5-28

SURELY, YOU DON'T HAVE TO WORRY ABOUT BEAUTY SLEEP, DO YOU, DEAR?

YES, I DO! I'M NOT SO FORTUNATE AS YOU ARE, HONEY!
AHEM... UH, WELL... LET'S GO! G'NIGHT, FOLKS!

THE CAT!

THE CAT!
WALT DISNEY

WELL... YOU PEOPLE SEEM TO BE EVERY-WHERE!
YES, MICKEY CERTAINLY KEEPS ME ENTERTAINED! I HAVEN'T HAD AN IDLE MOMENT!
AND DOES SHE PLAY A WICKED GAME OF TENNIS!
5-29

I SHOULDN'T WONDER... ALTHOUGH I KNOW NOTHING ABOUT THE GAME, MYSELF!

OH, I'M NOT REALLY GOOD! MICKEY EVEN BEAT ME IN A LOVE SET!
LOVE SET?! INDEED!!

HOW DISGUSTINGLY MUSHY!

OH, I SUPPOSE TENNIS IS ALL RIGHT IF YOU CARE FOR SOMETHING LIGHT AND TRIFLING!
BUT, OF COURSE, YOU PREFER RHUMBA DANCING!
5-30

HE DOES NOT! MONTY IS THE ATHLETIC TYPE... HE GOES IN FOR THE STRENUOUS, VIRILE SPORTS... LIKE BOWLING!

THAT'S RIGHT... THERE'S MY GAME! IF Y' WANT A REAL HE-MAN SPORT, WILBUR, JUST TRY BOWLING!

YES, IT'S VERY POPULAR! IT'S ALL THE RAGE BACK HOME... WITH MY MOTHER'S BRIDGE CLUB!

YOU KNOW WHAT I'D LIKE, MONTY? LET'S RENT SOME HORSES AND GO FOR A CANTER THROUGH THE PARK!
GREAT IDEA, TOOTS! SOUNDS KEEN!
BRIDLE PATH CROSSING
5-31

I JUST ADORE HORSES!!

YIPPEE! HI Y', FOLKS!
HELLO, THERE!

I WOULDN'T GO RIDING, IF THERE WAS NOTHING ELSE TO DO ON EARTH!

Chic
CHAPEAU
SHOP
WHAT A HEAVENLY NEW STYLE! I **MUST** HAVE IT TO WEAR TO THE BAZAAR TOMORROW!
6-2

HI, MINNIE!
Chic
CHAPEAU
SHOP
OH...GOOD MORNING! DON'T TELL ME YOU'RE SUDDENLY INTERESTED IN WOMEN'S HATS!

NOPE! JUST PICKIN' UP A LID THAT MILLICENT BOUGHT YESTERDAY... IT'S LIKE THAT ONE THERE!

Chic
CHAPEAU
SHOP
THAT LITTLE COUNTRY MODEL?
HOW QUAINT!
WALT DISNEY

OH-OH! LOOK WHO'S COMIN'!
GOOD GRACIOUS! CAN'T WE GO **ANYWHERE** WITHOUT SEEING MICKEY AND THAT... CREATURE?
6-3

HELLO, EVERYBODY! MY... ISN'T THIS A DELIGHTFUL BEACH?
YES, IT IS RATHER NICE...

...BUT I NEVER REALIZED BEFORE HOW **SMALL** IT IS!
WALT DISNEY

LAHHPY... DOOPY... DOOP-BEEP-BEEED!
OH-OH! I THINK I KNOW THAT BUGLE CALL!
6-4

!
HEY, Y' CAN'T **PARK** IN THE MIDDLE OF THE ROAD! KEEP MOVIN'! HA-HA-HA!!

DOGGONE SHOW-OFF! OF COURSE, I WOULDN'T STAND A CHANCE TRYIN' TO RACE HIM!
MICKEY, ...LOOK!

HOW DO Y' LIKE OUR TOWN BY NOW, MILLICENT?
I THINK IT'S LOVELY... AND I'M HAVING THE TIME OF MY LIFE!
6-5

HI THERE, MILLICENT! YOUR BOY FRIEND'S KINDA SLOW, ISN'T HE?

HE'S NOT AS SLOW AS YOU THINK... AND HE'S VERY SMOOTH!
OH! THAT...THAT HUSSY BURNS ME UP!
WALT DISNEY

I'M SO GLAD YOU CAME OVER, MICKEY...I HAVE WONDERFUL NEWS!
PROCEED! I'M ALL AGOG!
6-6

YOU KNOW MRS. VAN ASTOROCKS, WHO GIVES THE ANNUAL SOCIETY BALL FOR CHARITY?
I KNOW OF HER! WE DON'T EXACTLY MOVE IN THE SAME CIRCLES!

IN FACT, HER FUNCTIONS ARE RESERVED EXCLUSIVELY FOR THE TOP FRINGE OF THE UPPER LAYER OF THE ULTRA-ULTRA!

THEN THAT'S US... BECAUSE WE HAVE BEEN INVITED TO THE BALL!
NO! IT CAN'T ... IT'S... WHEEE-EW!
WALT DISNEY

Y' MEAN TO TELL ME MRS. VAN ASTOROCKS...THE MRS. VAN ASTOROCKS... WANTS ME TO COME TO HER BALL?
I SAW THE INVITATION... IT'S PROBABLY IN THE MAIL RIGHT NOW!
6-7

BUT, GOSH...THAT'S THE SNAZZIEST RUCKUS THERE IS! THERE'S PEOPLE THAT'D GIVE AN EYE TO GO TO IT!

JUST THE SAME, WE'RE INVITED, SO YOU MAY AS WELL GET USED TO THE IDEA!
ALL RIGHT... BUT THAT KIND OF ROYALTY SCARES ME! I WON'T KNOW WHETHER I SHOULD BREATHE IN OR OUT!

AND IN THE MEANTIME!

OH! MY GOODNESS GRACIOUS...!!
WALT DISNEY

HI Y', CUDDLE-CAT ...WHAT'S NEW?
GUESS WHAT! AN INVITATION TO MRS. VAN ASTOROCKS' SOCIETY BALL! IT'S ALMOST UNBELIEVABLE!
6-9

OH, THAT! SURE, I TAKE IN THAT HOP EVERY YEAR! QUITE THE THING, Y' KNOW!

BUT SHE DOESN'T EVEN KNOW ME...I'VE NEVER BEEN INVITED BEFORE! I CAN'T UNDERSTAND IT!

SIMPLE ENOUGH! Y' DIDN'T KNOW ME BEFORE, TOOTS! YOU'RE IN THE SWIM NOW!
OH, MONTY, YOU'RE WONDERFUL!
WALT DISNEY

WHAT HO, MINNIE! GONNA DOLL UP FOR SOMETHIN' SPECIAL?
WELL, AFTER ALL, ONE DOESN'T GO TO THE VAN ASTOROCKS' BALL EVERY NIGHT, YOU KNOW!
SNOOKUMS PROBABLY NEVER HEARD OF THE AFFAIR!
Le Swank GOWN SALON
6-10

SURELY, YOU'VE READ ABOUT IT... IT'S THE SOCIAL EVENT OF THE SEASON!
BUT STRICTLY BLUE-BLOOD, Y' SEE!
OH, SURE... I KNOW...!

WELL, SO LONG! IF I DON'T RUN INTO Y' BEFORE, I'LL SEE Y' AT THE BALL!

NOW, HOWEVER DID HE GET TO...??
ER...ULP! MUST BE... SOME... MIS-TAKE!
Distributed by King Features Syndicate, Inc.
WALT DISNEY

I'D JUST LIKE TO KNOW HOW MICKEY MOUSE GOT INVITED TO THE VAN ASTOROCKS' BALL! MONTY SAYS IT'S TERRIBLY EXCLUSIVE!
SPECIAL 98¢ CUT RATE
WHIZZO
RAZOR
DAILY BUGLE
BUGLE 3¢
6-11

WELL! HOW DO YOU DO, DARLING!
MY DEAR! HOW CHARMING YOU LOOK! MME. ZUZU IS REALLY WONDERFUL... I'VE HEARD!
MME. Zuzu's SALON DE BEAUTE'

YES, SHE'S VERY GOOD!
I SHOULD GO IN MYSELF, BUT I COULDN'T BE BOTHERED, REALLY!
SO GLAD TO HAVE SEEN YOU!
THANK YOU... GOOD-BYE!
SALON DE BEAUTE'

NOW I KNOW HOW MICKEY GOT HIS INVITATION! THAT SNIP, MILLICENT...!

...AND IF SHE THINKS SHE'S GOING TO OUT-SHINE ME...!!
MME. Zuzu's SALON DE BEAUTE'

GOSH, I ALMOST WISH I WASN'T GOIN' TO THAT BALL TOMORROW! SUPPOSE I PULL A SOCIAL BONER OF SOME KIND!

LET'S SEE, NOW... "AH, MRS. VAN ASTOROCKS, DELIGHTFUL PLACE YOU HAVE HERE!" HECK, NO...THAT'S TOO CORNY!
6-12

"PERFECTLY CHARMING OF YOU TO ASK ME," ... I MEAN ..."DELIGHTED TO BE HERE!"

AW, SHUCKS... SOUNDS TOO MUCH LIKE MONTY'S LINE OF TRIPE! GUESS I'LL JUST HAFTA BE MYSELF!

OH, HELLO, MILLICENT!
MICKEY, CAN YOU COME RIGHT OVER? I'VE GOT SOMETHING **PRICELESS** ON MONTY!
OH, BOY! I'M HALF-WAY THERE!

WHAT'S THIS... WHAT'S THIS? YOU'VE DUG UP SOME DIRT ON MONTY?
HAVE I! JUST WAIT TILL YOU HEAR!
6-13

AUNT AGATHA'S COOK GOT IT FROM THE SMYTHE'S BUTLER AND **HE** HEARD IT STRAIGHT FROM DE-KALE'S CHAUFFEUR..!

...I JUST HAPPENED TO BE IN THE KITCHEN AND... BZZ-Z...BZ-Z-Z-Z...!
NO! HONEST? WELL, WHADDYA KNOW...!

BOY-OH-BOY-OH-BOY! THIS CINCHES IT! THAT'S THE HOTTEST NEWS IN AGES!
WALT DISNEY

OH, BOY! HAVE I FINALLY GOT THE GOODS ON THAT GUY, MONTY! AND YOU CAN HELP ME PUT IT OVER!
YEAH? HOW COME?
6-14

Y' KNOW THE BIG SOCIETY BALL AT THE VAN ASTOROCKS' TONIGHT?
YEH, I HEERED OF IT, BUT I AIN'T GOIN'! THAT KINDER LIFE DON'T APPEAL TO ME!

LISTEN... HERE'S ALL Y' HAFTA DO... BZZ-Z... BZ-Z-Z...!

HAW-HAW-HAW! YUH KIN COUNT ON ME, MICKEY! AND WILL THAT TERMITE'S FACE GIT RED! HAW-HAW-HAW!

MICKEY IS SURPRISED TO GET A WARM RECEPTION FROM MRS VAN ASTOROCKS, WHO TELLS HIM HE ONCE SAVED THE LIFE OF A FRIEND!

THE EVENING WEARS ON... MUSIC AND GAIETY SPARKLE AMID THE DAZZLING SPLENDOR OF THE VAN ASTOROCKS' BALL!

ONE BY ONE THE CONTESTANTS ARE DROPPED OUT OF THE ELIMINATION DANCE, UNTIL ONLY TWO COUPLES ARE LEFT ON THE FLOOR!

Mickey and his partner, Millicent, have just won the elimination dance, the biggest event of the society ball!

Trying to regain the limelight after Mickey's victory in the elimination dance, Monty puts on an amateur magic show!

In the Van Astorocks' ballroom Monty is entertaining the guests with feats of magic!

IN THE MIDST OF MONTY'S SUCCESS AS AN AMATEUR MAGICIAN, HIS ACT IS INTERRUPTED BY THE ARRIVAL OF A SINGING TELEGRAM!

MONTMORENCY RODENT, YOU SURE ARE IN A JAM! YOUR BOSS IS COMING HOME TONIGHT, SO TAKE IT ON THE LAM!
6-26

BRING BACK HIS AUTO AND HIS CLOTHES... RETURN HIS MONEY, TOO, FOR IF HE EVER FINDS IT OUT, IT'S JUST TOO BAD FOR YOU!
YOU'RE JUST A CHAUFFEUR HERE, YOU KNOW... GET ON THE JOB, YOU CROOK!

AND FOR THIS TIMELY WARNING... KISS MEHITABEL, THE COOK!

THAT'LL BE $1.69, COLLECT, PLEASE!

WELL, DID YOU **EVER?**
ONLY A CHAUFFEUR!
USING HIS EMPLOYER'S CAR!
AND HIS CLOTHES, TOO!
A CHEAP IMPOSTOR!
WHAT NERVE!
$1.69 COLLECT, PLEASE!
6-27

HA-HA HA-HA HA HA HA HA-HA-HA-HA HA HA HA HA! HA HA HA HA

WE SHORE PUT IT OVER, DIDN'T WE?
AND HOW! THAT WAS A BLUFF ABOUT HIS EMPLOYER COMIN' BACK, BUT IT WORKED!

THAT PARASITE WON'T...
OH-OH!
WALT DISNEY

MINNIE! WAIT...!
6-28

AW, MINNIE, DON'T TAKE IT SO HARD!

I'M SORRY... BUT YOU WERE BOUND TO GET WISE TO THAT PHONY SOME DAY!
OHH! I WAS **NEVER** SO HUMILIATED! I HATE HIM! I **HATE** HIM!

PARDON ME... MAY I COME IN?
OH...!
WALT DISNEY

I HOPE YOU'RE NOT CRYING OVER MONTY ...HE'S NOT WORTH IT!
CERTAINLY NOT! I'M NOT CRYING AT ALL!
6-30

OHH, DEAR! I'VE... I'VE MADE A MESS OF...OF EVERYTHING!

NO, YOU HAVEN'T, MINNIE! YOU NEVER REALLY LIKED HIM, ANYHOW!
OF COURSE, I DIDN'T! I JUST WANTED TO MAKE MICKEY JEALOUS...AND... NOW LOOK HOW IT TURNED OUT! OHH-H...!

WELL... AHEM...I'M STILL WITH Y', MINNIE ...OR HADN'T Y' NOTICED?
WALT DISNEY

HONEST, MICKEY? YOU'RE NOT MAD... AFTER I'VE BEEN SO MEAN TO YOU?
AW, SHUCKS... FORGET IT, KID! EVERYTHING'S JUST LIKE IT USED TO BE!
7-1

BUT...BUT, WHAT ABOUT...?

Y' MEAN MILLICENT? YOU'LL BE SURPRISED!

I'D LIKE TO INTRODUCE MY COUSIN FROM THE CITY... MADELINE MOUSE!
!
WALT DISNEY

YOUR COUSIN MADELINE?? BUT I THOUGHT THIS WAS MILLICENT VAN GILT-MOUSE!
THAT'S JUST THE NAME SHE TOOK, WHILE SHE WAS HELPIN' ME WITH MY LITTLE PLOT TO SHOW UP MONTY!
7-2

Y' SEE, MADELINE IS REALLY A SOCIETY BUD IN HER HOME TOWN... EVEN IF SHE IS MY OWN COUSIN!

OH, YOU'RE A DEAR!
SMACK!

HEY, MINNIE, STOP...AWK... HEH-HEH ...HAVE A HEART...!
SMACK! SMACK! SMACK! SMACK! SMACK! SMACK! SMACK!
WALT DISNEY

THE DAY AFTER THE BIG BALL THAT ENDED MONTY'S "SOCIETY" CAREER, MICKEY'S COUSIN LEAVES FOR THE CITY!
7-3

GOOD-BYE, MILLICENT... I MEAN, MADELINE! COME BACK SOON!
HOPE I CAN! GOOD-BYE!
G.R.R.R.R.
2066⅓

SHE'S A DARLING! I'LL ALWAYS HATE MYSELF FOR BEING SO MEAN TO HER!
FORGET IT! LET'S GO HAVE A SODA!

OH... THANK YOU SIR!
SORRY MY CAR ISN'T A SUPER-DOOPER LIKE YOU'VE BEEN USED TO... BUT AT LEAST I OWN IT!

SILLY GOOSE! THIS IS JUST THE GRANDEST CAR I EVER RODE IN!

IT'S SO MUCH MORE FUN GOING PLACES WITH YOU THAN IT WAS WITH MONTY!
HONEST?
7-4

YES...HE WAS SUCH A SHOW-OFF! ALWAYS DOING THINGS TO ATTRACT ATTENTION!
I KNOW! IT MUST'VE BEEN EMBARRASSING!

I HATE TO BE CONSPICUOUS, DON'T YOU?
YEH, I SURE...??!
HA! HA HA HA HA HA HA HA HA HA HA HA!!

PARDON ME, FOLKS, BUT THE ORCHESTRA STOPPED PLAYING SOME TIME AGO!
WALT DISNEY

Ye DINKY DIMPLE NIGHT SPOT
WASN'T IT A GORGEOUS EVENING? LET'S WALK HOME AND MAKE IT LAST!
BETTER TAKE A CAB, I THINK... IT LOOKS LIKE RAIN!
7-5

MICKEY MOUSE, HAVE YOU NO ROMANCE IN YOUR SOUL?
SURE, I HAVE, BUT... SAY, WHAT'RE WE STOPPING FOR?

IS MY FACE RED! I'M OUTA GAS... AN' THE STATIONS IS ALL CLOSED UP!

ROMANTIC, EH, GAL?
I STILL SAY IT'S A GORGEOUS EVENING!
Distributed by King Features Syndicate, Inc.
WALT DISNEY

MICKEY MOUSE, SUPER-SALESMAN

JULY 7, 1941

–

OCTOBER 4, 1941

NEW JOBS, NEW ROLES, NEW MODELS

It is a cunning and enterprising Minnie who opens "Mickey Mouse, Supersalesman." Gottfredson has not always been kind to Mickey's girlfriend, often depicting her as frivolous and hare-brained. But here she is a brilliant strategist who masters "psychology... and propaganda... today's modern weapons," successfully manipulating the tearaway Mickey into taking a steady job as an assistant art director (!). It is a stark contrast with the Minnie of 1934's "Captive Castaways." This 1941 incarnation is sophisticated and cunning, but aspires to a steady middle-class life; whereas the younger Minnie was perhaps simpler, but had the spirit of a fighting heroine. Both still share an affection for Mickey; but other than that, they are practically two different characters.

As we note Minnie's evolving psychology, we should also remark on Mickey's graphical restyling, which with this story is essentially complete. Mickey is now slimmer, no longer built of two circles on top of each other; the official art references are clearly Fred Moore's model sheets for *The Little Whirlwind* (1941). It is a thoroughly more modern, slender look for our hero, even though he still wears his traditional two-button shorts.

The first few days of Mickey's job at the Hotflash Publicity Agency show us a very realistic workplace: Gottfredson was clearly knowledgeable about drawing boards, drawing tools, and art studios, and this experience shines through. The Hotflash setting reflects our own world, not the pulp-fiction realm of Mickey's more usual adventures. Making rent replaces fighting dinosaurs as the challenge of the moment. But Gottfredson's Mickey has always maintained a strong connection with everyday life; so his battle to succeed at Hotflash is as believable as his more fantastic battles.

Like those battles, of course, this one involves an antagonist. Joe Winderpaine, the bombastic rival salesman, is the kind of arrogant jerk that every sensible person hates with a passion. Yet what rarely happens in reality to such jerks happens to "Windy" here: in his competition with Mickey, the winner is the man who really deserves to win, while the social-climbing idea thief loses. Gottfredson and Merrill De Maris give readers a workplace victory of the sort we might wish for in real life, enabling us to overcome our own frustrations by identifying with Mickey.

The authors also introduce the figure of the Evil Speculator—here, a merciless landlord—whose defeat again allows us to live vicariously through Mickey. The effect is much like we might find in the films of Frank Capra, to whose blandly anti-capitalistic morals "Supersalesman" owes much.

While many Gottfredson stories from this period invoked conservative ideology, "Supersalesman" reflects an FDR-era progressivism, stressing the value of entrepreneurship and private enterprise over inherited wealth and financial capital. Everyone does their bit for the common good. Our individualistic Mouse, smart and audacious as well as creative, is the perfect flag-bearer for this philosophy.

—Francesco Stajano and Leonardo Gori

OH, DEAR, I'M GETTING WORRIED ABOUT MICKEY!
YOU MEAN HE'S GETTING ITCHY FEET AGAIN, I SUPPOSE!
7-7

EXACTLY! I KNOW THE SIGNS AND I CAN TELL HE'S GETTING RESTLESS TO GO OFF ON SOME WILD ADVENTURE!

HE'S SEEMED PRETTY QUIET TO ME... MAYBE YOU JUST IMAGINE IT!
MAYBE, BUT... OH, HERE HE COMES, NOW!

HELLO, GALS! SAY...Y' OUGHTA SEE THIS NEW ONE-MAN PLANE... Y' CAN REALLY **GO** PLACES WITH IT!
FLY
WALT DISNEY

WHAT A DAY! PERFECT WEATHER FOR SAILIN'! WISH I HAD A LITTLE SLOOP-RIGGED JOB AND...!
MICKEY...SIT DOWN AND RELAX!
R-RUM TA-TA TUMM
7-8
Copr. 1941, Walt Disney Productions World Rights Reserved

OH, SURE! I WAS JUST THINKIN' ...WOULDN'T IT BE FUN TO BE A DISCOVERER? YOU KNOW, LIKE BALBOA...!

YOU KNOW PERFECTLY WELL EVERYTHING'S **BEEN** DISCOVERED! PLEASE, MICKEY...!
YEH... UH-HUH ...WELL, I GOTTA BE GOIN'! SEE Y' TONIGHT, MINNIE!

I'M GOING TO HAVE TO DO SOMETHING QUICKLY...I CAN SEE **THAT!** AND I THINK I KNOW WHAT TO DO, TOO!

CLARABELLE, DO YOU KNOW WHAT I'VE DECIDED ABOUT MICKEY?
LAND SAKES, NO! ARE YOU STILL TRYIN' TO KEEP THAT WILD INDIAN ON THE RESERVATION?
7-9

YES, I AM! AND THE REASON I'VE FAILED BEFORE WAS THAT I USED THE WRONG TACTICS ...HE'S **SUCH** A STUBBORN MULE!
YOU'RE TELLING ME! BUT WHAT'S THE ANSWER?

LISTEN...BUT DON'T TELL A SOUL...BUZZ-Z-Z-Z... BZZ-Z-Z-Z...!
GOOD LAND!

PSYCHOLOGY, MY DEAR... AND PROPAGANDA... TODAY'S MODERN WEAPONS!
WALT DISNEY

WHERE'VE Y' BEEN, MINNIE? I WAS OVER AT YOUR HOUSE TWICE TODAY!
OH, DIDN'T YOU KNOW? I'M WORKING!
7-10

WORKING? UH... WHADDYA MEAN...?
I MEAN, I'VE GOT A JOB... I'M A SWITCHBOARD OPERATOR!

WH-WHAT'S THE BIG IDEA? Y' NEVER WORKED BEFORE ...Y' DON'T HAFTA!
I KNOW! BUT I JUST FELT THAT I HAD TO DO SOMETHING USEFUL... SOMETHING CONSTRUCTIVE!

AFTER ALL, WORK NEVER HURT ANYONE, BUT IDLENESS CAN GET SO TIRESOME AND BORING ... DON'T YOU THINK?
UH?... OH, YEH... THAT'S TRUE!
WALT DISNEY

HELLO!
HI Y', MINNIE! HOW ABOUT STEPPIN' OUT FOR A BIT OF FUN TONIGHT?
Copr. 1941, Walt Disney Productions
World Rights Reserved

I'M SORRY, BUT I'M REALLY TOO TIRED! HAVE YOU FORGOTTEN THAT I'M A WORKING GIRL NOW?

OH... YEH! YOU'RE STILL ...UH... SERIOUS ABOUT THAT?
OF COURSE! IT'S SUCH A WONDERFUL FEELING TO HAVE A USEFUL PURPOSE IN LIFE ...DON'T YOU THINK?
7-11

GOSH... I WISH MINNIE'D STOP HARPIN' ON THAT JOB! MAKES ME FEEL LIKE A TRAMP!
WALT DISNEY

OH, GOLLY... IF I DON'T CALL MINNIE RIGHT AWAY SHE'LL BE AT WORK!
7-12
Copr. 1941, Walt Disney Productions
World Rights Reserved

HELLO, MINNIE... HOW ABOUT A MOVIE TONIGHT?
OH, I CAN'T, MICKEY... TONIGHT I HAVE TO STAY OVERTIME!

BUT... GOSH, MINNIE...!
SORRY... I CAN'T TALK ANY LONGER OR I'LL BE LATE TO WORK! 'BYE!

WELL... IT MAY BE HER JOB, BUT IT'S SURE GIVIN' ME THE HEADACHE!
WALT DISNEY

HOW'RE THINGS GOIN', MINNIE... DO Y' STILL LIKE YOUR JOB?
OH, YES, INDEED! IT FEELS SO GOOD TO KNOW THAT I'VE REALLY ACCOMPLISHED SOMETHING!
7-14

IDLENESS GETS HORRIBLY BORING... DON'T YOU THINK?
YEH... OH, SURE... NOTHIN' LIKE KEEPIN' BUSY!

I S'POSE Y' THINK MAYBE I OUGHTA ...UH... HAVE A JOB, TOO?
I HADN'T THOUGHT ABOUT IT ...BUT THAT'S A WONDERFUL IDEA, MICKEY!

IN FACT, THERE'S AN OPENING AT MY PLACE! I CAN ARRANGE AN INTERVIEW FOR YOU TOMORROW... AREN'T YOU LUCKY?
OH... YEH... I SURE AM!
Distributed by King Features Syndicate, Inc.
WALT DISNEY

YOU'RE JUST LUCKY THERE'S A WONDERFUL POSITION OPEN AT MY PLACE! I CAN ARRANGE EVERYTHING AND...!
BUT, MINNIE, Y' NEVER DID TELL ME WHO YOU'RE WORKIN' FOR, OR WHAT THEY DO!
7-15

OH... DIDN'T I? WELL, IT'S THE HOTFLASH PUBLICITY AGENCY! THEY'RE GRAND PEOPLE TO WORK FOR ...I KNOW YOU'LL LOVE IT!

YOU KNOW WHAT A PRESS AGENCY DOES...THEY PLAN CAMPAIGNS AND...!
SURE... WRITE COPY, MAKE ILLUSTRATIONS AND STUFF! BUT WHERE DO I FIT IN?

YOU, MY DEAR, ARE TO BE AN ART DIRECTOR!
WHAT!!? MINNIE... ARE YOU GOIN' DAFFY?
Distributed by King Features Syndicate, Inc.
WALT DISNEY

NOTHING DOING! THINK I'M GONNA ASK FOR AN ART DIRECTOR'S JOB WHEN I CAN'T EVEN DRAW? THEY'D THINK I WAS BATS!
BUT YOU DON'T HAVE TO BE AN ARTIST TO HOLD THIS POSITION! I'VE ALREADY TALKED TO THE MAN IN CHARGE...
7-16

...I TOLD HIM ALL ABOUT YOU AND HE WAS SURE YOU WOULD FILL THE JOB PERFECTLY!
SO! THEN YOU HAVE BEEN AFTER A JOB FOR ME ALL THE TIME! I SHOULD'VE KNOWN!

JUST THINK...YOU'LL BE A BIG SHOT IN A THRILLING BUSINESS! THINK OF THE... THE GLAMOUR OF IT ALL!

OKAY! I'LL GO WITH YOU TOMORROW, BUT IF I MAKE A FOOL OF MYSELF, JUST REMEMBER IT WAS YOUR IDEA!
OH, I'M SO HAPPY!
WALT DISNEY

WITH MINNIE HAVING PULLED A FAST ONE ON HIM, MICKEY FINDS HIMSELF APPLYING FOR A JOB WITH THE HOTFLASH PUBLICITY AGENCY!

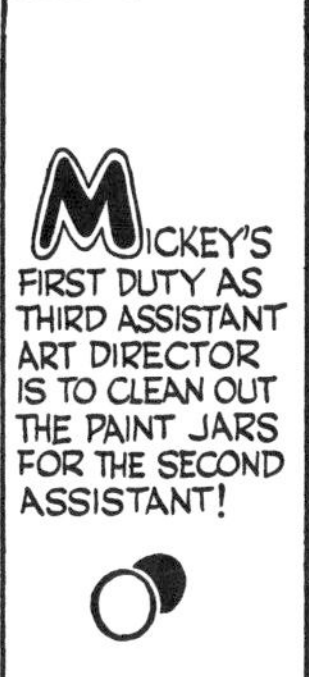
MICKEY'S FIRST DUTY AS THIRD ASSISTANT ART DIRECTOR IS TO CLEAN OUT THE PAINT JARS FOR THE SECOND ASSISTANT!

BE SURE AND GET 'EM GOOD AND CLEAN! THEY'RE STICKLERS AROUND HERE FOR KEEPIN' EVERYTHING SPIC AND SPAN!
OKAY... I'LL BE CAREFUL!
RACING
7-21

A HALF-HOUR LATER.
WELL... I THINK I'VE GOT 'EM THE WAY YOU WANT 'EM! WHAT DO I DO NEXT?
!
RACING

TAKE A BATH!
RACING
WALT DISNEY

NOW, SON, IF YOU'RE READY TO GO TO WORK, YOU'LL NEED A LOT OF PENCILS FOR THE NEXT JOB!
HONEST? AM I REALLY GONNA WORK WITH PENCILS?
7-22

SURE... AREN'T YOU THE THIRD ASSISTANT ART DIRECTOR? HERE... TAKE 'EM ALL!
GEE... THANKS!

HAVE Y' GOT 'EM GOOD AND SHARP?
YEH... THIS IS THE LAST ONE! NOW, HOW DO I START WORK?

START? YOU JUST FINISHED THE PENCIL JOB.. AND WELL DONE, TOO!
OH...!

HEY, SON, STEP IN HERE A MINUTE! WANT TO ASK YOUR PROFESSIONAL ADVICE!
7-23

WHAT DO YOU THINK OF THE PENCIL LINES UNDER THE INK LINES IN THAT DRAWING?
ER... THEY SEEM SORTA... WELL... WELL, UNNECESSARY NOW THAT IT'S INKED!

EXCELLENT JUDGMENT! THAT'S EXACTLY WHAT I THINK!
WALT DISNEY

TAKE THIS ART GUM AND ERASE EVERY ONE OF THEM!
Distributed by King Features Syndicate, Inc.

HERE'S THE SCRAP Y' WANTED FROM THE MORGUE, MR... UH, I MEAN, MAC!
GOOD... NICE WORK!
7-24

BY THE WAY, I JUST NOTICED YOU'RE NOT WEARIN' YOUR UNIFORM!
UNIFORM? WHAT KIND DO Y' MEAN?

YOUR THIRD ASSISTANT ART DIRECTOR'S UNIFORM! HOW'S ANYBODY GONNA KNOW WHO Y' ARE?
GOSH...I DIDN'T KNOW IT WAS CUSTOMARY! NEVER HEARD OF ANYTHING LIKE THAT!

SURE...ON IMPORTANT JOBS Y' GOTTA DRESS THE PART!
I'M GONNA ASK SOMEBODY ELSE... HE COULD BE JUST KIDDIN' ME!
WALT DISNEY

JUST IN CASE MAC WAS SPOOFING ME I'LL ASK THESE FELLOWS!
7-25

IS IT TRUE THAT A THIRD ASSISTANT ART DIRECTOR IS S'POSED TO WEAR A UNIFORM?
IS THAT THE $64-QUESTION?

WHO TOLD YOU THAT ONE?
MAC DID...BUT I THOUGHT HE MIGHT BE KIDDING!
OH... MAC TOLD YOU! THAT'S DIFFERENT!

SURE, MAC NEVER KIDS ANYBODY!
NO, IF HE SAID SO, Y' BETTER GET YOUR COSTUME, SONNY!
WALT DISNEY
Distributed by King Features Syndicate, Inc.

JUST TO MAKE CERTAIN, I'LL ASK MR. SQUEELE... I KNOW HE NEVER JOKES!
A.B SQUE
7-26

IS IT TRUE I SHOULD WEAR A UNIFORM, LIKE MAC TOLD ME?
EH...WHAT? OF COURSE, IT'S TRUE!
A.B.SQUEELE

YOU'RE WORKING UNDER MR. McCRACKENPOT! WHATEVER HE SAYS, GOES! UNDERSTAND?
YES, SIR!
A.B.SQUEELE

NOW... WHAT DID HE ASK ME?
SLAM!
A.B.SQUEELE
WALT DISNEY

SAY, PARDON ME, MAC, BUT ABOUT THAT...AH, UNIFORM I'M SUPPOSED TO GET! I...AH...WELL, I'M NOT JUST SURE WHAT A THIRD ASSISTANT ART DIRECTOR WEARS!
WELL, NOW, SON, YOU JUST RUN DOWN TO JONES' DEPT. STORE AND TELL MR. JONES I SENT YOU! HE'LL FIX YOU UP!
7-28

WHY, MICKEY, WHERE IN THE WORLD DO YOU THINK YOU'RE GOING? IT'S NOT LUNCH-TIME YET!
GOING OUT TO GET MY UNIFORM! I'LL BE BACK IN A FEW MINUTES!
Copr. 1941, Walt Disney Productions
World Rights Reserved

I'M THE THIRD ASSISTANT ART DIRECTOR UP AT THE HOTFLASH AGENCY! MR. McCRACKENPOT SAID YOU'D FIX ME UP!
WELL, WELL! ANOTHER NEW THIRD ASSISTANT, HUH? YOU BET I'LL FIX YOU UP! ANYTHING FOR A FRIEND OF MAC'S!
SECTION B

Jones'
DEPT. STORE
WALT DISNEY
Distributed by King Features Syndicate, Inc.

WELL. I'M BACK! GOSH, I HAD NO IDEA AN ART DIRECTOR HAD TO WEAR AN OUTFIT LIKE THIS! PRETTY SILLY, HUH?
SILLY! WHY, MICKEY, IT MAKES YOU LOOK GRAND! SO ROMANTIC! SO...SO CAPABLE!
7-29

GOSH, I DON'T KNOW ABOUT THAT! I KINDA FEEL LIKE... LIKE OLD MOTHER HUBBARD!
OLD MOTHER HUBBARD, NOTHING! YOU LOOK LIKE... LIKE, WELL, LIKE MICHELANGELO! WHY, YOU'RE A BORN ARTIST!

BY GOLLY, MINNIE, YOU MAY BE RIGHT AT THAT! I'M BEGINNING TO FEEL SORTA...SORTA ARTISTIC-LIKE!
OF COURSE I'M RIGHT! WHY...WHY, YOU SHOULD BE FIRST ASSISTANT ART DIRECTOR, NOT THIRD!

THAT DRAWING'S OUTA PERSPECTIVE, MY MAN! BETTER CHECK IT!
?
WALT DISNEY

YES?
7-30

GREAT JEEMINY...!!?

WOT WUZ DAT?
HE... IS THE THIRD ASSISTANT ART DIRECTOR! NOW, WHAT CAN I DO FOR YOU?

OH, I'M D' FOIST VICE-PRESIDENT IN CHARGE O' DELIVERIN' TELEGRAMS! SIGN HERE!
WALT DISNEY
Distributed by King Features Syndicate, Inc.

WELL? YOU'VE DELIVERED YOUR TELEGRAM... THERE'S NO NEED TO WAIT!
7-31

ABOUT A HALF-HOUR LATER

FOR GOODNESS SAKE... ARE YOU STILL HERE? GET OUT!

HOT DAWG! HAW-HAW-HAW!

HAW-HAW! DAT WUZ WORTH A SECOND LOOK! OHH, MY! HO! HO! HAW-HAW-HAW-W!
WALT DISNEY

THIS BIG NECKTIE, MAC ...DON'T Y' THINK IT MAKES ME LOOK... KINDA SILLY?
NONSENSE! IT'S THE PROPER THING FOR YOUR JOB! QUIT WORRYING AND GET ME THAT PAINT I SENT Y' FOR!
8-1

MAYBE IT'S ALL RIGHT, BUT IT DOESN'T SEEM PRACTICAL TO ME!

HEY! WHAT TH'...?!!

THE TIE!
GET RID OF IT! WHO TOLD Y' TO WEAR THE DARN THING, ANYWAY?

MORNIN', MAC! SAY...WHAT'S WRONG WITH EVERYBODY... THEY'RE ALL SO QUIET?
NOTHIN' MUCH! EXCEPT THE BOSS HAS BEEN OUTA TOWN AND HE'S COMIN' BACK TODAY!
8-2

THE BOSS...WHO'S HE?
I.Q. McFOOZLE... THE PRESIDENT OF THIS COCKEYED DUMP!
WHAT'S HE LIKE?

LOOK, SON! IF YOU WERE AT SEA IN A CAT-BOAT AND SAW A STORM WARNING HUNG OUT, Y' WOULDN'T ASK QUESTIONS, WOULD Y'?
NO...I'D JUST, UH...GET PREPARED FOR THE WORST!

CORRECT! START PREPARIN'!
WALT DISNEY

FROM WHAT THE BOYS SAY ABOUT MR. McFOOZLE HE MUST BE QUITE A CHARACTER!
QUITE!
8-4

IS HE KIND OF ORNERY AND BAD TEMPERED?
WELL, SEEING AS HE'S HEAD MAN OF THIS JOINT, WE'LL JUST SAY HE'S ECCENTRIC!

IN FACT, THERE'S ONLY ONE THING ABOUT OLD I. Q. THAT YOU CAN BE ABSOLUTELY SURE OF.
WHAT'S THAT?

...THAT Y' CAN'T BE SURE OF ANYTHING!
RACING
WALT DISNEY

SO MR. McFOOZLE'S COMIN' BACK TODAY! I'LL BET THINGS WILL START TO HUM NOW, EH?
YEH, WELL TAKE MY ADVICE, SON...IF Y' HEAR ANY HUMMIN', KEEP AWAY FROM THE BUZZ SAW!
RACING
8-5

DO YOU KNOW THAT OLD I. Q. ONCE FIRED THE BEST SECRETARY HE EVER HAD?
HE DID? WHY?

SHE HAD A HABIT OF GOING HOME EARLY TO COOK HER HUSBAND'S DINNER! HE GOT SORE AND CANNED HER!
I'D SAY HE HAD A RIGHT TO! AFTER ALL, A SECRETARY SHOULD...

BUT **HIS** SECRETARY WAS **ALSO** HIS WIFE!
HUH...OH...!
RACING

OH-OH! A CALL FOR ONE OF THE BOYS AND HE'S OUT! GUESS I BETTER ANSWER IT!
BRRRRR RINNGG!
8-6

SMITHERS, YOU BLASTED LOAFER, WHY IN TUNKET DON'T YOU ANSWER YOUR PHONE? THIS IS I. Q. SPEAKING!
GOLLY! MR. McFOOZLE, THE BIG BOSS!

I LEAVE TOWN FOR A FEW WEEKS AND THE BUSINESS FALLS TO PIECES! ALL ON ACCOUNT OF DRIVELING INCOMPETENTS LIKE YOU!
B-BUT, SIR... I'M NOT...!

SHUT UP! DON'T TRY TO ALIBI...COME INTO MY OFFICE RIGHT AWAY!
Y-YES, SIR...!
WALT DISNEY

MISTAKEN FOR ANOTHER EMPLOYEE OVER THE PHONE, MICKEY IS ORDERED INTO THE OFFICE OF THE HEAD MAN, WHO IS ON THE WAR PATH!

EVER SINCE MR. McFOOZLE HAS BEEN BACK HE'S BEEN CRABBING ABOUT THE CONDITION OF OUR BUSINESS!
YEH, HE'S BEEN BAWLIN' OUT EVERYBODY ABOUT IT!
8-11
Copr. 1941, Walt Disney Productions World Rights Reserved

DO YOU SUPPOSE THINGS ARE REALLY IN SUCH BAD SHAPE?
I DON'T KNOW... MAYBE IT'S JUST HIS WAY! I THINK I'LL TALK TO SOME OF THE BOYS ABOUT IT!

WHAT DO **YOU** THINK, MAC? ARE FINANCES IN A BAD WAY AROUND HERE?
THEY WERE, BUT THEY JUST IMPROVED!

HOW? WHAT HAPPENED?
I JUST WON $4.40 FOR A TWO-BUCK TICKET ON "SPINAWAY"!
RACING SHEET

MOUSE? SQUEELE SPEAKING! BRING THE "EL FUMO" CIGARETTE FILE INTO MY OFFICE! MR. McFOOZLE IS WAITING, SO STEP LIVELY!
YES, SIR... RIGHT AWAY!
8-12

NEXT TIME COME FASTER... MR. McFOOZLE ABHORS TARDINESS!
SNAP! SNAP! SNAP!
BUT I CAME AS FAST AS I COULD!
A B SQUEELE

TSK-TSK... YOU SHOULD HAVE STRAIGHTENED THESE UP... MR. McFOOZLE WON'T TOLERATE CARELESSNESS!

DANG IT... MR. McFOOZLE CAN **ALSO** DO HIS **OWN TALKIN'**! GET **THAT**!
YES... YES, OF COURSE... CERTAINLY...!
A B SQUEELE
WALT DISNEY

CONFOUND IT, SQUEELE, YOU DON'T HAVE TO RIDE THE EMPLOYEES JUST TO SHOW ME HOW DANGED EFFICIENT YOU ARE!
I ONLY TRY TO..
YOU MAY LEAVE, MOUSE!
YES, SIR!
A. B. SQUEELE
8-13

HEY! COME BACK HERE! WHO SAID YOU COULD GO? DO YOU TAKE ORDERS FROM SQUEELE OR ME?

YES, SIR ...I DO!
YOU DO **WHICH?** WHAT KIND OF AN ANSWER IS...?

...OH, I GET IT! HO-HO-HO! DIDN'T I TELL Y' HE'S SMART, SQUEELE? HO-HO-HO!
A.B. SQUEELE
WALT DISNEY

NOW THEN, LET'S GO INTO THIS "EL FUMO" ACCOUNT ... WHAT IN TUNKET'S WRONG?
WELL, AS I SEE IT, MR. McFOOZLE...!
8-14

HOW WAS I.Q.... STILL BUMPIN' AROUND THE CEILING?
YEH, HE'S PRETTY CRABBY! SEEMS TO BE MIGHTY WORRIED ABOUT THE BUSINESS!

I DON'T QUITE GET IT! A BIG ACCOUNT LIKE "EL FUMO" CIGARETTES SHOULD CARRY US ALONE!
GOOD REASONING, SON... IT WOULD.

... BUT WE JUST LOST "EL FUMO"! CONTRACT EXPIRED YESTERDAY ... AND WASN'T RENEWED!
OH!

GOSH... LOSIN' THE "EL FUMO" ACCOUNT MUST BE A TOUGH BLOW!
YOU CAN SAY THAT AGAIN! IT LEAVES US PEANUTS!
8-15

GEE, IF THERE WAS ONLY SOME OTHER CLIENT THAT COULD TAKE THE PLACE OF...
YEAH... LIKE THE NOISELESS POTATO CHIP CO.! THERE'S SOMETHIN' THAT AIN'T HAY!

THEY'RE PRETTY BIG, EH? SAY, IF A FELLA COULD LAND A CLIENT LIKE THAT...?
TURN OVER, SONNY BOY... YOU'RE DONE! WE'VE GOT SALESMEN, Y' KNOW... AND PUH-LENTY OF OUTSIDE COMPETISH!

NOW, LET'S HAVE A FEW PENCIL POINTS...AND LAY OFF THE DREAM, KID!
OH, SURE, SURE... BUT I CAN STILL THINK...!
WALT DISNEY

IN SPITE OF MAC'S DERISIVE WARNINGS, MICKEY IS BITTEN WITH THE BUG OF TRYING TO LAND A NEW CLIENT AND PULL THE HOTFLASH AGENCY OUT OF THE HOLE!

HERE COMES MR. McFOOZLE! CERTAINLY I COULDN'T GET IN TROUBLE JUST BY ASKIN' HIM!
8-16

UH...MR. McFOOZLE... I UNDERSTAND THAT WE NEED SOME NEW ACCOUNTS AND...!
EH? WHAT'S THAT GOT TO DO WITH YOU?

I MEAN, IF YOU'D LET ME GO OUT... JUST IN MY SPARE TIME, OF COURSE...!
WHAT!!? SPARE TIME? IF YOU'VE GOT ANY SPARE TIME AROUND HERE, YOU'RE NOT NEEDED!

YOU'RE FIRED!!

WHAT'S THE TROUBLE, SON PICK THE WRONG HORSE?
I.. I'VE BEEN ..FIRED!
8-18

OH! RAN INTO OLD I. Q., I SUPPOSE, AND DIDN'T SEE THE RED LIGHT!
YES, THAT'S IT! WELL.. I GUESS I WON'T SEE Y' AGAIN, SO ..!

FORGET IT, M' BOY! BE ON THE JOB TOMORROW MORNING!
BUT DON'T YOU UNDERSTAND...?

SURE, I DO! JUST GO HOME UNTIL HIS NECK STOPS SIZZLING, THEN COME BACK TOMORROW!
ULP... HONEST?

HOTFLASH PUBLICITY AGENCY
SEEMS CRAZY TO BE COMIN' BACK THE DAY AFTER I'M CANNED, BUT THAT'S WHAT MAC TOLD ME TO DO!
8-19

GOSH...SUPPOSE IT'S ANOTHER ONE OF HIS GAGS! I'M LIABLE TO GET BOOTED THROUGH A WINDOW!

WELL? ARE YOU GOING TO GO IN, OR JUST STAND THERE, BLOCKING THE DOORWAY?
Y-YES, SIR...!

WALT DISNEY

WELL, YOU WERE RIGHT, MAC... I'M NOT FIRED, AFTER ALL!
YOU'LL GET ONTO I.Q. AFTER A WHILE! WHY, I'VE BEEN CANNED SO OFTEN I FEEL LIKE A SARDINE!
RACING SHEET
8-20

SARDINE...THAT'S A HUNCH! IN THE FIFTH RACE... HMMM...!
JUST THE SAME, HE HAD NO RIGHT TO GET SORE, BECAUSE I WANTED TO TRY FOR SOME NEW BUSINESS!
RACING SHEET

SURE, WE HAVE SALESMEN...BUT THEY DON'T SELL ANYTHING, SO WHY NOT...?

WHO SAID THAT?

WHO SAYS I CAN'T SELL? WAS IT THIS TWERP?
AW, HE DIDN'T MEAN YOU, WINDY.. JUST SOME O' THE OTHER BOYS! PULL DOWN YOUR BACK!
8-21

MEET JOE WINDERPAINE, SON ..HE'S OUR STAR SALESMAN! WINDY, SHAKE HANDS WITH MICKEY MOUSE!
OH, SURE.. OKAY!
GLAD TO MEET Y', MR WINDERPAINE!

I'LL ADMIT WE GOT DUDS IN THE FIRM, BUT FIRST LET ME PUT Y' WISE TO A FEW THINGS ABOUT ME!

BETTER SIT DOWN, SON THIS IS A DOUBLE FEATURE!
QUIET, WISE GUY!
Distributed by King Features Syndicate, Inc.

MICKEY MEETS JOE WINDERPAINE, BETTER KNOWN AS "WINDY," THE AGENCY'S STAR SALESMAN!

Y' WANT TO KNOW THE KIND OF SALESMAN I AM, DON'T Y'? WELL, LISTEN, MY BOY!
I DIDN'T HEAR HIM ASK, BUT GO AHEAD!
8-22
Copr. 1941, Walt Disney Productions World Rights Reserved

WHO DO Y' THINK LANDED THE "EL FUMO" CIGARETTE ACCOUNT? NOT MY FAULT WE COULDN'T HOLD 'EM! AND WHO BROUGHT IN "ICKY-WICKY" CORN FLAKES ...?

...AND "MOLARGLO" TOOTH PASTE ...AND "FIREPROOF" HOSIERY... AND "BREEZO" OYSTER-OPENER? AND WHO GOT...?

AND WHO'S GONNA LAND "NOISELESS" POTATO CHIPS, WHILE YOU STAND AND BLOW?
RELAX, SISTER! I'VE GOT THAT COMPLETELY UNDER CONTROL!
HONEST? YIPPEE! THAT SAVES THE DAY!
Distributed by King Features Syndicate, Inc.

DID Y' HEAR THAT, MAC? WE'RE GONNA GET THE "NOISELESS" POTATO CHIP ACCOUNT! ISN'T THAT SWELL?
YEH... IT WOULD BE... IF WE GET IT!
8-23

LISTEN, WISE GUY ...THAT JOB IS IN THE BAG AND SEWED UP! SEE Y' LATER!

Y' DON'T THINK HE'S REALLY GOT IT? HE SEEMS VERY CONFIDENT!
SON, IF WE GOT EVERY ACCOUNT WINDY WAS CONFIDENT OF, WE'D HAVE TO TAKE OVER THE GRAND CENTRAL STATION!
-BRR-RR-RINGG-!

IT'S I.Q! CALLIN' A MEETING OF ALL EMPLOYEES! SOMETHING'S UP!

AN HOUR OR SO OF DISCUSSION HAS GONE BY AND, SO FAR, NOTHING VERY HELPFUL ADVANCED TO AID THE SINKING FORTUNES OF THE HOTFLASH AGENCY!

The HOTFLASH AGENCY HUMS WITH ACTIVITY ...ALL BENT ON LURING IN THE LUCRATIVE "NOISELESS" POTATO CHIP ACCOUNT!

TRYING TO GET THE BOSS TO OKAY SOME SKETCHES, WINDY'S HIGH-PRESSURE SALESMANSHIP HAS A REVERSE EFFECT ON THE OLD MAN!

PLAYING ON McFOOZLE'S PERVERSE NATURE, MICKEY GETS AN O. K. ON THE "NOISELESS" POTATO CHIP CAMPAIGN, AFTER WINDY'S HIGH-POWERED METHODS HAD NEARLY UPSET THE APPLE CART!

ARTISTS AND COPY WRITERS HAVE OUTDONE THEMSELVES ON THE "NOISELESS" CAMPAIGN! FROM NOW ON IT'S UP TO WINDY, THE STAR SALESMAN!

HERE COMES WINDY...HE'S BEEN OVER AT "NOISELESS" POTATO CHIPS ALL MORNING WITH OUR SAMPLES!
IT'S ABOUT TIME HE WENT TO WORK ON THOSE GUYS!
9-4

WELL, BOYS, IT'S IN THE BAG...ALL SEWED UP!
Y' MEAN...Y' REALLY GOT THE CONTRACT THIS TIME?

NOT YET! THEY DON'T GO FOR THIS PARTICULAR CAMPAIGN ...BUT WITH SOME CHANGES AND A FEW NEW LAYOUTS...

...AND A FEW MORE COCKTAIL PARTIES AND NIGHT CLUBS AT MY EXPENSE, YOU MIGHT GET 'EM SLIGHTLY INTERESTED! BAH!

WOW! THE BOSS SURE BLEW UP ON WINDY, DIDN'T HE?
I DON'T BLAME HIM! WINDY'S NO NEARER TO LANDING THAT ACCOUNT THAN HE WAS A YEAR AGO!
9-5

WELL, IT'S NO HELP FOR ME TO STEW ABOUT IT... I'D BETTER GET TO WORK!
EXCEPT, RIGHT NOW, THERE'S NOTHIN' FOR Y' TO DO!
RACING SHEET

NO? WELL, SAY...ANY OBJECTION IF I GO OUT FOR A WHILE?
NOPE... GO AHEAD!

IF YOU'RE GOIN' TO THE TRACK, "CORN PLASTER" IN THE FOURTH RACE LOOKS GOOD!
THANKS! SEE Y' LATER!
RACING SHEET
WALT DISNEY

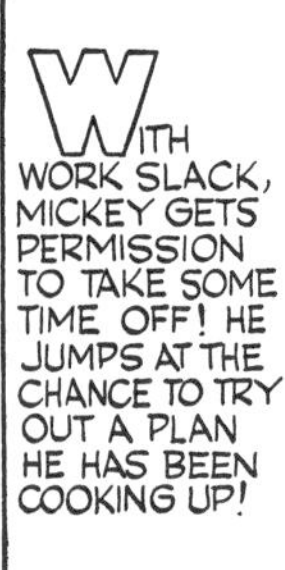
WITH WORK SLACK, MICKEY GETS PERMISSION TO TAKE SOME TIME OFF! HE JUMPS AT THE CHANCE TO TRY OUT A PLAN HE HAS BEEN COOKING UP!

THIS LOOKS LIKE AS GOOD A PLACE AS ANY TO START ON!
"U-DRIVE" HORSE-SHOE NAIL CO.
IRA BLOOP, MGR.
9-6

WHADDYAWANNASEEIMABOUT?
HORSE-SHOE NAILS!

IF YOU'RE TRYIN' TO SELL SOME-THIN', YOU'RE WASTIN' YOUR TIME! I'VE GOT NO MONEY TO...!
AH! THAT'S JUST IT! DO YOU REALIZE WHAT'S WRONG WITH YOUR BUSINESS, MR. BLOOP?
Distributed by King Features Syndicate, Inc.

LISTEN! THE PUBLIC...THE MAN IN THE STREET...IS NOT HORSE-SHOE NAIL CONSCIOUS!
EH? WHY... COME TO THINK OF IT... I DON'T BELIEVE THEY ARE!

HAVING A LITTLE TIME OFF, MICKEY GRABS THE OPPORTUNITY TO TRY HIS HAND AS A SALESMAN!

MAYBE YOU'VE GOT SOMETHING THERE, YOUNG MAN! THE PUBLIC DOESN'T **KNOW** ABOUT "U-DRIVE" HORSE SHOE NAILS!
OF **COURSE**, THEY DON'T! HOW CAN THEY KNOW HOW **SUPERIOR** THEY ARE IF Y' DON'T **ADVERTISE?**
9-8
Copr. 1941, Walt Disney Productions World Rights Reserved

WHY, MR. BLOOP, WE CAN HAVE YOUR PRODUCT ON EVERY **TONGUE**... A **HOUSEHOLD WORD**! THINK OF IT...!

EXCUSE ME, SIR... THAT'S OUR STANDARD LINE! SERIOUSLY, I'M JUST TRYIN' TO GET A LITTLE BUSINESS FOR MY FIRM...!
HMMM... A LITTLE BUSINESS IS WHAT **I** WANT, TOO... AND, YOUNG MAN, I'VE A NOTION TO GAMBLE WITH YOU!
Distributed by King Features Syndicate, Inc.

I'M SMALL... AND MIGHT BE SLOW PAY... BUT IF TERMS CAN BE ARRANGED...!
SHAKE, MR. BLOOP ...CONSIDER YOURSELF A CLIENT!

"U-DRIVE" HORSE SHOE NAIL CO.
IRA BLOOP, MGR.
BOY, WHAT A BREAK! IT'S PRETTY SMALL, BUT IT'S AN **ACCOUNT**! AND I'VE STILL GOT TIME TO TRY SOME MORE PLACES!
9-9

STUPID OLD DOPE! DOESN'T KNOW A GOOD THING WHEN IT'S SHOVED UNDER HIS NOSE!
COMFY-WUMFY TRACTOR CO. INC.

NEVERLEAK BATH SPONGE
"THE SPONGE WITHOUT A HOLE"
THERE WAS A BUSINESS MAN... HE'LL GO PLACES! NOW, TO SURPRISE THE BOSS!

SNOOKUMS, CONTACT I.Q. AND FIND OUT WHEN I CAN SEE HIM! I'VE GOT IMPORTANT BIZ!
MICKEY! ARE YOU **SERIOUS?**
WALT DISNEY

WELL, WHAT DO Y' WANT TO SEE ME ABOUT? IF IT'S A RAISE, YOU'RE CRAZY!
IT'S NOT THAT! MR. McFOOZLE, I'D LIKE A TRY AT GETTIN' THAT "NOISELESS" POTATO CHIP ACCOUNT!
9-10

NO! YOU LEAVE THAT TO WINDY! YOU DON'T KNOW THE ROPES AND COULDN'T LAND A CLIENT, ANYWAY!

BUT, MR. McFOOZLE, I'VE ALREADY LANDED ONE. IN FACT, TWO!
TOMMYROT! OF ALL THE BRAZEN CRUST ...TO TRY AND STUFF **ME** WITH SUCH FAT-HEADED DRIVEL!

WELL, I'LL BE A... DANGED IF THE INFERNAL YOUNG SCOUNDREL HASN'T ACTUALLY DONE IT!
Distributed by King Features Syndicate, Inc.
WALT DISNEY

WELL, WELL.. TWO NEW ACCOUNTS FOR US! WHEN DID YOU DO THIS, MY BOY?
JUST THIS AFTERNOON, SIR!
Copr 1941, Walt Disney Productions World Rights Reserved
9-11

FINE WORK! YOU'VE GOT THE MAKINGS OF A GO-GETTER, YOUNG MAN! WISH I HAD MORE EMPLOYEES LIKE YOU!

THANK YOU, SIR! THEN, HAVE I YOUR PERMISSION TO TRY FOR THE POTATO CHIP ACCOUNT?
WHAT!!?

CERTAINLY NOT! OF ALL THE INFERNAL CRUST... THAT'S BIG BUSINESS! YOU GET BACK TO YOUR WORK! UNDERSTAND?
WALT DISNEY

I JUST HEARD ABOUT YOU LANDING THOSE NEW ACCOUNTS! I THINK IT'S JUST WONDERFUL!
MUCH GOOD IT DID ME! THE BOSS STILL WON'T LET ME TRY FOR THE BIG MONEY!
9-12

CONGRATULATIONS, SON! Y' REALLY SHOWED US YOU CAN SELL!
THANKS! OF COURSE, I KNOW IT ISN'T MUCH...!
Y' CAN SAY THAT AGAIN! BATH SPONGES AND HORSE SHOE NAILS! PHOOEY!

Y' WOULDN'T FIND ME FOOLIN' WITH THAT KINDA SMALL CHANGE.. IT'S NOTHIN' BUT PEANUTS!

THERE'S MORE NOURISHMENT, SISTER, IN REAL PEANUTS THAN IN POTATO CHIPS BY HEARSAY!
Distributed by King Features Syndicate, Inc.
WALT DISNEY

HERE'S THE CONTRACT FOR THAT HORSE SHOE NAIL CO! IT'S YOUR ACCOUNT, MY BOY GO SIGN 'EM UP!
THANKS, MR. MCFOOZLE!
9-13

HE'S OUT ON A BIG HORSE SHOE DEAL! COME BACK IN AN HOUR!
OKAY... I'LL TAKE A STROLL THROUGH THE PARK WHILE I'M WAITING!
Copr. 1941, Walt Disney Productions World Rights Reserved

IT MAY BE PEANUTS, BUT AT LEAST IT'S AN ACCOUNT, AND I'M NOT GONNA LOSE IT!

GOOD GOSH... MR. BLOOP AND HIS BIG HORSE SHOE DEAL!
CITY PARK COURTS
WALT DISNEY

KILLING TIME WHILE WAITING FOR HIS CLIENT, MR. BLOOP, TO RETURN, MICKEY DISCOVERS THE GENTLEMAN PITCHING HORSE SHOES IN THE PARK!

I'M SURE GLAD TO HAVE HAD YOUR VIEWS ON SALES METHODS, MR CHIPPER!
I'VE ENJOYED YOUR VIEWS, TOO, MY BOY!
WELL, I'LL HAVE TO QUIT, CHARLIE...
9-18

...GOT TO GET BACK TO THE OFFICE!
THERE IT GOES! NOBODY EVER HAS TIME TO PLAY WITH ME!

SORRY, BUT Y' KNOW HOW IT IS! SO LONG!
SO LONG! HANG IT ALL...PEOPLE SPEND TOO MUCH TIME WORKIN'!

YOUNG MAN, YOU'VE GOT SOME MIGHTY SOUND THOUGHTS ON SALESMANSHIP! I'D LIKE TO DISCUSS IT WITH YOU... OVER A CROQUET COURT!
UH...THANKS...I DON'T KNOW IF I SHOULD...!

I MAINTAIN YOU CAN'T FORCE PEOPLE INTO BUYING ANYTHING JUST BY A LOUD VOICE!
YOU'RE RIGHT, MR. CHIPPER! JUST SHOW 'EM WHAT YOU'VE GOT AND LET 'EM DECIDE FOR THEMSELVES!
9-19

MEANWHILE, BACK AT THE HOTFLASH AGENCY!

YOU WISH TO SEE MR. McFOOZLE? IS IT IMPORTANT BUSINESS?
IT MOST CERTAINLY IS! I HAPPEN TO BE THE OWNER OF THIS BUILDING!

GOODNESS! I WONDER WHAT'S WRONG, NOW... HE LOOKED ORNERY!

YOUNG MAN, YOU PLAY A FINE GAME OF SALESMANSHIP...I MEAN YOU TALK GOOD CROQUET! HOW ABOUT PICKING UP AGAIN TOMORROW?
FINE! I'LL MEET Y' DURING MY LUNCH-HOUR!

MICKEY SPENDS MOST OF HIS SPARE TIME IN THE CITY'S RECREATION PARKS WITH HIS NEW FRIEND, MR. CHIPPER!

I DON'T KNOW WHY I GO AROUND WITH HIM SO MUCH. BUT HE SEEMS TO LIKE MY COMPANY!
AH... THERE YOU ARE, MY BOY!
9-20

MEANWHILE, AT THE OFFICE, THINGS ARE NOT SO GOOD!
JUST BECAUSE Y' OWN THE BUILDING YOU CAN'T SCARE ME! I'VE TOLD Y' BEFORE, I WON'T GIVE UP MY LEASE!
VERY WELL, McFOOZLE! BUT LET ME TELL YOU ONE THING...

...YOU PAY YOUR RENT ON THE DOT, OR OUT YOU GO!
DON'T WORRY... YOU'LL GET IT!

FROM WHERE? THE DANGED RENT'S DUE NEXT WEEK AND I CAN'T RAISE A REASONABLE FACSIMILE OF A DIME!

HAVE YOU HEARD THE WORST? IF MR. McFOOZLE CAN'T PAY THE RENT BY TOMORROW NIGHT, WE'RE GOING TO BE KICKED OUT!
SO MAC WAS TELLIN' ME! BOY, WE'RE SURE IN A TOUGH SPOT!
9-22

ARE YOU..UH..GOING TO LUNCH, NOW?
UH-HUH! GOT A DATE WITH MR. CHIPPER! SEE Y' LATER!

LOOK, ROMEO...I JUST TALKED TO THE BANK AND THEY'LL GIVE ME A LOAN COVERING THE PAYROLL AND RENT IF ...WE GET ONE MAJOR ACCOUNT!
BUT LISTEN, I.Q...WITH THE PETTY EX-PENSES YOU ALLOW ME, HOW DO Y' EXPECT...?

LISTEN, ALIBI IKE...IF YOU DON'T SEW UP THAT POTATO CHIP DEAL BY TOMORROW AFTERNOON, WE'RE THROUGH! AND YOU'LL BE THE FIRST ONE!
UH.. YEAH.. YEAH..!
WALT DISNEY'S

NOON OF THE FATEFUL DAY ARRIVES! MICKEY HAS ANOTHER DATE WITH THE SPORT-LOVING MR. CHIPPER, BUT ISN'T VERY GOOD COMPANY!

SORRY, MR. CHIPPER, BUT I GUESS I'VE GOT TOO MUCH ON MY MIND!
THAT SO? SUPPOSE Y' TELL ME ABOUT IT!
9-23

GOSH...DO Y' THINK I.Q. RAISED THE DOUGH?
I HEARD THE BANK WON'T KICK IN UNLESS WE LAND THE ACCOUNT! LOOKS LIKE WE'RE SUNK!
WINDY'S OVER AT "NOISELESS" NOW, MAKIN' A LAST STAB AT IT! MAYBE HE MIGHT...!

OH, YEAH? IF WE GOTTA DEPEND ON THAT BALONEY-SLINGER, I'M STARTIN' TO READ THE WANT ADS!

YOUNG MAN, I ADMIRE YOUR SPUNK AND I LIKE YOUR SALES IDEAS! I THINK I'LL GIVE YOU THE POTATO CHIP ACCOUNT!
YOU'LL GIVE ME.. ...? BUT...HOW CAN YOU, UH... ULP??

THAT'S WHAT I SAID... I'M GOING TO GIVE YOU THE "NOISELESS" POTATO CHIP ACCOUNT!
BUT... BUT HOW CAN YOU? YOU'RE NOT THE PROMOTION MANAGER!
9-24

OF COURSE NOT...I'M THE PRESIDENT! I OWN THE PLACE! DIDN'T YOU KNOW?
G-GOSH!

WELL, LET'S NOT WASTE ANY MORE TIME...COME ON OVER TO MY OFFICE!
!
?

THE CONTRACT'S READY... ALL I HAVE TO DO IS SIGN IT!
BOY-OH-BOY! IF THIS IS A DREAM, DON'T WAKE ME UP!
"NOISELESS" POTATO CHIP CO.
WALT DISNEY'S

MICKEY IS OVERJOYED WHEN HIS FRIEND, MR. CHIPPER, TURNS OUT TO BE THE PRESIDENT OF "NOISELESS" POTATO CHIPS AND OFFERS HIM THE ACCOUNT!

I SUPPOSE YOU'RE WONDERING WHY THE OWNER SHOULD COME IN THE BACK DOOR!
WELL...IT DID SEEM KINDA FUNNY!
9-25

PRIVACY, MY BOY! IF I CAME THROUGH THE FRONT OFFICES SOME PESKY HOT-SHOT SALESMAN WOULD BE WAITIN' TO NAB ME!

MATTER OF FACT, YOUR FRIEND, WINDERPAINE'S BEEN OUT THERE YAPPIN' HIS FOOL HEAD OFF ALL DAY!
BOY! WHAT A SURPRISE HE'S GONNA GET!

YIPPEE! OUR BIG ACCOUNT! MR. CHIPPER, YOU'VE SAVED THE DAY!
WALT DISNEY

TWENTY-FIVE MINUTES TO THREE! THINGS LOOK VERY DARK TO I.Q. McFOOZLE, WHO DOES NOT YET KNOW THAT MICKEY HAS THE BIG CONTRACT!

YOU'RE LICKED, McFOOZLE ... WHY NOT ADMIT IT? Y' HAVEN'T GOT THE RENT AND Y' CAN'T RAISE A NICKEL!
THE BANK DON'T CLOSE TILL THREE! IF I GET THAT CONTRACT IN TIME...!
9-26

THAT YOU, WINDY? ARE Y' GETTIN' ANY PLACE WITH THOSE PEOPLE OVER THERE?
I'VE GOT 'EM PRETTY WELL SOLD, I.Q! NOW, IF Y' COULD STRETCH THAT TIME LIMIT...!

BAH!
NO DICE, EH? LOOKS LIKE YOU'RE MOVIN' OUT!
MR. McFOOZLE, I'VE...!
SLAM!

...OH, EXCUSE ME! I'LL COME BACK LATER!

WISH THAT GUY IN WITH THE BOSS WOULD LEAVE, WHOEVER HE IS! I'LL BUST, HOLDIN' BACK THE GOOD NEWS THAT I'VE GOT THE "NOISELESS" POTATO CHIP CONTRACT!
I.Q. McFOO
PRIVATE
9-27

QUARTER TO THREE! NO CHANCE OF YOUR RAISIN' THE RENT TODAY, McFOOZLE, SO Y' MIGHT AS WELL START MOVIN'!
GOOD DAY, SHYLOCK!
I.Q. McFOO
PRIVATE

I'VE GOT IT! POISELESS NIPS.. CHIPPERS, UH...THIS IS IT!
WHAT? YOU...YOU'VE GOT...??

BY TUNKET, IT IS!
RUN AFTER THAT MAN AND BRING HIM BACK...NO MATTER HOW!
GET ME THE BANK... QUICK!
WALT DISNEY
Distributed by King Features Syndicate, Inc.

Mickey pops up with the life-saving potato chip contract in the nick of time, but the building owner has just left, confident that the lease is broken!

DON'T JUST STAND THERE! RUN AFTER HIM AND BRING HIM BACK!
BUT WHAT'LL I TELL HIM?
9-29

TELL HIM ANYTHING! GET GOING!
YES, SIR!

HEY, MISTER! URGENT MESSAGE IN MR. McFOOZLE'S OFFICE! YOUR WIFE BURNT DOWN... I MEAN, YOUR HOUSE HAD TRIPLETS...!
?

IT'S PLAIN TO SEE YOU'RE AS BATTY AS A COOT, BUT I'LL GO BACK AND SEE WHAT IT'S ALL ABOUT!
YES, SIR... THAT'S THE MAIN IDEA!

LOOK HERE, McFOOZLE... WHAT'S THE IDEA OF BRINGING ME BACK HERE WITH SOME COCK AND BULL STORY?
CALM YOURSELF, MY DEAR FELLOW... I HAVE SOME INTERESTING INFORMATION FOR YOU!
9-30

YOU'D LIKE US TO VACATE THESE QUARTERS, SO YOU COULD RENT TO SOMEONE ELSE AT A HIGHER RATE WOULDN'T YOU?
WHICH IS JUST WHAT I'M GOING TO DO! WE'VE BEEN THROUGH ALL THAT, BLAST IT!

THINGS HAVE CHANGED, MY DEAR MAN! HERE'S YOUR RENT... IF YOU THINK IT'LL BOUNCE, CALL THE BANK!

JUST ONE MORE DISAPPOINTMENT...THE RENT WILL BE PAID PROMPTLY EVERY MONTH! GOOD DAY!
BLANKETY BLANK!
LUCKY FOOL!
WALT DISNEY

HELLO, WINDY, MY BOY! HOW ARE Y' MAKING OUT OVER THERE ON THE "NOISELESS" ACCOUNT?
WELL... Y' SEE, IT'S LIKE THIS, I.Q. ...I'VE GOT 'EM INTERESTED, SEE? BUT, ER...!
10-1

WELL, LISTEN, Y' BIG WINDBAG! MICKEY MOUSE GOT THAT CONTRACT RIGHT FROM UNDER YOUR NOSE...IT'S ON MY DESK NOW!

WHY, THE DOUBLE-CROSSING LITTLE SHRIMP! THAT'S SABOTAGE ... I'VE BEEN SCUTTLED!
I RESIGN!

THANK YOU VERY MUCH!
WALT DISNEY

AND NOW, MY BOY, I GUESS I'VE FINALLY GOT TIME TO THANK YOU FOR SAVING MY BUSINESS!
Y' DON'T HAFTA, MR. McFOOZLE... IT'S BEEN A LOTTA FUN!
10-2

IT WAS A FINE PIECE OF WORK! NOW I WONDER WHAT I CAN DO FOR **YOU**?
SHUCKS...I DON'T EXPECT ANYTHING, SIR!

HOW'D Y' LIKE TO HAVE WINDY'S JOB?
I DON'T BELIEVE I'D CARE FOR THAT, FULL TIME!

THEN, I GUESS YOU'LL JUST HAVE TO GO BACK AND WORK FOR MAC UNTIL I THINK WHAT TO DO FOR YOU!
OKAY! THANK Y', SIR!
WALT DISNEY

GREAT WORK, M'BOY! IT SURE SAVED OUR JOBS FOR US!
YOU BETCHA! THAT'S WHAT I CALL BRINGIN' HOME THE OLD BACON!
THANKS FELLAS! UH...EXCUSE ME... MR. SQUEELE WANTS TO SEE ME!

ORDINARILY WE FROWN ON EMPLOYEES STEPPING OUTSIDE THEIR REGULAR CAPACITIES BUT UNDER THESE CIRCUMSTANCES YOUR ACTION WAS VERY CREDITABLE!
THANK YOU, SIR!
10-3

NICE GOIN', SON! THAT DEAL LOOKED AS SWEET TO ME AS A HUNDRED TO ONE SHOT COMIN' HOME IN FRONT!
GLAD Y' THINK SO, MAC! SEE Y' LATER!

OH, MICKEY, YOU **WONDERFUL...**!
LAY OFF...**PLEASE!** I DON'T WANTA HEAR ANY MORE ABOUT THAT CONTRACT! I JUST WANT A DATE FOR TONIGHT!
WALT DISNEY
Distributed by King Features Syndicate, Inc.

I DON'T CARE IF YOU **DON'T** LIKE TO BE PRAISED, I THINK YOU DID THE GRANDEST THING...
AHEM... BRRMPH-H..!
10-4

YOUNG MAN, THIS IS DISGRACEFUL! FOR SUCH UNSEEMLY CONDUCT I SENTENCE YOU TO TAKE THIS BONUS AND A WEEK'S VACATION!

AND FOR AIDING AND ABETTING THE OFFENSE, YOUNG LADY, YOU ALSO WILL RECEIVE THE SAME PUNISHMENT!

DO I MAKE MYSELF CLEAR?
YES, SIR! THANK YOU VERY MUCH!
WALT DISNEY
Distributed by King Features Syndicate, Inc.

MYSTERY AT HIDDEN RIVER

OCTOBER 6, 1941
–
JANUARY 17, 1942

WOODMAN, SPARE THAT ALIBI

When cartoon characters change design, as frequently took place at the Disney studio, the audience is expected to accept the alterations without question. But what do you do when a change renders the character's name meaningless?

Such was the case with Pegleg Pete, Walt Disney's oldest recurring cartoon star. Pete's peg leg was conspicuously absent from the animated cartoons beginning in 1936, but Gottfredson didn't seem to get the memo to mask the cat's handicap until 1941's "Mystery at Hidden River."

Mickey arrives at the shady Hidden River lumber camp to search for the missing Clarabelle Cow and investigate a logwood theft plot. He immediately encounters Pete, taking note that his foe has adopted a French-Canadian identity and dropped the peg leg. When Mickey asks about the limb, Pete responds that he's gotten a new-model artificial leg. "Pierre, she's now streamline lak' modern design, eh?"

As Tom Andrae has noted earlier in this volume, Pete's "Pierre" alias and costume are derived from the Donald Duck short *Timber* (1941). Among the better Jack King–directed cartoons written by Carl Barks and Jack Hannah, *Timber* was still making its rounds in theaters at the time "Hidden River" was published. What better moment for a tie-in—and as long as we're following cartoon continuity, why not explain what happened to Pete's leg? The process had begun by which, in non-Gottfredson stories, Pegleg Pete was rechristened Black Pete. Or Sneaky Pete. Or Big Bad Pete. Or he might even regain his peg leg. So much for consistency.

Sylvester Shyster re-emerges in "Hidden River"—quite ceremoniously, after a seven-year absence from the strip—as Pete's partner in the logwood scam. Yet there is no convincing reason for Shyster to be "the brains in this deal," as he calls himself; for he employs neither the legal vernacular nor the skulduggery that he utilized in 1930s strips. He is here merely to bark orders at Pete, a role suitable for any number of ciphers.

And thus "Hidden River" is, appropriately, a farewell to the prewar Gottfredson adventure model: one that employed more recurring characters than we would see after this. After "Hidden River," Pete would remain the strip's sole regular villain; Clarabelle would never again figure so pivotally into the plot; and Shyster would be dropped entirely. Minnie, too, would be resigned to walk-on "girlfriend" roles in due time; but Gottfredson and friends still had a few shining moments left for her.

More predominant in the 1940s *Mickey* strip were Native American caricatures who spoke in thick, broken English, and one persistent "Indian princess" is critical to Mickey's victory in "Hidden River." Since her fractured language is ultimately revealed to be a put-on, the portrayal could almost be read as progressive. But the strip still remains as much a product of its time as the work of a craftsman at his peak.

Culture students note: when Pete, at one point, speaks of settling down to grow "marihuana" (sic), it doesn't mean he's a stoner. The drug simply didn't carry that association in 1941. Like Pete's cargo of opium in the earlier "Captive Castaways" (1934), it was perceived as merely something a crook was likely to smuggle—not necessarily use.

—Thad Komorowski

GOSH, WHAT A STORM! THE FIRST DAY OF MY VACATION, AND IT HAS TO POUR CATS AND DOGS!
Distributed by King Features Syndicate, Inc.

NO USE ASKIN' MINNIE TO GO OUT IN THIS WEATHER!
10-6

EEEE-EEEK MICKEY!!

SOMETHING TERRIBLE HAS HAPPENED TO CLARABELLE!
WH-WHAT'S WRONG ... IS SHE MARRIED?
WALT DISNEY

THIS IS AWFUL! CLARABELLE...LOST IN THE WOODS...WAY UP NORTH...!!
N-NOW, MINNIE... B-BE BALM...CALM! TELL ME EVERYTHING!
TELEGRAM
10-7

IT'S FROM A TRAVEL BUREAU! SHE WAS ON A CONDUCTED TOUR AND DISAPPEARED...!
YEH, I SEE...AT A LUMBER CAMP THEY WERE VISITIN'! GOSH!

C'MON...NO TIME TO LOSE! GOTTA GET THE F.B.I.!
BETTER TAKE... UMBRELLA!

WON'T NEED IT! WE'LL TAKE THE CAR AND KEEP DRY!
Copr 1941, Walt Disney Productions World Rights Reserved

"GETTING A WIRE SAYING THAT CLARABELLE HAS MYSTERIOUSLY DISAPPEARED WHILE ON A VACATION TOUR, MICKEY AND MINNIE RUSH FRANTICALLY THROUGH A RAINSTORM TO THE LOCAL F.B.I. OFFICE!"

...AND SHE'S OUR DEAREST FRIEND AND YOU'VE JUST GOT TO FIND HER!
SHE MIGHT'VE BEEN KID-NAPED, OR...!
JUST A MINUTE, PLEASE ...ONE AT A TIME! LET'S GET OUR FACTS STRAIGHT AND ORDERLY!
10-8

FIRST...WHEN AND WHERE WAS THE VICTIM LAST SEEN ALIVE? PLEASE BE ACCU-RATE!
IT SAYS RIGHT HERE IN THE TELEGRAM...!
TELEGRAM

AH, YES...HIDDEN RIVER LOGGING CO.! HMMM...CURIOUS, THIS! ALWAYS LOSING MY MEN UP THERE... GOOD MEN, TOO!

WE'RE NOT LOOKING FOR MEN...IT'S CLARABELLE!
IF Y'KNOW THE PLACE..!
IF YOU YOUNG PEOPLE WOULD SIT DOWN, THE INVESTIGATION WOULD PROCEED QUICKER...AND DRIER!

At the F.B.I. office Mickey and Minnie learn that the G-Men have already been active at the lumber camp where Clarabelle disappeared!

AY YUST SEE YOU BAN FOR HIDDEN RIVER! GOT BIZZNESS HEY?
I HOPE SO... I WANT TO GET A JOB AT THE LUMBER CAMP! IS THAT WHERE YOU'RE GOIN'?
10-13

YA! AY BAN WORK DERE LONG TIME... MORE FOOL ME!
TELL ME, IS IT TRUE ABOUT THE SABOTAGE GOIN ON... I MEAN, THE LOGS' DISAPPEARIN'?

BAD BIZZNESS! WHEN FOUR HUNNERD LOGS SHE START DOWN CHUTE AND T'REE HUNNERD SHE COME OUT BOTTOM END... WOT YOU T'INK?
GOLLY... I WOULDN'T KNOW!

WELL, AY T'INK ANY MAN BIG FOOL TO TAKE YOB DERE... MORE FOOL ME!

HIDDEN RIVER LOGGING CO.
EMPLOYMENT OFFICE
SO THIS IS THE LUMBER CAMP WHERE SOLID LOGS DISAPPEAR!
YA! IF A FALLER BAN CRAZY ENOUGH TO WANT A YOB HERE, ASK INSIDE! AY BAN GO WORK NOW!

GOSH, I HOPE THEY TAKE ME! I'VE GOT A HUNCH THAT THIS MYSTERY AND CLARABELLE'S DISAPPEARANCE ARE CONNECTED!
10 14

YUH WANTER DO **WHAT**? HEY, FELLERS, ...GIT A LOAD O' WHAT WANTS TO BE A **LUMBERJACK**!
HAW-HAW-HAW! SINCE WHEN ARE WE CUTTIN' TOOTHPICKS?
HE'S BRUNG A SATCHEL TO CARRY HIS SILK HANKIE'S!
OH HAR! HAR! HAR! HAR!
WALT DISNEY

I STILL WANTA GET A JOB, IF THERE'S AN OPENING!
YOU BETTER SEE THUH STRAW BOSS ...HE'S OUT ON THUH SOUTH TRAIL! MEBBE HE MIGHT PUT Y' ON!
10-15

THAT IS, IF HE DON'T EAT YUH FIRST! HE LIKES **SHRIMPS** FOR LUNCH!
HAW-HAW-HAWR!
HAR! HAR!

GOSH! I HOPE THAT FOREMAN ISN'T AS TOUGH AS HE SOUNDS!

LEESTEN, YOU! **NEX'** TIME PIERRE HAV' TO BREAK A GOOD AXE OVER A MAN, BY GAR, SHE'S GONNA GET **MAD**...SEE?
!
WALT DISNEY

BACK TO CAMP, DOG OF A PEEG, AN' BREENG PIERRE NEW AXE... QUEEK, BY GAR!
PARDON ME, SIR... COULD I SPEAK TO Y' A MINUTE?
10-16

WOTTA YOU WANT?
PEG-LEG PETE!!

YOU 'AVE MADE WAN BEEG MEESTAKE, MY FRAN'! YOU ARE TALK TO PIERRE DE LA POOCH!
AW, DON'T HAND ME THAT STUFF, PETE... I KNOW Y'!

SO WOTTA YER INTEND TO DO ABOUT IT, HUH?
N-NOTHING! JUST WANTED TO S-SAY ...HELLO!
WALT DISNEY

LISSEN, YUH LI'L RUNT! AROUND HERE I'M PIERRE DE LA POOCH AND YOU AIN'T SPILLIN' NO BEANS, SEE?
WHY, SURE NOT, PETE! ANYTHING YOU SAY!
10-17

NOW, DAT'S TALKIN' SENSE!

SA-A-AY... YOU MUST'VE BROKEN JAIL! YOUR STRETCH UP THE RIVER HAS ABOUT FIVE YEARS TO GO YET!

COME TO THINK OF IT, I RECALL A COUPLE OF OTHER TERMS Y' DIDN'T FINISH! AND THEY SAY THERE'S G-MEN AROUND HERE, TOO! TSK! TSK!
AW, NOW LISSEN, PAL! REMEMBER ALL OUR GOOD TIMES TOGETHER? YOU WOULDN'T SQUEAL ON YER OL' BUDDY... WOULD YUH, PAL?
WALT DISNEY

NOW, YOU AIN'T TALKIN' TO NO G-MEN ABOUT YER OL' BUDDY'S PAST... ARE YUH, PAL?
NOT A WORD! AND, BY THE WAY... I CAME OUT HERE TO GET A JOB AS A LUMBERJACK! HOW'S ABOUT IT?
10-18

WOT? YUH MEAN YUH WANTER DO TIMBER WORK... WITH AN AXE?
YEH... IT'S FOR MY HEALTH! I NEED TO GET OUTDOORS AND EXERCISE!

WHY, SURE... YOU KIN HAVE A JOB, PAL!
THANKS! I'LL GO GET FIXED UP AT THE OFFICE!
YEAH, I'LL BE GLAD TO GIT YUH HEALTHY...

... REAL HEALTHY.

OF ALL THUH BLINKIN' BLASTED LUCK! MICKEY MOUSE MEDDLIN' IN MUH PRIVATE AFFAIRS AGAIN!
10-20

WELL, I DON'T HAVE TO BE CLAIRVOYANT TO KNOW WHO'S THE VILLAIN IN THIS MYSTERY! THE TRICK IS TO GET THE GOODS ON HIM!

AND I GOTTER GIVE THUH PESKY LI'L RAT A JOB JEST TO KEEP 'IM QUIET ABOUT MUH PAST! THERE AIN'T NO JUSTICE!

CHUNK!
WELL, HE'LL BE WORKIN' ON A MIGHTY DANGEROUS JOB...AND ACCIDENTS KIN HAPPEN!
WALT DISNEY

COM' ON, LEETLE WAN! PIERRE, SHE'S GOIN' TAK' YOU TO BEEG TREES!
OKAY, I'M READY!
HEY! THAT'S FUNNY... NO PEG-LEG!
TOOL SHED
10-21

HOW COME, PETE...WHAT ABOUT THE OLD WOODEN KICKER?
AH...I HAV' REPLACE HEEM WEETH NEW MODEL STORE LEG! PIERRE, SHE'S NOW STREAMLINE LAK' MODERN DESIGN, EH?

BE YOURSELF, PETE! WHY PRATTLE THAT CHINOOK ACCENT WHEN WE'RE ALONE?
OH, NO YOU DON'T! YOU LAK' SEE PIERRE GET OUT OF PRACTISE AND MAK' SLEEP-UP IN CAMP! NAUGHTY... NAUGHTY!

BUT, GIT DIS, MUGG...I AIN'T FALLIN' FER IT...SEE?
WALT DISNEY

NOW, LEETLE WAN, PIERRE, SHE'S GONNA SHOW HOW TO NOTCH THE TREE... LIKE THEES! STAN' WELL BACK, FOR CHEEPS, THEY FLY!
10-22

EEF THE LEETLE WAN GET HURT, PIERRE FEEL VER' BAD...
CHUNK!

...HE FEEL TERR'BLE ...OOPS!

OH...SO SORRY! PIERRE, SHE'S FORGET TO SPIT ON HEES HANDS!

THERE SHE GOES!
TIMBER!

DON' STAN' TOO CLOSE...WHY, WHER' DEED HE GO?
10-23

CRASH! KA-THUD!

WUMP!

NOW, LEETLE WAN, PIERRE, SHE'S GEEVE YOU SPECIAL PREEVILEGE ...YOU CAN TOP THE TREE!
UH..ULP...Y' MEAN I GOTTA CLIMB WAY UP THERE?
10-24

SHUCKS! I GUESS THIS IS SAFER THAN BEIN' ON THE GROUND!
Copr. 1941, Walt Disney Productions
World Rights Reserved

AT LEAST, NOTHIN' CAN FALL ON ME OR... OMIGOSH!
CHUNK! CHUK! CHUNK!

HAPPY DAYS ARE HERE AGAIN...

GOOD GOSH! PETE'S CUTTIN' DOWN THE TREE! HEY! STOP!
CHUNK! CHOCK! CHUNK!
10-25
Copr. 1941, Walt Disney Productions
World Rights Reserved

CUT IT OUT! PETE! STOP! DO Y' HEAR ME?
SHE WAS ONLY A BIRD IN A GILDED...
I CAN'T HEAR A THING!

TIM-B-E-R!
WALT DISNEY

TIM-B-E-R!
10-27

BAM! KA-RASH!
HAWR! HAWR! I RECKON DAT FINISHED THUH LI'L PEST!

WELL, I'LL BE... HE'S ALIVE!
HEY, WHAT'S THE IDEA... CUTTIN' THE TREE DOWN WHILE I WAS IN IT? I COULD'VE BEEN HURT!

BUT, PIERRE, SHE'S GEEVE FAIR WARNING ...HE CALL, "TIM-B-E-R"!

BOY, WHAT A TRICK! CUTTIN' DOWN THE TREE WITH ME IN IT THEN HOLLERIN' TIMBER AFTER IT STARTS TO FALL! I'VE GOTTA WATCH THAT GUY!
10-28
Copr 1941, Walt Disney Productions World Rights Reserved

MAYBE A LITTLE OF HIS OWN MEDICINE...!

THUH LI'L RUNT'S LUCKIER THAN A CROSS-EYED RABBIT... BLAST 'IM!

YOW-W!
T-HUD!

TIM-B-E-R-R-R!

BOY... WHAT A DAY! I ONLY HOPE MY LUCK WILL HOLD, FOR OLD PETE'S SURE OUT TO GET ME!
HIDDEN RIVER LOG
TOOL SHED
10-29

NOW, I THINK I'LL DO A LITTLE SCOUTING AROUND FOR SOME CLUES ON WHAT COULD'VE HAPPENED TO CLARABELLE!

THERE'S ONE THING I ADMIT I LIKE ABOUT PETE! WHEN A MYSTERIOUS CRIME HAPPENS IN HIS VICINITY, Y' HAFTA HUNT FOR THE EVIDENCE ALRIGHT..
Distributed by King Features Syndicate, Inc.

...BUT Y' DON'T HAFTA HUNT FOR "WHODUNIT"!

SO FAR, I HAVEN'T SEEN ANYTHING THAT WOULD GIVE ME THE FAINTEST CLUE ABOUT CLARABELLE'S DISAPPEARANCE!
10-30
Copr. 1941, Walt Disney Productions World Rights Reserved

ANOTHER PUZZLER IS WHAT THE STOLEN LUMBER HAS TO DO WITH IT... BUT I'LL BET MY EYE THEY'RE CONNECTED!

I HEAR THERE'S INDIANS LIVIN' IN THIS FOREST... WONDER IF THEY'D KNOW ANY... OH-OH! THERE'S SOMEBODY, NOW!

GOOD GOSH! IT... IT'S MINNIE!
Distributed by King Features Syndicate, Inc.
WALT DISNEY

MINNIE!
YES? YOU WANT-UM ME, WHITE MANS?
Copr. 1941, Walt Disney Productions World Rights Reserved

OH... SORRY! I THOUGHT YOU WERE SOMEONE I KNEW! BUT HOW COME YOU ANSWERED TO THE NAME?
ME NAMED MINNIE-TEE-HEE, BUT SOMETIMES CALL-UM MINNIE FOR SHORT!
10-31

OH, I SEE! QUITE A COINCIDENCE... UH, ISN'T IT?
ME GOT-UM OTHER NAME... PRETTIER, TOO! FRIENDS CALL-UM "LITTLE STAR"!

WOULD YOU LIKE TO CALL-UM "LITTLE STAR," HANDSOME WHITE MANS?
UH... ULP... THANKS... OH, SURE... ULP!
WALT DISNEY

WHAT YOU DO IN FOREST, WHITE MANS? YOU MIGHTY HUNTER, MAYBE... SLAY-UM GRIZZLY?
UH, NO... I WORK OVER AT THE CAMP... A LUMBERJACK!
11-1

OOOOO! YOU SWING-UM AXE-HATCHET... GET HEAP BIG MUSCLE! MUCH NICE!
ULP!

"LITTLE STAR" LIKE BIG, STRONG...!
YEH... UH, THANKS! WELL... I GOTTA BE GOIN' NOW!

YES? GOOD! WHERE WE GO, HUH?
WALT DISNEY

WHO AREY', ANYWAY, "LITTLE STAR"? ...WHERE DO Y' COME FROM?
ME DAUGHTER OF BIG CHIEF, "SNOOZE-ON-UM-JOB," TRIBE OF PALUMAWALSY!
COME...ME SHOW-UM TEPEE!
11-3

BUT THAT TRIBE LIVES WAY UP NORTH!
YES! ME COME DOWN, VISIT AUNT... HELP-UM WITH CORN HARVEST! HEAP MUCH WORK!

MY AUNT CALLED "RISING-FULL-MOON"! SHE MUCH NICE LIKE ME! COME... YOU MEET-UM!
OKAY, "LITTLE STAR"!

AUNTIE, ME WANT YOU MEET-UM HANDSOME WHITE MANS! ME FIND-UM... ISN'T HE PRETTY?
HOW?
AND HOW!
WALT DISNEY

YOU LIKE-UM CORN PONE AND CIDER, WHITE MAN? AUNTIE MAKE-UM GOOD, HUH?
UMM... SWELL!
GEE, SHE'S KINDA CUTE! AND THE OLD SQUAW SEEMS TO BE A FRIENDLY SORT, TOO!
11-4

SAY! WONDER IF THEY'D KNOW ANYTHING ABOUT CLARABELLE? MAYBE THEY'VE SEEN HER, IF I GIVE 'EM HER DESCRIPTION!

...AND THEN SHE'S GOT A BIG NOSE, AN'..AN' SHORT HORNS AND A PROMINENT FRONT TOOTH! REMEMBER SEEIN' ANYONE LIKE THAT RECENTLY?
NO! WE NO SEE-UM, HAVE WE, AUNTIE?

ME SEE-UM! KNOW RIGHT WHERE SHE IS!
HONEST? TELL ME... QUICK!
WALT DISNEY

WHAT A BREAK! THE OLD SQUAW RECOGNIZED MY DESCRIPTION OF CLARABELLE AND KNOWS RIGHT WHERE SHE IS!
HURRY, AUNTIE!
NO GOOD, HURRY! SHE NO GET AWAY!
11-5

WHAT DO Y' MEAN?
ME SEE-UM PALEFACE TIE HER TO TREE TWO NIGHTS AGO!

THIS IS AWFUL! POOR CLARABELLE TIED TO A TREE ALL THIS TIME! SHE MAY BE DEAD FROM EXPOSURE!

WALT DISNEY

YOU COME SEE-UM "LITTLE STAR" AGAIN, HANDSOME WHITE MANS?
OH, SURE! AND THANKS FOR THE EATS! SO LONG!
11-6

NEXT DAY.
I SURE HATE TO BE WASTIN' SO MUCH TIME EVERY DAY, WHEN I WANTA BE DOIN' DETECTIVE WORK!

AND WITH PETE TRYIN' TO BUMP ME OFF "BY ACCIDENT," I SURE HAFTA....
GOOD GOSH!
L-LEM... MEE-E... OOOOOWW...

THAT'S CLARABELLE'S VOICE... I'D KNOW IT ANYWHERE! SHE'S LOCKED UP AND YELLIN', "LET ME OUT"!

L-LEM... MEEE... OOOOOWW-W!!
!
WALT DISNEY

BOY... I'M GLAD TO HAVE PETE WORKIN' IN ANOTHER SPOT TODAY! DONT HAFTA WATCH FOR "ACCIDENTS"!
WONDER WHAT THIS OLD BUCK WANTS?
11-7

ME HEAR-UM YOU LOOK-UM FOR WHITE SQUAW LOST IN WOODS!
YES! DID YOU SEE HER?

ME SEE-UM... BUT YOU TOO LATE! EVIL PALE-FACE MURDER HER... THROW BODY IN RIVER!
GOOD GOSH! POOR CLARABELLE... WHAT A TERRIBLE END!

ARE... ARE Y' SURE THAT... THAT...?
CERTAIN ME SURE! INJUN REMEMBER PERFECT...

...IT HAPPEN ONLY TEN YEAR AGO!
OH-H-H-H-H!

ANOTHER DAY GONE AND PETE HASN'T GOT ME YET! BUT NO CHANCE TO WORK ON CLARABELLE'S CASE, EITHER, DOGGONE IT!
HEY! MR. AXE-MAN!

YOU WANT-UM KNOW ABOUT WHITE LADY WHAT GET LOST?
BOY... THAT CERTAINLY GETS AROUND AMONG YOU INDIANS!
11-8

YOU GIVE-UM TWO BITS, ME TELL-UM ALL ME KNOW!
HERE Y' ARE! SHOOT!

ME KNOW NOTHIN', MISTER... THAT'S ALL ME KNOW!
TAKEN!
WALT DISNEY

11-10
Copr. 1941, Walt Disney Productions World Rights Reserved

FASTER, LEETLE WAN... SHE'S POOTY BEEG TREE, BY GAR!

YEOWW!! HEY, LOOK! HADN'T I BETTER...?
PAH! NO REAL LUMBERJACK SCAIRT OF HEES OWN SHADOW! PIERRE, SHE'S DEESGOOSTED!

BUT I GUESS HE HAV' TO BABY THE LEETLE WAN... THERE!
Distributed by King Features Syndicate, Inc

FASTER, LEETLE WAN... YOU SOON BE FEENISH!
CHOP! CHOP! CHUNK! CHOP! CHUNK!
11-11
Copr. 1941, Walt Disney Productions World Rights Reserved

AND HOW! THERE WON'T BE ENUFF LEFT OF 'IM TO PASTE A STAMP ON AND SEND HOME!

THERE Y' ARE, BOSS, I'M ALL... HEY!!

WH-WHAT DO I DO, NOW?
Distributed by King Features Syndicate, Inc

?
F' GOSH SAKES...IT DIDN'T FALL! WHAT'S WRONG?
Copr. 1941, Walt Disney Productions World Rights Reserved

OHO-O...!

...SO DAT'S IT!
11-12
Distributed by King Features Syndicate, Inc.

VEREE SIMPLE! THE LEETLE WAN, HE WEEL GO UP AND CUT EET OFF SO EET CAN FALL! EES ONLY 'BOUT 200 FEET!
ULP... ME? Y-YES, SIR!
WALT DISNEY

GO UP 'BOUT 200 FEET, LEETLE WAN, AND CUT OFF THE TOP...THEN THE TREE, SHE WEEL FALL!
ULP... Y-YES, SIR!
Copr. 1941, Walt Disney Productions World Rights Reserved

THUH DUMB L'IL RUNT DON'T SEE THAT HE'LL COME DOWN WITH IT! AND IF A 200-FOOT DROP DON'T FINISH 'IM...!
11-13

HAW-HAWR -HAWR! DAT DOES IT!
CRASH!!
Distributed by King Features Syndicate, Inc.

HEY! WHAT DO I DO, NOW...?

...I CAN'T GET MY AXE LOOSE!
WALT DISNEY

WELL, IF DAT SHRIMP DON'T BEAT ALL FER LUCK! I SEND HIM UP TO CUT A 200-FOOT TREE OUT FROM UNDER 'IM AND WHEN IT FALLS HE STICKS UP DERE!
Copr. 1941, Walt Disney Productions World Rights Reserved

HEY! HOW'M I GONNA GET MY AXE LOOSE? IT'S STUCK!
11-14

HMMM...SHE IS WAN BEEG PROBLEM, BY GAR...
WHOOEE-E-OOT!
OH-OH ...TOO BAD! ...THUH QUITTIN' WHISTLE!

I GO HOME AN' THEENK ABOUT IT!

NICE GUY, THAT PETE! GOES HOME AND LEAVES ME WITH MY AXE STUCK 200 FEET IN THE AIR!
11-15

200 FEET! GOOD GOSH... WHAT AM I DOIN'?

WHEW... THAT WAS A HECK OF A SPOT! IT'S ME FOR OVER THE ROOF TOPS...
ZIPPP!

...AND DOWN THE FIRE-ESCAPE! FOILED AGAIN, BROTHER PETE!
Distributed by King Features Syndicate, Inc.

TONIGHT'S A SWELL CHANCE TO SHADOW OLD PETE AND SEE WHAT HE DOES IN TOWN! HE'LL THINK I'M STILL STUCK UP IN THAT TREE!
HIDDEN RIVER MEAT MARKET - AND - POST-OFFICE
11-17

I'LL BET HE'S GOT A HIDE-OUT OR SOME CRONIES THAT HE MEETS! IF HE DOES, I'M SURE GONNA GET ME AN EARFUL!

OH-OH! HERE COMES LITTLE LORD FAUNTLEROY, NOW!

FISH
GENERAL STORE
AHA! VILLAINY IS AFOOT... NO DOUBT ABOUT IT!
PICKLED HERRING
WALT DISNEY

GENERAL STORE
PSST!
JUST AS I THOUGHT ...PETE'S DOWN HERE TO MEET ONE OF HIS HENCH-MEN!
11-18

!
DOGGONE...I WISH HE'D TALK LOUDER! I'VE GOTTA FIND OUT WHAT HE'S COOKIN' UP!
FLOUR XXX
Copr. 1941, Walt Disney Productions World Rights Reserved

YOU DON'T MEAN...?
YES! GEEVE ME WAN BEEG SIZE PACKAGE OF BUBBLE BATH...UH...GARDENIA FLAVOR!

I JEST LOVES TO TAKE BUBBLE BATHS!
PFLOFF!!
FLOUR XXX
Distributed by King Features Syndicate, Inc.

HOT DOG! PETE'S GOT A DATE WITH SOMEBODY IN THAT CABIN! MAYBE IT'S HIS HEAD-QUARTERS!
11-19
Copr. 1941, Walt Disney Productions World Rights Reserved

WELL, THEY CAN'T KEEP LI'L ROLLO OUTA THE PARTY... OH-OH! PETE'S GIVIN' HIM SOME MONEY!

I DON'T KNOW IF I OUGHTA, PIERRE... THE SHERIFF'S BEEN WATCHIN' ME!
AW, COME ON... JUS' THEES WANCE MORE...

...PICK ME OUT WAN GOOD HORSE FOR TOMORROW'S RACE!
URP!
Distributed by King Features Syndicate, Inc.

DOGGONE THAT PETE! I TRAIL HIM ALL OVER TOWN, AND WHAT'S HE DO? BUYS BATH-SALTS...

HARDWARE
STORE
...AND BETS ON A HORSE RACE! WELL, HERE WE GO AGAIN!
11-20

PSST! PIERRE!
AND I SUPPOSE THIS GUY'LL ASK FOR A DIME FOR A CUP O' COFFEE!

OLD SQUINT-EYES WANTS TO SEE YUH DOWN AT THE HOLE!
VER' GOOD... I WEEL BE THERE RIGHT AWAY!
WALT DISNEY
Distributed by King Features Syndicate, Inc.

BOY, WHAT A BREAK! AM I GLAD I SHADOWED PETE BACK IN TOWN TONIGHT AND HEARD HIM GET THAT MESSAGE!
11-21
Copr 1941, Walt Disney Productions World Rights Reserved

NOW HE'S GONNA LEAD ME STRAIGHT TO THE HIDE-OUT AND I'LL PROB'LY FIND CLARABELLE AND...

HELLO, HANDSOME WHITE MANS!
WHO, ME?
...OMIGOSH ...LITTLE STAR!
Distributed by King Features Syndicate, Inc

NOT YOU, FAT-ONE... I MEAN-UM PRETTY MANS BEHIND YOU!
SO!
WALT DISNEY

SO! THE LEETLE WAN TAKES A WALK IN THE WOODS AT NIGHT, EH?
I... UH... I WAS GONNA SEE LITTLE STAR! SHE LIVES RIGHT OVER HERE!
YOU COME SEE-UM ME? HOW NICE!
11-22

ANYWAY... Y' SEEM TO BE WALKIN' IN THE WOODS, YOURSELF!
YES... A LEETLE STROLL HELPS THE SLEEP! I GO TO BED, NOW!

I DON'T SUPPOSE Y' UNDERSTAND WHAT Y' GUMMED UP TONIGHT!
ME GUM-UM UP? NO SAVVY!

TRAILIN' ME, HUH? THAT BLASTED RUNT'S LIVED TOO LONG! TOMORRER I FINISHES 'IM!
WALT DISNEY

...SO, Y' SEE, IF YOU'D KEPT QUIET I COULD'VE TRAILED PETE TO HIS HIDE-OUT AND UNCOVERED THE WHOLE MYSTERY!
OH, ME SO SORRY! NO CATCH-UM WISE IN TIME!
Copr. 1941, Walt Disney Productions World Rights Reserved

BUT LITTLE STAR MAKE IT UP... ME DO DETECTER WORK AND HELP-UM WHITE MANS!
OH, NO! NO, I'VE GOT A GIRL BACK HOME I HAD TO TALK OUT OF IT! THEY JUST GUM THINGS UP!
11-24

HUMPH! SHE WHITE GIRL... DUMB LIKE BUNNY! INJUN GIRL **SMART** ...LIKE FOX!

ANYWAY, NO USE TALK-UM! LITTLE STAR JUST **LOVE** TO HELP-UM HER PRETTY WHITE MANS!
OH... HEAP MUCH!
WALT DISNEY

PLEASE LET LITTLE STAR DO DETECTER WORK AND HELP-UM PRETTY WHITE MANS!
HEY... LET GO... NOTHIN' DOIN'...!

I JUST **TOLD** Y' I'VE GOT A GIRL BACK HOME AND...!
IS SHE NICE GIRL? IS SHE ANYTHING LIKE ME?
11-25

NO, SHE'S NOT LIKE YOU! SHE'S... WELL, WHAT'S THAT GOT TO DO WITH IT, ANYWAY?
LITTLE STAR VERY NICE... DON'T YOU THINK?

MEANWHILE, PETE KEEPS A MYSTERIOUS APPOINTMENT!

WONDER WHAT OL' SQUINT-EYES WANTS OF ME HERE AT THUH HOLE THIS TIME O' NIGHT!

WELL, LOOK WHO'S HERE! MICKEY'S OLD TIME ARCH ENEMY AND PETE'S PARTNER IN CRIME, SYLVESTER SHYSTER! THEY MEET IN A SECRET HIDE-OUT, KNOWN AS THE HOLE!
11-26

WOT'S ON YER MIND, SHYSTER?
I WANT TO WARN YOU NOT TO GET CARELESS! THERE'S INDICATIONS THAT THE G-MEN ARE GETTING PRETTY HOT!
Copr. 1941, Walt Disney Productions World Rights Reserved

THE TIMBER WE'RE HIGHJACKING IS MIGHTY IMPORTANT TO THE DEFENSE PROGRAM AND THEY'RE WORKIN' ON IT **HARD**!

ANOTHER THING... I'M WORRIED ABOUT THAT PESKY FEMALE YOU KIDNAPED! IF SHE EVER GOT AWAY, THE JIG WOULD BE UP FOR **US**!
YEAH? WELL, LEAVE THAT TO ME! I'VE DECIDED TO END **THAT** RISK ...TONIGHT!

YOU'VE DECIDED! **I'M** THE BRAINS IN THIS DEAL, YOU FOOL! SIT DOWN!
Distributed by King Features Syndicate, Inc.

YOU FOOL. THAT WOULD BE A CRAZY THING TO DO, BUMP OFF THE DAME BEFORE WE'RE READY TO CLEAR OUT!
OKAY, OKAY! WE'LL LET HER LIVE A LITTLE LONGER, THEN!
Copr. 1941, Walt Disney Productions World Rights Reserved
11-27

..BUT, BY GAD, I'LL FINISH OFF DAT LITTLE **RAT** TOMORROW!

YOU LET ME HELP-UM WITH DETECTER WORK! INJUN GIRL SMART...TRACK 'EM DOWN, YOU BETCH-UM!
NOTHIN' DOIN'... AND THAT'S FINAL! I DON'T WANT ANY **GIRLS** WORKIN' WITH **ME**! THEY'RE TOO...

...RATTLEBRAINED AND... **OOPS**!
TEE-HEE-HEE!
WALT DISNEY

LISTEN, STUPID...YOU CAN'T RISK A MURDER RAP NOW, WITH THE PRISON RECORD **YOU'VE** GOT! IT HAS TO LOOK LIKE AN ACCI-DENT!
YEH, BUT THESE ACCIDENTS AIN'T CLICKIN'!

HERE'S ONE YOU NEVER THOUGHT OF ...BZZ-Z ...BZZ...!
HEY, DAT'S **GOOD**! I'LL TRY IT TOMORROW!
Copr. 1941, Walt Disney Productions World Rights Reserved
11-28

WELL! WONDER WHAT THAT LUMBERJACK'S DOIN' OUT SO LATE?

OH-OH! I GET IT!

PRETTY TOUGH CASE TO CRACK, ISN'T IT, G-MAN?
EH??
WALT DISNEY

I'LL ADMIT YOU GUESSED RIGHT, BUT HOW DID YOU KNOW I'M A G-MAN?
THAT'S EASY...
11-29

...ANYBODY WITH FEET THAT FLAT MUST'VE BEEN A COP FOR A LONG TIME!

AND A COP WOULDN'T BE WORKIN' HERE AS A LUMBERJACK UNLESS HE'D BECOME A G-MAN AND WAS ASSIGNED TO THIS CASE!
REMARKABLE, MR. HOLMES! WELL, I KNOW WHO YOU ARE, TOO, AND WHAT YOU'RE HERE FOR!

HAVE YOU HAD MUCH...ER, SUCCESS?
OH, YES... WONDERFUL! I'VE RAISED A GRAND APPETITE ...AND A **SWELL** SET OF MUSCLES!

YES, I HAVE TO ADMIT THAT I HAVEN'T UNCOVERED ONE SINGLE CLUE EITHER ABOUT CLARABELLE OR THE STOLEN TIMBER!
WE'RE NOT DOING SO HOT, EITHER! AND THE SHORTAGE OF THOSE MOLIGNUMITE LOGS IS GETTING MIGHTY SERIOUS!
12-1

BUT I NEVER KNEW A GANG OF CROOKS THAT DIDN'T SLIP UP SOMETIME! WE'LL GET THE GOODS ON 'EM YET!
BOY, I HOPE SO! G'NIGHT!

NEXT MORNING, AS MICKEY REPORTS FOR WORK!

WELL, BOSS, WHAT DO I DO TODAY?
TODAY, PIERRE, SHE'S GOT VEREE SPECIAL JOB... WAN HE NOT TRUST TO ANNYBODY BUT THE LEETLE WAN!

OKAY... LET'S HAVE IT!
HMM... SOMETHING TELLS ME THERE'S WORMS IN THIS APPLE!
WALT DISNEY

WHAT'S THIS VERY SPECIAL JOB YOU'VE GOT FOR ME TODAY?
PIERRE TELL YOU A SECRET... SOM' VALUABLE TIMBER, SHE'S HIJACKED ON WAY TO THE MILL, SEE?
12-2
Copr. 1941, Walt Disney Productions World Rights Reserved

YEH; THAT'S NO SECRET ...BUT WHAT'S IT GOT TO DO WITH...?
THE LEETLE WAN, HE'S POOTY GOOD DETECTIVE, AND PIERRE GONNA GEEVE HEEM BEEG CHANCE! COM' ALONG!

YOU WEEL STAY WEETH WAN LOG ALL THE WAY THROUGH THE MILL! MAYBE YOU FIND THE TROUBLE, YES?
WHAT'S THIS? INVITIN' ME TO UNCOVER HIS OWN RACKET! THERE'S A CATCH SOMEWHERE!

...AND DON' GET OFF 'TIL SHE COM' CLEAR OUT OTHER SIDE OF THE MILL!
OKAY, BOSS!
DARNED IF I SEE HIS GAME, BUT I'LL NEVER FIND OUT, IF I DON'T TRY IT!
WALT DISNEY
Distributed by King Features Syndicate, Inc.

REMEMBER... STAY WEETH THEES LOG EV'RY MINUTE 'TIL SHE'S COM' OUT THE MILL!
OKAY... TURN 'ER LOOSE!
12-3
Copr. 1941, Walt Disney Productions World Rights Reserved

YEAH, STICK WITH IT TO THE END... HIS END, THUH LI'L DOPE!
PLOCK!
WHATEVER HIS GAME IS I'LL SOON FIND OUT!
I THOUGHT THIS WOULD BE TOUGH GOIN', BUT IT'S AS EASY AS...

...AS FALLIN' OFF A LOG!
Distributed by King Features Syndicate, Inc.

I DON'T KNOW WHAT PETE SENT ME DOWN HERE FOR, BUT IT'S NOT TO FIND OUT HOW THESE LOGS GET STOLEN!
12-4
Copr. 1941, Walt Disney Productions
World Rights Reserved

I'M DARNED IF I SEE HOW THEY DO! IT'S IMPOSSIBLE FOR THE LOGS TO LEAVE THE CHUTE...

...OOPH!... PRACTICALLY IMPOSSIBLE...
SPLASH

...UNTIL THEY GET TO THE END... AND HERE IT IS! MIGHTY MYSTERIOUS!

I STARTED WITH THIS LOG TO THE END OF THE CHUTE, AND NO SIGN OF... GOOD GOSH! I COULD GET HURT!!
Copr. 1941, Walt Disney Productions
World Rights Reserved

12-5

THUH BLASTED LUCKY FOOL! RID THUH WHOLE LENGTH O' THUH CHUTE WITHOUT GITTIN' KILLED! WELL, HE AIN'T THROUGH YET!

GOLLY...I GOTTA CATCH IT! I'M S'POSED TO STICK WITH IT RIGHT THROUGH THE MILL!

GOTCHA! EVERYTHING UNDER... CONTROL ...NOW!
WALT DISNEY

OMIGOSH! I'M GOIN' OVER A FALLS!
12-6
Copr. 1941, Walt Disney Productions
World Rights Reserved

SHUCKS! JUST A BABY ONE!

DOGGONE IT... I'LL R-RIDE THIS...TH-THING TO THE ...MILL, IF I BU-BREAK EVERY...B-BONE IN MY BODY!

DON'T DARE FALL OFF N-NOW... WOULD L-LOSE...TRACK... OF MY LOG!

HOT DOG! WE'RE COMIN' INTO QUIET WATER!
Copr. 1941, Walt Disney Productions World Rights Reserved

THUD!
12-8

GOLLY! NOW I'VE LOST TRACK OF MY LOG ... AND WILL PETE BE SORE!

OH-OH... THAT'S IT! I'D KNOW IT ANYWHERE ... THE WILDEST DOGGONE LOG ON THE RIVER!

WHEW! THAT WAS A ROUGH TRIP, BUT I DID WHAT PETE TOLD ME TO... I STAYED WITH THIS LOG CLEAR TO THE MILL!
Copr. 1941, Walt Disney Productions World Rights Reserved
12-9

ONLY HE SAID TO STAY ON IT 'TIL IT CAME OUT OF THE MILL! I WONDER WHY?

NOTHIN' CAN HAPPEN ONCE IT GETS IN... OMIGOSH!!

I GET IT! THAT BLOODTHIRSTY WEASEL WAS TRYIN' TO BUMP ME OFF!
Distributed by King Features Syndicate, Inc.

THUH CUSSED, PESKY LI'L RAT... I MIGHT 'A KNOWN HE WOULDN'T GIT KILT, BLAST 'IM!
WELL, I STAYED WITH THAT LOG ALL THE WAY, LIKE Y' TOLD ME, BUT NOTHIN' EVER HAPPENED TO IT!
Copr. 1941, Walt Disney Productions World Rights Reserved

NO? SHE'S WAN BEEG MEESTERY, BY GAR! YOU CAN KNOCK OFF NOW... PIERRE, HE'S GOT OTHER PLANS TODAY!
OKAY... I'LL JUST LOAF AROUND!
12-10

I WISH IT WAS NIGHT, SO I COULD TRAIL HIM! I KNOW DARN WELL HE'S GOIN' TO HIS HIDE-OUT!

AT LEAST, IT GIVES ME A CHANCE TO DO SOME MORE INVESTIGATING!

LOOK HERE, SHYSTER, YUH CAN'T KILL DAT BLASTED RUNT BY ACCIDENT! IT'S GOTTER BE DONE ON PURPOSE... AND FREQUENT!
WALT DISNEY

I TELL YUH I AIN'T GONTER FOOL WID DAT LI'L PEST NO LONGER!
I'LL WRING HIS DANGED NECK!
NOW DONT FLY OFF THE HANDLE! SIT DOWN AND LISTEN!
Copr 1941, Walt Disney Productions World Rights Reserved
12-11

I'VE FIGURED IT OUT! A FEW HUNDRED FEET MORE OF THAT TIMBER AND WE CAN PULL FREIGHT WITH A NEAT NEST EGG!
NO KIDDIN'? AND THEN I KIN BUMP 'IM OFF... AND THUH DAME, TOO! OH, HAPPY DAY!

PSST!
OH-OH... THAT'S THE G-MAN! WONDER WHAT'S UP?

THERE'VE BEEN NEW DEVELOPMENTS! IF YOU WANT TO SAVE YOUR FRIEND'S LIFE, YOU'LL HAVE TO WORK FAST!

WHAT'S NEW? WHAT MAKES Y' THINK I'VE GOTTA WORK FAST TO SAVE CLARABELLE?
THE DAILY PERCENTAGE OF THAT HIGHJACKED TIMBER HAS SUDDENLY INCREASED!
Copr. 1941, Walt Disney Productions World Rights Reserved

THAT MEANS THINGS ARE GETTIN' TOO HOT FOR THE GANG ...THEY'RE GOIN' TO GRAB ALL THEY CAN AND PULL OUT!
GOSH... AND I HAVEN'T EVEN THE FAINTEST CLUE WHERE CLARABELLE IS!
12-12

WHY DIDN'T I THINK? IF SHE WAS NABBED FOR SEEIN' TOO MUCH, SHE MUST'VE BEEN DOWN BY THE CHUTE! THOSE LOGGERS ARE HONEST ...THEY'D TELL ME, IF THEY SAW HER!

SON, OUTSIDE OF INJUNS, TH' ONLY FEMALES I'VE SEEN THIS YEAR IS A COW, TWO COTTONTAILS AN' A JAYBIRD!
WALT DISNEY
Distributed by King Features Syndicate, Inc.

THOUGHT I HAD SOMEP'N THERE! I'VE JUST GOTTA FIND CLARABELLE... IF PETE'S PULLIN' OUT SOON, HE WON'T LEAVE HER ALIVE TO TALK!
12-13

AND YOU'RE NOT WRONG THERE, MICKEY!

I KIN HARDLY WAIT! JEST A LI'L MORE TIMBER TO COMPLETE THUH DEAL... THEN I BUMPS OFF THEM TWO PESTS!
CAN'T COME TOO SOON FOR ME... I'M FED- UP WITH THAT MOONSTRUCK FEMALE!

AND THEN I BUYS ME A LI'L FARM AN' SETTLES DOWN AND GOES STRAIGHT THUH REST O' ME LIFE!
GOIN' STRAIGHT, EH? WHAT KIND O' CROPS YOU FIGURIN' ON RAISIN'?

SOMETHIN' REAL PROF'TABLE, LIKE MARIHUANA ... MAYBE!

YEP, IT'S A GRAND FUTURE! I BUMP OFF MICKEY AN' THUH OL' MAID... COLLECK MUH SHARE OF THUH TIMBER DEAL...!
...AND THEN Y' GO STRAIGHT ON A LITTLE FARM... RAISIN' POPPIES ...Y' ALREADY TOLD ME THAT! WAKE UP, Y' FOOL!
12-15
Copr. 1941, Walt Disney Productions World Rights Reserved

WE'VE GOT WORK TO DO... AND FAST! A MATTER OF HOURS, AND WE HAVE TO MAKE A GETAWAY... AND NO SLIP-UP!
SURE... I KNOW! BUT WHEN WE LAM, I'M LEAVIN' TWO BIRDS THAT AIN'T TELLIN' NO TALES!

IF I ONLY KNEW WHERE TO LOOK FOR CLARABELLE! OR IF SHE COULD FIND A WAY TO...
ME GOT-UM NOTE... FROM SQUAW IN TROUBLE!
HUH?

B-BOY! HOPE IT'S NOT TOO LATE! WHY COULDN'T Y' HAVE BU-BROUGHT ME THIS D-DAYS AGO?
UGH! PALEFACE HEAP SPEEDY... MEBBE COULD DELIVER BEFORE WRITTEN! INJUN SLOW ...NO CAN DO!
WALT DISNEY

A NOTE FROM A WOMAN IN TROUBLE! IT MUST BE CLARABELLE... SHE'S FOUND A WAY TO REACH ME!
12-16

OH, GOSH... IT'S ONLY LITTLE STAR! "HEAP MUCH TROUBLE IN DETECTER WORK! HANDSOME WHITE MANS PLEASE COME TO HELP! HURRY!"

WHAT KINDA JAM IS SHE IN? I TOLD HER NOT TO HELP... BUT MAYBE SHE'S REALLY RUN ONTO SOMETHING!

ME SEND-UM FOR DETECTER OUTFIT... BUT LOOK! GLASS TO MAKE THINGS BIG ONLY MAKE-UM SMALLER!
AW, PHOOEY!
WALT DISNEY

WHERE YUH BOUND, RED?
DON'T GIMME AWAY... I'M GONNA SNEAK DOWN TO THE HOLE FER A WHILE!
OH, BOY... HE MUST BE ONE OF PETE'S GANG! THEY CALL THEIR HIDE-OUT THE HOLE!
Copr. 1941, Walt Disney Productions. World Rights Reserved
12-17

THIS IS THE CHANCE I'VE BEEN LOOKIN' FOR! HE'LL LEAD ME RIGHT TO HEADQUARTERS!
Distributed by King Features Syndicate, Inc.

GOOD NIGHT... HOW FAR IS IT, ANYWAY? WE'VE BEEN HIKIN' FOR MILES!

YEP... OUGHTER BE PLENTY O' FISH IN TH' OLD SWIMMIN'-HOLE, TODAY!
URP!
WALT DISNEY

I'M GOIN' BUGS FROM FOLLOWIN' FALSE CLUES...IT'S TIME I PUT A LITTLE SCIENCE TO WORK!
Copr. 1941, Walt Disney Productions World Rights Reserved
12-18

WITH THIS UMBRELLA RIB AS AN AUDIATOR I SHOULD HAVE A FIRST CLASS FOOTPRINT DETECTOR!

IT'S A WELL-KNOWN FACT THAT HOURS AFTER A PERSON HAS PASSED, THE GROUND STILL VIBRATES!

IF PETE PASSED THROUGH HERE, THE CRYSTAL PICK-UP SHOULD CATCH... OH-OH!

HOT DOG! A FOOTPRINT!
TWANG-G-G!!
WALT DISNEY

HOT DOG! THIS FOOTPRINT DETECTOR WORKS SWELL! PICKS UP VIBRATIONS HOURS AFTER PETE PASSED HERE!
FWANG-G-G...!
12-19

IT CAN'T HELP BUT LEAD ME TO THE HIDE-OUT! CLARABELLE, HERE I COME!

I NOTICE THE SOUND VARIES, DEPENDING ON HOW HEAVY PETE'S STEPS... HEY! WHAT TH'...?
WHIZ-Z-Z-Z

!
!
WHANG!!

GOSH DARN IT! HE MUST'VE TRIPPED ON THAT ROOT AND FALLEN!
WALT DISNEY
Distributed by King Features Syndicate, Inc.

HUMPH...WHITE MANS THINK GIRL NO GOOD! PICK-UM UP TRAIL ALREADY! ME SHOW-UM!
12-20
Copr 1941, Walt Disney Productions World Rights Reserved

NOT SO FAST, BOSWELL...! OH!!
SNAP!

GIRL NO GOOD, EH? PLENTY SMART, YOU BETCH-UM!
ARR... ARF! GRRR... ARRH!
Distributed by King Features Syndicate, Inc

OH, ME SORRY! WRONG MANS!
RRR-R-R!
WALT DISNEY

I MIGHT'VE KNOWN IT WAS YOU AND YOUR SLEUTH HOUND! GIRLS ARE SURE A BIG HELP!
LITTLE STAR AWFUL SORRY! DIDN'T KNOW BOSWELL WAS TRAIL-UM PRETTY WHITE MANS!
Copr. 1941, Walt Disney Productions World Rights Reserved
12-22

ME TAKE-UM HOME, SO YOU CAN COME DOWN!

HAWR! HAWR! HO-HO-HAWR!
? ?

SO! OUR BUSY LEETLE DETECTIVE, HE'S KINDA UP A TREE, EH?
Distributed by King Features Syndicate, Inc

THE FOLLOWING NIGHT, AT A SECRET MEETING PLACE WITH THE G-MAN!

YES, MICKEY, I'M AFRAID THIS CASE HAS GOT US LICKED! THERE'S SIGNS THAT THE CROOKS MAY PULL A GETAWAY TONIGHT OR TOMORROW!
GOOD GOSH! AND THEY WON'T LEAVE CLARABELLE ALIVE!
12-23

THERE'S ONE LAST CHANCE! PETE'S STILL IN CAMP AND HASN'T GONE TO HIS HIDE-OUT YET!

WHEN HE DOES, I'VE GOTTA TAIL HIM, AND NO BUNGLING THIS... OH-OH! HERE HE COMES, NOW!

HE SURE LOOKS SILLY CARRYIN'... HEY! HE'S LEAVIN' FOR GOOD!
WALT DISNEY

IT'S NOW OR NEVER! PETE'S BOUND FOR HIS HIDE-OUT AND THEN THE GETAWAY ... BUT HE'S NOT LOSIN' ME THIS TIME!
12-24

ARF-ARF ARF-ARF ARF!!
HEY... WOT THUH...?!!
OMIGOSH! IT'S THAT HOUND OF LITTLE STAR'S AGAIN!

HA, HA, HO HO, HAW-HA-HA, WISE GUY! WHO'S UP A TREE NOW!
?
Distributed by King Features Syndicate, Inc.

GOOD GOSH... WHAT AM I DOIN'?
WALT DISNEY

FOLLERIN' ME AGAIN, HUH? WHY, YUH BLASTED LI'L RUNT, I ORTA WRING YER DANGED NECK!
12-25

I GOT STRICKLY PRIVATE BIZZNUSS, AN' IF YUH TAKE **ONE** STEP AFTER ME IT'LL BE YER **LAST!** SEE?

SEE WHAT YOU'VE DONE, LITTLE STAR...SPOILED PROB'LY MY LAST CHANCE TO DISCOVER HIS HIDE-OUT!
BUT **ME** NO SPOIL-UM...
Distributed by King Features Syndicate, Inc.

...PRETTY WHITE MANS GIVE-UM **SELF** AWAY!
WHA...ER... WELL WE HADN'T OUGHTA DONE IT... I MEAN...!

AH, THERE YOU ARE, ALL SET! EVERYTHING'S GOING AS PLANNED ...SMOOTHEST JOB WE EVER PULLED!
THUH PESKY LI'L **RAT** STARTED TAILIN' ME, BUT I SCAIRT 'IM BACK!
WHEN WE LAMMIN'?
12-26

TOMORROW MORNIN'! NEED A FEW MORE LOGS TO COMPLETE THE DEAL!
GOOD! IT'LL JEST GIMME TIME TO CHOP DAT RUNT INTO FISH BAIT BEFORE I GO!

OH-OH! I JUST HEARD THOSE GUYS TALKIN' ABOUT TAKIN' SOMETHING TO EAT AT THE HOLE!
WILL THE BOYS BE THERE?
YEAH, I PASSED THE WORD ALONG!

WOW...WHAT LUCK! I NEVER THOUGHT I'D GET ANOTHER CHANCE!
WALT DISNEY

BOY...WAS I LUCKY TO HEAR THOSE BIRDS SAY THEY WERE TAKIN' SOME EATS TO THE HOLE! IT'S ONE LAST CHANCE TO FIND THE PLACE!
OLD SAM CAN SURE STOW 'EM AWAY!
YEP, BUT HE AIN'T GONNA WIN **THIS** BET!
Copr. 1941, Walt Disney Productions
World Rights Reserved

WILL HIS FACE TURN RED!
JUST WHEN HE THINKS HE'S WON, WE SAY...

...YEAH, WE SAW Y' EAT THE DOUGHNUTS, BUT WE DIDN'T SEE Y' **EAT THE HOLES!** HAW-HAW-HAW!
GOOD GOSH... ANOTHER DUD!
12-27

WELL, PETE, TOMORROW WE'RE RICH! TOO LATE NOW FOR THE LAW TO CATCH UP WITH US!
YEP! MUH POCKETS WILL BE FULL O' DOUGH AND TWO **BEEOOTIFUL** MURDERS BEHIND ME! WOT A DAY!
WALT DISNEY

DAYLIGHT...AND STILL NO SOLUTION! EVERY CLUE TURNS OUT TO BE A DUD...IT'S PROB'LY TOO LATE NOW, ANYWAY ...HOPE-LESS...!
Copr. 1941, Walt Disney Productions World Rights Reserved
12-29

YES, SIR... THE PERFECT CRIME! WITHIN AN HOUR WE'LL BE MILES AWAY FROM HERE! HEH-HEH-HEH!
WHERE ARE WE GOING BIG... B-O-Y!

WHERE I'M GOIN' IS NONE O' YER BLASTED BIZZNUSS...!

...WHERE YOU'RE GOIN' DEPENDS ON WHETHER YUH'VE LIVED RIGHT OR NOT!
Distributed by King Features Syndicate, Inc.

I'LL MAKE ONE LAST SEARCH AROUND THE LOG CHUTE! IF I DON'T FIND A CLUE NOW, I MIGHT AS WELL GIVE UP!
12-30

DAT'S ONE PEST WOT AIN'T GONTER GO MEDDLIN' IN MUH PRIVATE AFFAIRS NO MORE!
SPR-RANNGGG!!

STOP IT, Y' FOOL! I'LL HAVE NOTHING SO DANGED CRUDE... AND MESSY!

WE'LL DO THIS THE SMOOTH, GENTEEL WAY!
AW, YUH NEVER LET A GUY GIT ANY FUN OUTEN HIS WORK!
Distributed by King Features Syndicate, Inc.

I'M LICKED! NOT ONE SOLITARY CLUE! PETE'S REALLY GOTTEN AWAY WITH IT THIS TIME!
12-31

HEY! WHAT'S THIS? LOOKS LIKE A TRAP-DOOR TO AN UNDERGROUND SHAFT!

IT IS! THERE'S A LADDER! IT'S THE ENTRANCE TO THE "HOLE"! I'VE FOUND IT!

IF I'M NOT TOO LATE, I CAN STILL... WHA---??
HELLO, PRETTY WHITE MANS!

EEEK!
GOOD GOSH... SHE'S FALLIN' INTO THE CHUTE!

EEEK!
1-1

HELP! HELP! ME!
WHAT A SPOT...!

...JUST AS I FIND THE WAY TO PETE'S HIDE-OUT! SHOULD I GO TO CLARABELLE OR...?

EEEEEEEK!
HELP!
HELP!
Distributed by King Features Syndicate, Inc.

HELP! OH. HELP!
HANG ON, LITTLE STAR... I'M COMIN'!
1-2
Copr 1942, Walt Disney Productions World Rights Reserved

I DON'T KNOW WHAT I CAN DO, IF I CATCH HER, BUT I'VE GOTTA TRY!

HOLD TIGHT... AND WATCH OUT FOR THAT CURVE AHEAD!

OMIGOSH! WE'RE DONE FOR NOW!
EEEK!
Distributed by King Features Syndicate, Inc.

TRYING TO RESCUE LITTLE STAR, WHO HAS FALLEN IN THE LOG CHUTE, MICKEY JUMPS AFTER HER! SUDDENLY A SECTION OF THE CHUTE SWINGS OPEN AND THEY ARE HURLED INTO SPACE!

WOW! WE'RE GONERS!
1-3

MINNIE!! HOW IN THE WORLD...!??
F-FOOLED YOU... DIDN'T I?
WALT DISNEY

MINNIE! DO Y' MEAN TO TELL ME THAT LITTLE STAR... THE INDIAN GIRL... WAS **YOU** ALL THE TIME?
IT CERTAINLY WAS! ME FIX-UM GOOD DISGUISE, EH, PRETTY WHITE MANS?
1-5

WELL, OF ALL THE... BUT.. BUT **WHY?**
YOU WOULDN'T LET ME COME WITH YOU TO HELP! I HAD TO **SHOW** YOU I COULD BE A DETECTIVE... AND I DID!

Y' SURE FOOLED **ME**, MINNIE! BUT LET'S GET OUTA THE WATER AND...
SAY!!

LOOK, DO Y' KNOW WHERE WE ARE? IT'S THE "**HOLE**"! I'VE FOUND PETE'S HIDE-OUT **AT LAST!**
WALT DISNEY

HOW DO YOU **KNOW** THIS IS PETE'S HIDEAWAY?
I CAN SEE THE WHOLE THING, NOW! WHEN THAT GATE OPENED IN THE SIDE OF THE FLUME, WE WENT THROUGH IT...
1-6
Copr. 1942, Walt Disney Productions World Rights Reserved

...THE SAME WAY THE MISSING LOGS HAVE BEEN GOIN'! THE GATE OPENS AND CLOSES AT INTERVALS, ALLOWING PART OF THE LOGS TO DROP DOWN IN HERE!

WELL, WHAT OF IT? IF CLARABELLE'S IN THERE... **DO** SOMETHING!
THAT'S RIGHT! I'VE GOTTA FIND A WEAPON AND WORK FAST! IT MAY BE TOO LATE!

THIS IS SO MUCH MORE GENTEEL! WE'LL BE FAR AWAY AND WON'T WITNESS THE, ER... BITTER END!
YEAH, THAT AIN'T SO GOOD ...BUT I KIN **IMAGINE** IT!

OH, I JUST **HOPE** IT'S NOT TOO **LATE** TO SAVE CLARABELLE!
WE'LL FIND OUT, SOON AS I GET SOMEP'N TO USE FOR A WEAPON!
1-7
Copr. 1942, Walt Disney Productions World Rights Reserved

SO LONG, TOOTS! SORRY I CAN'T STAY FER THUH FINISH... I KNOW IT'S GONTER BE A BANG-UP SUCCESS!
CUT THE CHATTER, PETE, AND GET A MOVE ON!
HAW! HAWR!

IF THIS WUZ A MOVIE, THUH MARINES WOULD BE LANDIN' ABOUT NOW...

...BUT NUTHIN'S GONTER SAVE... **OOF!**
PARDON ME! MIND IF I PUT MY OAR IN?
Distributed by King Features Syndicate, Inc.

WHY, YOU LI'L ... RAT-FACED RUNT... I'LL...!
THE JIG'S UP, PETE! PUT OUT THAT FUSE BEFORE I BRAIN Y'!
1-8
Copr. 1942, Walt Disney Productions World Rights Reserved

OH, YEAH? I'LL SLICE THUH GIZZARD OUTEN ANYBODY WOT GOES NEAR THAT FUSE! HAW! HAW! YUH THOUGHT YUH SAVED HER...

...BUT SHE'S GONTER GIT BLOWED HIGHER'N A KITE... SEE?
YEH, AND YOU ALONG WITH HER!
WOT???!

YOWW! WHYN'T YUH TELL ME?
Distributed by King Features Syndicate, Inc.

SO YUH THINK YUH GOT ME, DO YUH? WHY, YOU'RE JEST WALKIN' INTO...OOF!
1-9
Copr. 1942, Walt Disney Productions World Rights Reserved

WANTA FIGHT, EH? OKAY...YOU ASKED FER IT!

CR-RUNCH!

HERE! I DON'T WANT IT EVER SAID THAT I KILLED AN UNARMED MAN!
WALT DISNEY

SO YUH THINK YUH KIN FIGHT ME, HUH? WHY YUH DOPEY LI'L WART, I'LL MAKE FERTILIZER OUTER YUH!
Copr. 1942, Walt Disney Productions World Rights Reserved
1-10

THUNDER! I'LL HAVE TO GO BACK AND SEE WHAT'S DELAYIN' PETE! THAT DUMB OX WILL GET BLOWN UP WITH THE DAME!

OH, MINNIE... IT'S YOU! I'M SAVED!
YES, BUT-QUICK... WE'VE GOT TO HELP MICKEY WITH PETE!

WHAT TH'...??

NEVER MIND PETE ...HERE'S ONE FOR US!
Distributed by King Features Syndicate, Inc.
WALT DISNEY

UG-GLUGG...!
NO DRATTED FEMALE'S GOIN' TO...**OUCH!** HEY! **OUCH!**
Copr. 1942, Walt Disney Productions World Rights Reserved
1-12

TAKE THAT... AND **THAT!** AND **THAT!**
I AIN'T DOIN' NO MORE FOOLIN' WITH **YOU!**
REMEMBER YOUR AGE, PETE... DON'T STRAIN YOURSELF!

CRACK-

YOU... WHY, I'LL... I'LL...!
CAREFUL, OLD BOY... YOU'RE TRIPPIN' ON YOUR BLOOD PRESSURE!
Distributed by King Features Syndicate, Inc.
WALT DISNEY

BLASTED LI'L BLANKETY-BLANK DASH BLANK...!
BE CALM, PETE! REMEMBER YOUR APOPLEXY!
Copr. 1942, Walt Disney Productions World Rights Reserved
1-13

Y' GOTTA KEEP COOL...!
FIRE ONLY

WHEN I GIT MUH HANDS ON YER NECK, I'LL...!
MAYBE **THIS** WILL HELP YOUR TEMPERATURE!

YIPPEE! A BASKET!

CLANG! CLANG! CLANG! THE ANVIL CHOR-US...!
Distributed by King Features Syndicate, Inc.

DAT WAS D' LAST STRAW! YUH'VE WENT AND HOIT M' DIGNITY! **NOW** I'M GOIN' **ALL OUT** ATCHA!
Copr. 1942, Walt Disney Productions World Rights Reserved
1-14

DIS'LL MAKE A NEAT LITTLE SWITCH T' SPANK YUH WIT'! **UNHH!!**

PETE! STOP! LOOK WHAT YOU'RE...!
BOP!
Distributed by King Features Syndicate, Inc.

WELL, I'LL BE DOGGONED! SAMPSON'S PULLED THE TEMPLE DOWN ON HIS OWN HEAD!
WALT DISNEY

YOU'D BETTER HURRY, IF YOU WANT TO CATCH THE REST OF THE GANG! MR. SHYSTER TOLD ALL SIX OF THEM TO WAIT AT GRANITE POINT FOR HIM AND PETE!
BOY, SIX OF 'EM! I'D LIKE TO HAVE A FEW HUSKY G-MEN WITH ME WHEN I TACKLE **THEM!**
1-15

MICKEY! LOOK... THE G-MEN!

WE WERE JUST GOING TO INVESTIGATE THAT CAVE, BUT LOOKS LIKE YOU BEAT US TO IT! HOW'D YOU EVER FIND IT, SON?
EXPLANATIONS LATER, CHIEF! FIRST GET A SQUAD OF YOUR HUSKIEST MEN DOWN TO GRANITE POINT, QUICK! THE REST OF THE GANG ARE WAITING THERE FOR THE RINGLEADERS!

WE BEAT YOU THERE, MICKEY! WE NABBED THEM ON THE WAY UP HERE! WHAT WE WANT ARE THE **RINGLEADERS!**
WELL, THERE THEY ARE!
RUB-A-DUB-DUB, TWO CROOKS IN A TUB, AND ALL WASHED UP!
WALT DISNEY

WELL, GOODBYE, MICKEY! THANKS A MILLION AND CONGRATULATIONS ON THE WAY YOU BUSTED THAT GANG UP!
SAME TO YOU! I'D PROB'LY NEVER HAVE CAUGHT THE REST OF THAT CREW BY MYSELF!
SPEAKING OF CONGRATULATIONS, IT SEEMS TO ME I HAVE A FEW COMING!
1-16

YEAH, CONGRATULATIONS ON THE WAY YOUR BLOODHOUND TREED ME AND THE WAY...
WELL, SMARTY, AFTER ALL, IF **I** HADN'T FALLEN IN THE LOG CHUTE **YOU'D** NEVER HAVE FOUND THEIR HIDEOUT!

OH, LET'S NOT ARGUE! ALL I WANT TO DO NOW, IS RELAX! PHEW! I'VE FOUGHT ENOUGH TODAY!

WELL, THEN, DON'T LET ME HEAR YOU ...**OH**-OH...THE ONE O'CLOCK WHISTLE!
WHOOOOOOOWOOT!

RELAX LATER! WE'VE JUST GOT TIME TO CATCH THE **2:45** TRAIN FOR HOME!
SWEET HOME!
WALT DISNEY

OH! DID ANYONE THINK TO WIRE GOOFY WHEN WE'D ARRIVE HOME?
I DID! TOLD HIM
WE'D HAD A **TERRIFIC** BATTLE CATCHING THE CROOKS, BUT WOULD ARRIVE HOME TODAY AT THREE!
AS IF YOU HAD TO TELL GOOFY YOU'D CAUGHT THE CROOKS ...THE WAY HE HERO-WORSHIPS YOU!
Copr. 1942, Walt Disney Productions World Rights Reserved

SHUCKS, CAN I HELP IT, IF GOOFY HAS CONFIDENCE IN ME?
WELL, I HOPE HE DOESN'T HAVE A BRASS BAND DOWN AT THE STATION TO WELCOME YOU! TOO MUCH HERO-WORSHIP ISN'T GOOD FOR THE WORSHIPEE!
WELL, YOU'LL KNOW IN A MINUTE! WE'RE PULLING IN!
1-17

AMBULAN
OXYGEN
Distributed by King Features Syndicate, Inc.
WALT DISNEY

THE GLEAM

JANUARY 19, 1942

–

MAY 2, 1942

A GLEAM IN GOTTFREDSON'S EYE

Hypnosis, according to *Encyclopedia Britannica*, is "a psychological state with physiological attributes superficially resembling sleep, and marked by an individual's level of awareness other than the ordinary conscious state."

Deception, meanwhile, is defined by Merriam-Webster as "the act of making someone believe something that is not true: the act of deceiving someone."

Thus, it would be fair to say that Floyd Gottfredson's "The Gleam," while ostensibly an adventure dealing with hypnosis, is far more a tale of deception—for the readers as well as for the cast of characters.

Indeed, the deceptions begin when the very first strip immediately propels us into a shocker, the likes of which Mickey's audience—be they moviegoers or daily strip readers—had never seen before: Minnie is *dead*!

And, as per the often-agonizing timing of newspaper continuities, dead she remains—at least for the next twenty-four hours—until she simply isn't, leaving poor Goofy with alarmist egg on his face.

The deceptions in "The Gleam" are furthered by the Disney characters' ubiquitous gloves. Hiding more than just fingerprints, they conceal the identity of the Gleam's inside accomplice—as the gloves (and only the gloves!) reach beyond an identity-hiding door to hand the Gleam his first ill-gotten gain.

Finally, deception comes calling in the form of the comics medium's biggest cheat: the notion that, on a soundless page of art and text, the reader will only *read* a mysterious voice—but never *hear* it and, thus, possibly identify it. If we could *hear* the Gleam, his identity might very well be deduced by his tonal similarity to a "character we've met before," despite his best efforts to disguise his voice. Alas, the very medium we cherish limits our arsenal of mystery-solving techniques.

For those who have already read "The Gleam," the tale's ultimate deception comes in the identities of one or more of our central players; but we will refrain from dispensing spoilers here.

So deception would seem to trump hypnosis as the story's central feature—were *we* not so "hypnotized" by Gottfredson's skilled narrative. "The Gleam" makes the perfect transitory midpoint between the classic mystery of "The Phantom Blot" (1939) and the more modern intrigue of "The Atombrella and the Rhyming Man" (1948) yet to come. In "The Gleam" you will see artistic and storytelling techniques reflective of each tale—past and future—and observe first-hand the evolving talents of Floyd Gottfredson and his collaborators.

...If this is hypnosis, don't wake me!

—Joe Torcivia

YEP, IT'S AN INVITE TO A "COME-AS-YOU-WERE-WHEN INVITED-WELCOME-BACK-PARTY" I'M GIVIN' FER CLARABELLE!
WELL, GOTTA GET ALONG AND DELIVER MINNIE'S!
SAY, THAT SOUNDS LIKE QUITE A PARTY! I'LL BE THERE, AND THANKS, GOOFY!
1-19

HOWDY, STRANGER!
MINNIE MOUSE

OKAY, SOURPUSS, DON'T ANSWER ME, IF...

...YOU DON'T ...EEEAWK!! MINNIE!!

HALP! MICKEY! SOMETHIN' AWFUL'S HAPPENED TO MINNIE!
1-20

WHAT IS IT, GOOFY? WHAT'S HAPPENED, QUICK?
SHE'S BEEN KILLED OR SOMETHIN'! I FOUND HER STRETCHED OUT ALL LIMP AND HORRI-BLE-LIKE ON THE BACK PORCH!

G-G-G-GAWRSH, SHE'S... SHE'S GONE!

AREN'T YOU BOYS RATHER OLD TO BE PLAYING TAG LIKE THAT?
WALT DISNEY

B-B-BUT...BUT GOOFY SAID YOU WERE DEAD...OR...OR SICK ...THAT YOU WERE ...ARE YOU SURE YOU'RE ALL RIGHT?
DOGGONE IT, MINNIE, YOU'RE SUPPOSED TO BE LAYIN' OVER THERE-DEAD!
WHAT ARE YOU TWO TALKING ABOUT? DEAD? I NEVER FELT BETTER IN MY LIFE!
1-21

OH, YEAH? WELL, WHAT ABOUT THET THERE FURRINER THAT COME OUTA YER GATE? I SUPPOSE HE DIDN'T STAB YOU OR SOMETHIN'!
FOREIGNER? WHAT FOREIGNER? REALLY, I HAVEN'T THE...
GOT A WIRE FOR MINNIE MOUSE.. ..YOU HER?
Copr. 1942, Walt Disney Productions
World Rights Reserved

"...AND WILL ARRIVE FOR A VISIT TODAY. STOP. LOVE, AUNT AND UNCLE DUDLEY MOUSEGOMERY."

JUST LIKE THIS SHE WAS... ONLY... ONLY, WELL, MORE SO!
WALT DISNEY

MICKEY AND GOOFY ARE AT THE STATION TO MEET MINNIE'S AUNT MARTHA AND UNCLE DUDLEY MOUSEGOMERY! MINNIE, WHO HAS BEEN ACTING STRANGELY OF LATE, DIDN'T DESCRIBE THEM VERY WELL!

1-23

INSIDE IS LAUGHTER, MUSIC AND DANCING AT GOOFY'S "COME-AS-YOU-WERE-WHEN-INVITED-PARTY" BUT OUTSIDE IS..

!

AT THE HEIGHT OF THE FESTIVITIES AT GOOFY'S PARTY THE LIGHTS SUDDENLY ARE BLACKED OUT! MICKEY THINKS A FUSE HAS BLOWN, BUT...!

BUT, I TELL Y', GOOFY, MINNIE WAS SLUMPED ON THE KITCHEN FLOOR NOT TWO MINUTES AGO! AND OUT COLD!
YEAH? WELL I DON'T BELIEVE IT! YUH DIDN'T BELIEVE ME ABOUT FINDIN' HER ON TH' STEPS THIS MORNING!
1-29

KEEP CALM, EVERYBODY! THE POLICE SHOULD BE... OH, HERE THEY ARE, NOW!
KNOCK! KNOCK! KNOCK!

IT'S ROBBERY, CHIEF... MAYBE KIDNAPING! MINNIE'S MISS...!
DETAILS LATER, MICKEY... CAN'T WORK IN THE DARK! GET THOSE LIGHTS FIXED, JOE!

THERE! THEY'LL WORK NOW!

EEEEEEEEEEKK!!
Distributed by King Features Syndicate, Inc.

QUICK... THAT'S CLARABELLE SCREAMING!
EEEEEKK!!
Copr. 1942 Walt Disney Productions World Rights Reserved

LOOK... IT'S MINNIE!
WHAT TH...? MINNIE!!
1-30

YOU'VE HAD US SCARED TO DEATH! DOGGONE IT, MINNIE, WHERE HAVE YOU BEEN?
YEAH, AND DON'T SAY OUTSIDE HANGIN' UP CLOTHES!

BEEN? WHY... WHY, I'VE BEEN CHILLY, THAT'S WHERE I'VE BEEN! SO, NATURALLY, I GOT MY WRAP!
WALT DISNEY

BUT, MINNIE... CAN'T Y' REMEMBER? Y' PASSED OUT ON THE KITCHEN FLOOR!
NONSENSE! IF THIS IS SUPPOSED TO BE A GAG, IT'S VERY UN-FUNNY!
'TAIN'T NO GAG THET SOMEBUDDY PINCHED YER AUNT MARTHY'S NECKLACE AN' TARARA!
1-31

WHICH IS WHAT WE WERE CALLED FOR! NOW, FIRST, IS EVERYBODY PRESENT WHO WAS HERE WHEN THE CRIME WAS COMMITTED?

YES! THERE'S MINNIE AND CLARABELLE... GOOFY... AUNT MARTHA...!

DUDLEY! MY HUSBAND! HE'S MISSING!

OHH... MY **POOR** DUDLEY! HE'S GONE!
AN OPEN AND SHUT CASE, CHIEF! THE ONLY ONE MISSIN'... HE'S OUR MAN ALL RIGHT!
2-2

USE YOUR NOODLE, CASEY! A MAN DOESN'T ROB HIS OWN WIFE! COME ON... SEARCH THE PREMISES!
YES, CHIEF!

WE'VE GOTTA LOOK EVERY-WHERE, GOOFY! I'LL GO TRY THE REST OF THE HOUSE!
GAWRSH, I HATE TO BE SNOOPIN' IN PEOPLE'S PRIVATE.. ..OH, I FERGOT.. ..THIS IS **MY** HOUSE!
Distributed by King Features Syndicate, Inc

WELL, F'R...!!?
ZZZZ-Z-Z-Z-
BZZ-Z
ZOOP
BZZ-Z..
WALT DISNEY

WAKE UP, UNCLE DUDLEY! DON'T Y' REALIZE EVERYBODY'S BEEN LOOKIN' FOR Y'?
EH? MFF-FTT... WHAT...?
2-3
Copr 1942, Walt Disney Productions World Rights Reserved

HERE HE IS, FOLKS! I FOUND HIM ASLEEP!
WELL... IT WAS LATE... NEARLY NINE-THIRTY, AND...
OH, OF **COURSE**... HE ALWAYS DOES THAT AT PARTIES! I SHOULD HAVE KNOWN, IF I WASN'T SO UPSET ABOUT MY JEWELS BEING STOLEN!

...HE'S ALWAYS R'ARIN' TO GO PLACES AT NIGHT ...THEN CAN'T KEEP HIS EYES OPEN!
WELL, DADGUMMIT, IT WAS TOUGH TRYIN' TO SLEEP TONIGHT! ALL THAT SCREAMIN' AN' SHOUTIN'.. ...

..A PARTY DON'T NEED TO BE SO NOISY AS.. WHAT'D YOU SAY ABOUT YOUR JEWELS? **STOLEN?** CALL THE **POLICE**, SOMEBODY!

THE POLICE **HAVE** BEEN CALLED, UNCLE DUDLEY ...THEY'RE WORKIN' ON THE CASE RIGHT NOW!
BUT WHY DIDN'T SOMEBODY **TELL** ME? MY WIFE'S JEWELS STOLEN AND NOBODY EVEN WAKES ME UP!
2-4

WE'VE SEARCHED THE HOUSE AND GROUNDS, MICKEY, AND NOT A SHRED OF EVIDENCE! IT'S AN OUTSIDE JOB AND **PLENTY** SMOOTH!
WELL, STAY WITH IT, WILL Y', MR. O'HARA? THOSE JEWELS ARE WORTH A LOT OF MONEY!

MY DIAMOND TIARA! MY BEST EMERALD NECKLACE! MY... OHHHH!!
I FEEL TURRIBLE, MA'AM! HONEST... IN **TWENTY YEARS** NO GUEST O' MINE EVER LOST **ONE** SINGLE JOOL! IN FACT...

...THEY NEVER EVEN **WORE** ANY!

IT'S THE DAY AFTER GOOFY'S PARTY AND AT MINNIE'S HOME THE DISAPPEARANCE OF AUNT MARTHA'S JEWELS IS STILL A MYSTERY!
?

DIDN'T YOU GET A LOOK AT THE SCOUNDREL AT **ALL**, MARTHA?
NO, OF COURSE NOT! THE LIGHTS WERE ALL OUT AND HE WAS GONE IN A FLASH!
2-5
Copr 1942, Walt Disney Productions World Rights Reserved

WELL, I'D JUST LIKE TO GET MY HANDS ON HIM FOR A FLASH!

WELL, I **STILL** DON'T BELIEVE THE LIGHTS WENT OUT, OR THERE EVER **WAS** A ROBBERY! IT'S JUST **SOMEONE'S** IDEA OF A JOKE!
DON'T BE SILLY! WHO'D GO TO ALL THAT TROUBLE FOR A GAG?

YOU WOULD! YOU'VE BEEN ACTING **VERY** PECULIAR LATELY!
ULP... **I** HAVE??
WALT DISNEY

I CAN'T UNDERSTAND MINNIE! SHE FAINTED LAST NIGHT IN THE EXCITEMENT, BUT JUST **WON'T** BELIEVE IT!
YEH, SHE'S GOT ME WORRIED!
RRRINGGG
THERE'S THE DOOR-BELL... I'LL GET IT!
2-6

HOWDY, FOLKS! AUNTY MARTHY, I FEEL TURRIBLE OVER YOU GITTIN' ROBBED IN MY HOUSE, SO I WANT YUH TO LET ME REPLACE...
OH, DEAR, NO! I COULDN'T THINK OF IT, MR. GOOFY!

BUT, I INSIST, MA'AM! I DOUBT IF THESE HERE IS QUITE AS GENUWINE AS YOUR'N WUZ...

...BUT THEY'RE ABSOTOOTLY THUH MOST EXPENSIVE THUH DIME STORE CARRIES!
Distributed by King Features Syndicate, Inc.

NO, MICKEY, WE'RE STILL STYMIED ON THAT JEWEL CASE, BUT WE'RE GIVIN' IT ALL WE'VE GOT!
WELL, WHAT I CAME DOWN FOR... I'D LIKE TO WORK WITH YOU! I FEEL KINDA... WELL, THEY'RE MINNIE'S FOLKS AND...!
2-7

SURE! SURE... I UNDERSTAND! BUT IT WOULD BE BETTER IF YE WORKED ON YOUR OWN AND LET NOBODY KNOW ABOUT IT!
Y' MEAN, SO THE CROOK WOULDN'T GET SUSPICIOUS OF ME! YEH... I GET THE POINT!

WELL, NOBODY KNOWS I CAME HERE BUT MINNIE, AND SHE...!
AND **SHE'S** ON THE 'PHONE RIGHT NOW! AIN'T LOVE WONDERFUL?

OH, MICKEY... THE MOST WONDERFUL, **EXCITING** NEWS... I **COULDN'T** WAIT TO TELL YOU... YOU'D NEVER GUESS...!
WELL, **TELL** ME QUICK... WHAT IS IT?

YOU'D NEVER GUESS, MICKEY... IT'S SO THRILLING...!
WELL, TELL ME! HAVE THEY FOUND THE JEWELS... IS THE CROOK CAPTURED...?
2-9

WHAT ARE YOU TALKING ABOUT? I'M TRYING TO TELL YOU THAT THE VAN SWANKS ARE GIVING A PARTY IN HONOR OF AUNT AND UNCLE! ISN'T IT MARVELOUS?
YEH, IT'S PRACTICALLY STUPEFYING!

HMM! EVIDENTLY A DUD, EH?
ALL THAT FRANTIC FUROR WAS JUST OVER AN INVITE TO THE VAN SWANK'S!

YES, THAT'S WOMEN! MY WIFE'S THE SAME WAY ABOUT THE McGINTY'S CLAMBAKE! WELL, GOOD LUCK, MICKEY!
THANKS, MR. O'HARA! I'LL KEEP IN TOUCH WITH YOU!
Distributed by King Features Syndicate, Inc.
WALT DISNEY

I'M SO THRILLED TO BE GOING TO THE VAN SWANK'S PARTY!
AREN'T WE LUCKY THAT YOU KNOW SUCH ENTERTAINING PEOPLE, MINNIE?
YEP... CAN'T HAVE TOO MANY PARTIES TO SUIT ME, DADGUMMIT!
2-10
Copr 1942, Walt Disney Productions
World Rights Reserved

THEN, SUPPOSE YOU TRY STAYING AWAKE FOR A CHANGE!
DON'T WORRY ABOUT ME... I'M AS FRISKY AS A COLT!

A COUPLE OF HOURS AFTER THE PARTY HAS GOTTEN UNDER WAY IN ALL ITS STUFFY SPLENDOR!

I DON'T KNOW ABOUT UNCLE DUDLEY, BUT I'M BEIN' BORED TO SLEEP! GIMME AIR!
Distributed by King Features Syndicate, Inc.
WALT DISNEY

WELL, I SUPPOSE I'VE GOTTA GO BACK IN! I'VE NEVER SEEN ANYTHING DULLER THAN THIS PARTY IN MY LIFE!
2-11

WHY, MR CASEY... I DIDN'T SEE Y' BEFORE! WHAT'RE Y' DOIN' HERE?
CAN'T YUH SEE? I'M MINGLIN' WITH TH' GUESTS!

ROUTINE ASSIGNMENT! THEY ALWAYS CALL FOR A DICK AT THESE E-LITE BRAWLS TO GUARD THE DAMES' ICE! DON'T GIMME AWAY!
I WON'T! AND NO ONE WOULD EVER GUESS!

OH, HELLO, MINNIE! I WAS... SAY! WHAT'S THE MATTER? ...ARE Y' SICK?
NO... NOT AT ALL! I JUST FEEL... SORT OF... QUEER!

YOU'RE SICK, MINNIE! C'MON...LET ME TAKE Y' HOME!
NO! I'M ALL RIGHT! I JUST... FEEL...FUNNY!
2-12

COME ON...IT'S A GOOD EXCUSE TO LEAVE THE PARTY! WE CAN GET MORE EXCITEMENT OUT OF A GAME OF DOMINOES!
NO.. WE HAVE TO STAY... IT'S FOR AUNT MARTHA AND...!

I KNOW, BUT ...HEY??!
THE LIGHTS!
THIS IS TERRIBLE!
GOOD GRACIOUS! WHAT HAPPENED?
IS IT A BLACKOUT?

EEEEEEEEKK!! MY JEWELS! HELP, POLICE! I'VE BEEN ROBBED!!
GOOD GOSH! JUST LIKE GOOFY'S PARTY!
WALT DISNEY

TURN ON THE LIGHTS, SOMEBODY!
MY JEWELS! HELP ...DO SOMETHING!
QUIET, PLEASE! STAY WHERE YUH ARE ...EVERYBODY! THIS IS TH' LAWR TALKIN'!
2-13

THE CURRENT'S COMPLETELY OFF, SIR, BUT I'LL HAVE SOME CANDLES IN A MOMENT!
OKAY! THESE'LL DO TO START!

OH, DEAR... THIS IS AWFUL!
HORRIBLE!
POSITIVELY SPINE-CHILLING!
QUIET, I SAID! HERE, MOUSE ..CALL HEADQUARTERS FOR THE RADIO SQUAD!
YES, SIR!

BOY! WHAT A PEACH OF A PARTY! AND TO THINK I ALMOST WENT HOME!
WALT DISNEY

OH-H! THE HORROR OF IT! ROBBED ...IN MY OWN HOUSE! MY PRICE-LESS PEARL NECKLACE SNATCHED FROM UNDER MY NOSE...!
CALM YERSELF, MRS. VAN SWANK! I'M IN CHARGE HERE AND YUH GOT NOTHIN' TO WORRY ABOUT!
2-14

WHAT HAPPENED? WHY ARE THE LIGHTS OUT?
DIDN'T Y' KNOW? THE SAME THING AS AT GOOFY'S PARTY! THE LIGHTS WENT OUT, THEN SOME-BODY GRABBED MRS. VAN SWANK'S NECKLACE!

OH, DEAR...AGAIN? I MUST HAVE FAINTED... WHEN I CAME TO EVERYTHING WAS BLACK!
YEH...POOR KID, Y' HAVEN'T BEEN WELL LATELY!

WHEEE-E-U... WHEE-E-E-E-U..
S'CUSE ME, MINNIE! THERE'S THE POLICE ...I'LL HAFTA GET BUSY!

I SEE YUH GOT THE LIGHTS ON! WHAT DID YUH FIND?
NOTHIN', SO FAR... EXCEPT THAT THE LEAD-IN WIRES WERE CUT JUST OUTSIDE THE HOUSE!
Copr 1942, Walt Disney Productions World Rights Reserved
2-16

THE REST OF THE BOYS ARE OUT NOW, SEARCHIN' THE GROUNDS FOR CLUES!
OKAY, HOGAN...GO JOIN 'EM! I'LL CARRY THROUGH INSIDE HERE!

NOW, MRS. VAN SWANK, IF YUH'LL ROUND-UP THE SUSPECTS... EVERYBODY THAT WAS HERE TONIGHT... I'LL GET ON WITH THE INVESTIGATION!
OH, DEAR! THIS IS VERY AWKWARD! I DON'T EVEN KNOW HALF OF THEM!

EEEEEEEEEEEK!!
BUT I'LL HAVE TO...EH!??
OMIGOSH! WHO'S THAT?
WALT DISNEY

EEEK! OH, IT'S 'ORRIBLE! OHH-H...!
CALM YOURSELF, GIRL! WHAT'S SCARED YUH?

YOU'D BE S-SCARED, TOO... THAT Y' WOULD, S-SOR! IT'S A D-DEAD BODY... IN THE L-LIBRARY, SOR!
2-17

SOMETHIN' WRONG HERE! SMELLS LIKE FOUL PLAY!
G-GOSH!

OH, F'R...IT'S ONLY MINNIE'S UNCLE DUDLEY! HE NEVER CAN STAY AWAKE AT PARTIES!
ZZZZ-ZZ Z-Z

SO THAT'S OUR DEAD BODY! JUST SOME JERK ASLEEP!
I KNOW! HE DOES THAT AT EVERY PARTY... AND HERE COMES HIS WIFE, PLENTY MAD!
Z-Z Z!
2-18
Copr 1942, Walt Disney Productions World Rights Reserved

SO HE'S UP TO HIS OLD TRICKS, EH? WELL, THE FLOWER IS A NEW AND CHARMING TOUCH!
YESH, I PUT IT THER'! LOOKSH PURTY, AIN'T IT?

BRRM-FSK... WHAT... WHERE AM I? WHAT HAPPENED?
PLENTY! BUT THERE'LL BE MORE WHEN I GET YOU HOME! DISGRACING ME LIKE THIS EVERY TIME! IT'S MORTIFYING!

SAVE IT FOR HOME, LADY! I WANT EVERYBODY IN THE LIVING-ROOM FOR QUESTIONING! MAKE IT SNAPPY!

OKAY, EVERYBODY, YOU'RE ALL IN THE CLEAR! THE ROBBERY WAS UNQUESTIONABLY AN OUTSIDE JOB!
WELL... MR. CASEY, I **MUST** SAY THAT'S A BIG HELP TO RECOVERING
MY PRICELESS PEARL NECKLACE!
2-19

THE VERY THING YOU WERE SENT HERE TO PREVENT! A FINE DETECTIVE! WHY, I COULD HAVE BEEN **KIDNAPED** FOR ALL YOU...!
MADAM, A JEWEL THIEF MIGHT SLIP BY ME IN THE DARK...

...BUT NOT A TRUCK! GOOD NIGHT!

MICKEY! WHAT ARE YOU MUTTERING ABOUT?
LIGHTS CUT OFF... JEWELS SNATCHED LESS THAN A MINUTE LATER! OUTSIDE JOB? HMMM!
WALT DISNEY
Distributed by King Features Syndicate, Inc

HEY, MICKEY! DID YUH READ ABOUT LAST NIGHT AT MRS. VAN SWANKS? SHE...!
I KNOW... I WAS THERE!
DAILY BLAM
2-20

BUT IT WUZ EGGZACKLY LIKE AT **MY** HOUSE... MUSTA BEEN THUH SAME CROOK!
UNDOUBTEDLY! BUT THAT'S NO HELP TO US!

THE POINT IS... HOW CAN A MAN CUT THE WIRES IN BACK OF THE HOUSE, GET TO THE FRONT ROOM IN PITCH DARKNESS...

...GRAB THE JEWELS AND ESCAPE ALL IN ABOUT FIVE SECONDS?
HE **COULDN'T**! AIN'T NO MAN LIVIN' COULD DO THAT! UH... HE SHORE DONE IT SLICK, DIDN'T HE?
HMM...I WONDER...!
WALT DISNEY

YES, SIR, I'M CONVINCED! THESE ROBBERIES MAY BE AN OUTSIDE JOB, BUT THEY COULDN'T BE PULLED WITHOUT A **CONFEDERATE** ON THE **INSIDE**!
Copr 1942, Walt Disney Productions
World Rights Reserved

WHAT'S MORE, I'VE GOT A SWELL IDEA HOW TO NAB 'EM! SEE Y' LATER, GOOFY!
2-21

I DUNNO WHUT YER IDEAR IS, MICKEY, BUT YOU'RE WRONG ABOUT THAT INSIDE MAN...!

...THEM CIVIL WAR VETERANS IS TOO OLD FER THAT!

SO Y' SEE, MR O'HARA, IT WOULD BE **IMPOSSIBLE** TO PULL THOSE JEWEL ROBBERIES WITHOUT AN ACCOMPLICE ON THE INSIDE!
YES, I SEE WHAT YE MEAN!
2-23

BUT I'VE GOT A SWELL PLAN TO TRAP THE CROOKS, WITH THE HELP OF YOU AND YOUR MEN!
ALL RIGHT, MICKEY... LET'S HEAR IT!

MY BOY, IT'S A LULU! JUST LET US KNOW WHEN AND WE'LL DO OUR PART!
THANKS, MR. O'HARA! I'LL CALL Y' LATER!

H'LO, MINNIE! IS YOUR AUNT MARTHA IN? I GOTTA SEE HER RIGHT AWAY!
WHY, YES... BUT WHAT IN THE WORLD...?

EXPLAIN YOURSELF! WHY THIS SUDDEN FRENZY TO SEE MY AUNT MARTHA?
IT'S A PLAN I'VE THOUGHT UP TO NAB THE JEWEL THIEF! SHE CAN HELP ME PUT IT OVER!

Y' SEE, LOCAL SOCIETY WILL BE THROWIN' **MORE** PARTIES FOR YOUR AUNT AND UNCLE AND...!
I KNOW THAT!
IN FACT, WE'RE INVITED TO MRS. UPPACRUST'S TOMORROW NIGHT!
2-24

NO KIDDIN? JUST A MINUTE... I'VE GOTTA USE THE 'PHONE!

IT'S TOMORROW NIGHT, MR. O'HARA ... AT THE UPPACRUST'S HOUSE!
OKAY, MICKEY! I'LL HAVE EVERYTHING SET THE WAY YE PLANNED IT!
WALT DISNEY

I SEE WHAT YOU MEAN... YOU WANT ME TO ACT AS A DECOY AT THE PARTY!
THAT'S IT! WEAR ALL THE JEWELRY YOU CAN STAGGER UNDER! AND I'LL BE STICKIN' TO YOU LIKE A SHADOW!
Copr. 1942, Walt Disney Productions World Rights Reserved
2-25

WE'LL HAVE PLENTY OF CANDLES ALREADY LIT, SO WE CAN'T BLACK-OUT! AND THE COPS ARE GONNA SURROUND THE PLACE!

DADGUMMIT, SON... IT CAN'T MISS! AND I WANT TO BE THE FIRST TO GET MY HANDS ON THE THIEVIN' RASCAL!

I'LL CALL FOR Y' AT EIGHT, MINNIE! AND, BOY... THIS IS **ONE** PARTY I'M GLAD TO GO TO!
OH, DEAR... I ONLY **HOPE** NOTHING GOES WRONG!
Distributed by King Features Syndicate, Inc.
WALT DISNEY

ANOTHER SOCIAL EVENT GETS UNDER WAY! THIS TIME WITH PREPARATIONS TO FOIL THE BLACKOUT BURGLAR WHO HAS STRUCK TWICE BEFORE!

OH, DEAR...I'M SO NERVOUS WITH ALL THESE JEWELS! EVERY MINUTE I EXPECT THE LIGHTS TO GO OUT!
JUST WHAT I'M HOPING FOR! THOSE CANDLES WILL GIVE SOMEBODY THE SURPRISE OF HIS LIFE!
2-26

MY! THERE'S DUDLEY STILL AWAKE... WHAT AN EVENT!
EXCUSE ME A MINUTE... I WANT TO ASK HIM SOMETHING!

YEP, THEY'RE GUNS! AND I'M JUST ITCHIN' FOR A CHANCE TO USE 'EM, TOO!
WELL, I HOPE...GOSH, WOULDN'T IT BE AWFUL IF THERE WASN'T ANY ROBBERY TONIGHT?
WALT DISNEY

DOGGONE, I'M AFRAID THE CROOK'S BEEN SCARED OFF! MY PLAN WAS JUST A LITTLE TOO GOOD!
I FEEL ...CHILLY! THERE SEEMS TO BE A DRAFT...
2-27

YES, THERE IS A...OH-OH! THERE GO THE LIGHTS! WATCH OUT!

!

F'R GOSH SAKES! HOW DID...??
GOOD GRACIOUS!
WHAT HAPPENED?
WHO DID THAT?

EEEEK! HELP! HELP! MY JEWELS!!
OMIGOSH! AGAIN!
WALT DISNEY

MY JEWELS! MY PRECIOUS JEWELS!
D-DON'T GET EXCITED ...L-LET'S GET SOME LIGHTS ON HERE!
ROBBERS!
CALL THE POLICE SOME-BODY!
2-28

RIGHT IN MY OWN DRAWING-ROOM! OHH-H!
DREADFUL!
THERE OUGHT TO BE A LAW!
THE COPS ARE OUTSIDE! I'LL GO SEE IF...!

...OH! HERE'S MR. CASEY, NOW! DID Y' GET HIM?
NOT EXACTLY! BUT...

...I GOT A SWELL CLOSE-UP! WE'LL KNOW HIM THE NEXT TIME!
Distributed by King Features Syndicate, Inc.

FINE POLICE PROTECTION WE HAVE! A LADY'S DIAMOND TIARA SNATCHED FROM UNDER HER NOSE! HUMPH!
REMEMBER, I WASN'T INSIDE, MRS. UPPACRUST! MOUSE, HOW DID THOSE CANDLES GO OUT?
JUST WHAT I'D LIKE TO KNOW!
Copr 1942, Walt Disney Productions World Rights Reserved
3-2

WHEN THE CURRENT WENT OFF I WAS STANDIN' RIGHT BESIDE 'EM! THEN THERE WAS A SUDDEN DRAFT AND...

...OH-OH! GET A LOAD OF THIS, MR. CASEY ...AN ELECTRIC FAN RUN BY A STORAGE BATTERY!
AHA! NOW, WE'RE GETTIN' SOME-WHERE... WE GOT EVIDENCE!

YEH! EVIDENCE THAT WE'RE UP AGAINST SOMEBODY TOO DARN SLICK FOR US!
WALT DISNEY

WHAT I DON'T SEE, MR. CASEY... IF YOU WERE CLOSE ENOUGH TO PHOTOGRAPH THE CROOK, WHY DIDN'T Y' NAB HIM?
SURE... AHEM... I WAS JUST GOIN' TO BUT, ER... MY FLASHBULB BLINDED ME AND HE GOT AWAY!
Copr 1942, Walt Disney Productions World Rights Reserved

NOW THEN... LET'S GET ON WITH THE CASE! WHICH LADIES WAS ROBBED?
NO ONE BUT ME, MR. CASEY! THE OTHERS WERE NOT MOLESTED!
3-3

THAT ROBBER MUST BE TERRIBLY SMART, MICKEY...
THAT'S ANOTHER QUEER THING! I THOUGHT SURE HE'D MAKE A PASS AT THE HEAVY SUGAR YOU'RE PACKING, AUNT MARTHA!
Distributed by King Features Syndicate, Inc.

...TO HAVE KNOWN THAT THESE ARE ALL IMITATION!
THEY ARE?

DARN IT! JUST LIKE BEFORE... NOT A SUSPECT IN THE LOT!
OKAY... INVESTIGATION CLOSED! YUH CAN ALL GO HOME NOW!
3-4
Copr 1942, Walt Disney Productions World Rights Reserved

COME ON, DUDLEY, WE'RE GOING... GOOD GRIEF! IS HE AT IT AGAIN?
I THINK I HEARD SNORING FROM THE HALL A WHILE AGO!

ALL RIGHT... COME ON! THE PARTY'S OVER!
BONK!
HUH? A PARTY? WHERE? LET'S GO!
WALT DISNEY

NO QUESTION ABOUT IT, WE'RE UP AGAINST A MASTER CROOK! ANY GUY THAT USES A PORTABLE ELECTRIC FAN TO BLOW OUT CANDLES...

AND HOW DID HE KNOW THEY WERE THERE? WE NEVER FIND A TRACE OF AN INSIDE MAN!
3-5

THE GUESTS HAVE BEEN DIFFERENT AT ALL THREE PARTIES! NOBODY WAS WEARIN' A DISGUISE...!
RRRRR RRINGG!!

O'HARA SPEAKIN'! IF YE'D LIKE TO RUN DOWN TO HEADQUARTERS, I'VE GOT SOME NEW DOPE ON THE JEWEL THIEF!
OH, BOY! I'M ON MY WAY!

WONDER WHAT CHIEF O'HARA'S NEWS IS... HE SOUNDED LIKE IT WAS BIG!
3-6

NO, WE HAVEN'T CAUGHT THE THIEF, MICKEY! BUT YE'LL REMEMBER THAT CASEY GOT A FLASH OF HIS MUG LAST NIGHT!
SURE! BUT WHY DIDN'T HE SHOOT WITH HIS GUN INSTEAD OF A CAMERA?

ER, YES... HE SHOULD! BUT, ANY-HOW... WE SENT THAT SHOT OUT OVER THE WIRE PHOTO, AND YE'LL BE PROUD TO KNOW...

...THAT OUR FAIR CITY IS HONORED BY AN INTERNATIONAL MASTER CRIMINAL!
!
Distributed by King Features Syndicate, Inc.

Y' MEAN THIS SNAPSHOT OF THE JEWEL THIEF HAS BEEN IDENTIFIED IN OTHER CITIES?
NOT ONLY IN THIS COUNTRY, BUT ABROAD! OUR MAN IS WANTED ALL OVER THE WORLD!
3-7
Copr. 1942, Walt Disney Productions
World Rights Reserved

HE'S KNOWN AS THE "GLEAM", FROM THE DAZZLING JEWEL IN HIS TURBAN! HE'S NEVER BEEN CAUGHT, AND IF WE CAN DO IT...
BUT WHY WOULD A BIG-TIMER PICK ON OUR LITTLE TOWN?

HERE'S WHY! SOME WAY HE LEARNED THAT MINNIE'S RICH AUNT AND UNCLE WERE COMIN' HERE, AND KNEW THAT SOCIETY WOULD SPLURGE FOR 'EM!
GOSH! Y' THINK THAT'S IT?

YES, M' BOY ...WE'RE DEALIN' WITH A MASTER MIND!
UH...SEE Y' LATER, MR. O'HARA!
GOOFY DESCRIBED A MAN LIKE THIS VISITIN' MINNIE! BUT ...IT COULDN'T BE! IT'S... THERE'S SOME MIS-TAKE...!

I'LL GO SEE IF GOOFY RECOGNIZES THAT PICTURE OF THE JEWEL THIEF! BUT, DOGGONE IT, I **CAN'T** BELIEVE MINNIE'S MIXED UP IN IT!
3-9
Copr 1942, Walt Disney Productions World Rights Reserved

DO Y' RECOGNIZE HIM, GOOFY?
'COURSE I DO! IT'S THUH JERK THET COME OUTA MINNIE'S HOUSE AN' WOULDN' SPEAK TO ME! DURN SNOB!

YOU **COULD** BE MISTAKEN!
OH, YEAH? I S'POSE MAIN STREET'S **FULL** O' GUYS DRESSED IN BATH TOWELS...

...AND WEARIN' A JEWEL THET KNOCKS YER EYE OUT!
I GUESS YOU WIN! BUT, I'M GONNA SETTLE THIS, RIGHT NOW!

LOOK, MINNIE... DO YOU KNOW THIS MAN?
WHY, NO! **SHOULD** I?
3-10

ARE Y' **SURE** Y' NEVER SAW HIM ANYWHERE?
OF COURSE I DIDN'T! WHY SHOULD **I** KNOW THE SULTAN OF BANSHEE, OR WHOEVER HE IS?

MINNIE, YOU'RE WONDERFUL!
MICKEY **MOUSE**! WHATEVER HAS COME **OVER** YOU?

HOT DOG! I KNEW ALL ALONG SHE HAD NOTHIN' TO DO WITH THAT CROOK!

BUT...IF IT **WERE** TRUE, NATURALLY, SHE WOULDN'T ADMIT IT! I'M GETTIN' **NOWHERE**!
WALT DISNEY

HEY, MICKEY, I GOT A HOT CLUE ON THESE HERE JOOL ROBB'RIES ...THAT IS, IF YOU'RE STILL INTERESTED!
I SURE AM! WHAT'S NEW?
Daily BLAST
3-11

I REMEMBER YUH TOLE ME THERE MUST BE AN **INSIDE** MAN ON THEM JOBS... AND I GOT TO THINKIN' ...!

WELL, I FIGGERED IT OUT! THERE'S **ONE** GUY THAT'S BEEN PRESENT AT **EV'RY** ROBB'RY!
YEH... WHO?

YOU!
Distributed by King Features Syndicate, Inc.

ANOTHER GLITTERING PARTY IS THROWN FOR MINNIE'S AUNT AND UNCLE! AGAIN ELABORATE PLANS ARE MADE TO FOIL THE "GLEAM"! BUT...
3-12

EXT MORNING!
YUH MEAN, THAT THERE JOOL SLICKER DONE IT AGAIN?
HE SURE DID ...BLAST HIM! LIGHTS CUT OFF AND... ZOWIE! SAME OLD STORY!
Copr. 1942, Walt Disney Productions World Rights Reserved

WE HAD CANDLES ALL OVER THE ROOM ...SCATTERED SO THEY COULDN'T BE PUT OUT! SO, WHAT HAPPENED?
YOU TELL ME... YOU WUZ THERE!

THE HOSTESS WAS CALLED TO THE PHONE IN THE HALL...THE ONLY SPOT WE'D OVERLOOKED... AND ZIP! HER JEWELS WERE GONE!
GAWRSH! SEEMS LIKE THAT GUY KNOWS EVER-THING!

BUT, WHAT'S DRIVIN' ME DAFFY IS, WHO TIPS HIM OFF EVERY TIME?
'TAIN'T ME! I DON'T GIT INVITED!

HEY, MICKEY, I JEST HEERED THAT ANOTHER PARTY LAST NIGHT AT THUH GILTMORE'S...!
I KNOW! THE "GLEAM" FOOLED US AGAIN! Y' DON'T NEED TO REMIND ME!
FOR SALE
3-13

THAT'S TWO MORE THIS WEEK, CASEY, AND THE WHOLE TOWN'S ON OUR NECK! WHAT'S THE MATTER WITH YE?
IT'S THAT INSIDE ACCOMPLICE, CHIEF ...HE MUST BE INVISIBLE! EVERY DOGGONE TRAP WE SET IS TIPPED OFF! I'M GOIN' BUGHOUSE!

Daily BLAST
FRIDAY MARCH 13, 1942
THE "GLEAM" STRIKES AGAIN!
RICHROX DIAMONDS SNATCHED BY BLACKOUT FIEND!
POLICE BAFFLED!
JEWELS VALUED AT $75,0
HAUL TO DATE $450,00
"THE GLEAM"

NO USE PUTTING IT OFF! AT TOMORROW NIGHT'S PARTY I'M GONNA SETTLE THE QUESTION!
WALT DISNEY

WHAT I CAME FOR... THERE'S ANOTHER PARTY TONIGHT AT THE VAN SNOOT'S AND I'D LIKE Y' TO HAVE NO COPS...NO PRECAUTIONS ...!
HMM...THIS IS PRETTY IRREGULAR, M' BOY! THIS JEWEL THIEF IS SURE TO TURN UP! WHAT'S THE ANGLE?
Copr. 1942, Walt Disney Productions World Rights Reserved

I'D RATHER NOT SAY! BUT IT WILL PROVE SOMETHING!
WELL... YOU'VE HELPED US OUT BEFORE, SON, SO, OKAY! BUT I DON'T GET IT!
3-14

HAVIN' A GOOD TIME, MINNIE?
WONDERFUL! BUT, WHAT MAKES YOU SO ATTENTIVE TONIGHT? YOU HAVEN'T BUDGED FROM MY SIDE ALL EVENING!

OH, IT'S JUST ... WHY MINNIE, WHAT'S WRONG!
YOU'RE HOLDING ME TOO TIGHT! LET ME GO... LET ME GO!
WALT DISNEY

MICKEY! LET GO... YOU'RE HURTING ME!
PLEASE... LET ME GO!
SHHH...YOU'RE ATTRACTIN' ATTENTION! I'VE GOTTA HOLD ON TO Y', MINNIE... YOU'RE SICK!
3-16

EEEEEEK!!
THERE GO THE LIGHTS!
IT'S THE "GLEAM" AGAIN!
MINNIE! HOLD STILL...!??

QUICK, JEEVES... THE CANDLES!
Y-YES, MODDOM!

EEEEEEK! MURDER!
JUST GET ME A LITTLE WATER, PLEASE! SHE'S FAINTED!
WALT DISNEY

ARE Y' ALL RIGHT, MINNIE?
I...I THINK SO!
NO WONDER SHE FAINTED, POOR DEAR!
YES...THE LIGHTS ALL OUT ...AND THAT HORRID JEWEL THIEF ...!
3-17

OH, DEAR! WHO DID HE ROB THIS TIME, MRS. VAN SNOOT?
NO ONE! THAT'S THE STRANGEST THING, MY DEAR! HE SEEMS TO HAVE LEFT COMPLETELY EMPTY HANDED!

I FEEL TERRIBLY FORTUNATE... BUT WHAT FOILED THE MAN NONE OF US HAVE THE SLIGHTEST IDEA!

I'M AFRAID I KNOW ...BUT, I JUST...I CAN'T BELIEVE IT!

MINNIE...AN ACCOMPLICE TO A THIEF! IT CAN'T BE TRUE... IT JUST CAN'T!

AND YET, IT MUST BE! I HELD ON TO HER WHEN THE LIGHTS WENT OUT AND NOT A THING WAS STOLEN!
3-18

SHE'S BEEN ACTIN' QUEER EVER SINCE HER AUNT AND UNCLE CAME...BUT, WHO'D EVER THINK SHE'D COME TO THIS?

I'LL HAFTA TELL THE POLICE... IT'S MY DUTY! BUT, GOSH! THEY'D PUT HER IN JAIL!
RRRRING RRR G!

CHIEF O'HARA SPEAKIN' DID YE PROVE WHAT YE WANTED TO AT THE PARTY LAST NIGHT?
Y-YES...I MEAN, NO! I MEAN, UH ...NOTHIN' EXACTLY DEFINITE!

IT'S LIKE THIS, MR. O'HARA... I DIDN'T WANT ANY COPS AT THE PARTY LAST NIGHT, SO I COULD PROVE... I MEAN...!
LOOK, MICKEY... MAYBE YE BETTER COME DOWN AND EXPLAIN WHAT YE MEAN! I DON'T GET IT!

Y' SEE... IT WAS ABOUT THIS INSIDE ACCOMPLICE! I HAD MY SUSPICIONS ABOUT A CERTAIN ...UH PERSON, AND...!
SO, WHY NOT TELL US AND HAVE THE CERTAIN PERSON UNDER SURVEILLANCE?
3-19

WELL, Y' SEE... SHE...ULP ...I MEAN, THIS PERSON... I COULDN'T BE SURE...!
WELL, I'M SURE CONFUSED! BUT, REMEMBER ONE THING, M'BOY! IF YOU'RE PROTECTIN' SOMEBODY OR WITHHOLDIN' INFORMATION...

...YE MIGHT GET YOURSELF IN TROUBLE!
YES, SIR! THANK Y', SIR! G'BYE!
WALT DISNEY

I DON'T KNOW WHAT TO DO TO PROTECT MINNIE, BUT I JUST CAN'T TURN HER OVER TO THE COPS!
FOR DEFENSE
BUY
3-20

OH, MICKEY, LOOK! THE GLITTERBY'S ARE GIVING A PARTY IN HONOR OF AUNT AND UNCLE!
I WAS JUST THINKIN', MINNIE... Y' OUGHTN'T TO GO TO ANY MORE SOCIETY PARTIES! THESE JEWEL ROBB'RIES AND ALL... IT'S, UH...DANGEROUS!

DON'T BE RIDICULOUS! WHAT WOULD PEOPLE THINK IF I STAYED AWAY? WHY, THEY MIGHT EVEN IMAGINE...
Distributed by King Features Syndicate, Inc

...THAT I HAD SOMETHING TO DO WITH THE ROBBERIES!
!

THE VERY IDEA! WOULDN'T I LOOK SILLY STAYING AWAY FROM PARTIES GIVEN FOR MY OWN AUNT AND UNCLE?
BUT, MINNIE, Y' HAVEN'T BEEN WELL, AND...
HERE'S HER AUNT AND UNCLE, NOW! MAYBE THEY CAN HELP ME OUT!
3-21

STUFF AND NONSENSE, SONNY! PARTIES NEVER HURT ANYONE! I FIND THEM VERY STIMULATING...VERY STIMULATING, INDEED!
FOR DEFENSE
BUY

AND HE OUGHT TO KNOW... HE'S SLEPT THROUGH THE BEST OF 'EM!

HOPELESS TO DO ANYTHING WITH MINNIE... ONLY ONE THING LEFT... I'VE GOTTA GET THE "GLEAM," HIMSELF!
WALT DISNEY

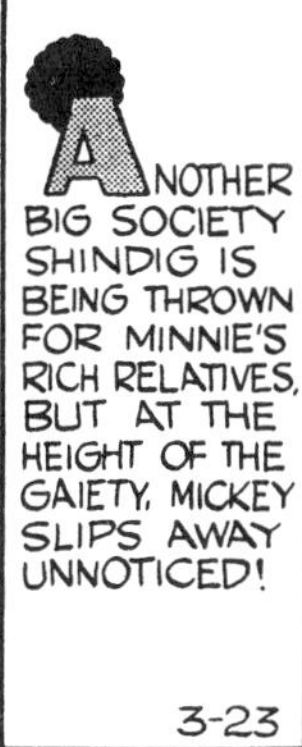
ANOTHER BIG SOCIETY SHINDIG IS BEING THROWN FOR MINNIE'S RICH RELATIVES, BUT AT THE HEIGHT OF THE GAIETY, MICKEY SLIPS AWAY UNNOTICED!
3-23

GOSH, I HOPE I CAN NAB THAT JEWEL THIEF BEFORE THE COPS EVER GET WISE TO MINNIE!
Copr. 1942, Walt Disney Productions World Rights Reserved

OH-OH! THERE GO THE LIGHTS!

THERE HE IS! AND, DOGGONE ...THAT'S MINNIE, ALL RIGHT!

STICK 'EM UP, MR. "GLEAM"! YOUR PROWLIN' DAYS ARE OVER!
WALT DISNEY

YOU HEARD ME! STICK 'EM UP AND HAND OVER THOSE JEWELS!
YOU HAVE MADE A MISTAKE, MY FRIEND... YOU SEE NO JEWELS!
3-24

UH... THAT'S RIGHT! SORRY TO HAVE TROUBLED YOU! GOOD NIGHT!

!

PARDON ME! I NEARLY WALKED OFF WITH YOUR GUN!
WALT DISNEY

SORRY ABOUT MY MISTAKE, MR....ER, GLEAM! HOPE YOU'LL PARDON ME...!
CERTAINLY, MY FRIEND! THINK NOTHING OF IT!
3-25

MICKEY... WHERE HAVE YOU BEEN? THERE'S BEEN ANOTHER SENSATIONAL ROBBERY!
NONSENSE! THERE WASN'T ANY ROBBERY AT ALL!

THE "GLEAM" TOLD ME SO, HIMSELF! AND, ANYWAY, HOW COULD I KNOW ABOUT IT...?

...I'M ONLY A CHIMPANZEE!
WALT DISNEY

MICKEY... WHAT'S COME OVER YOU? HANGING FROM THE CHANDELIER LIKE THAT!
YES MOUSE, THERE'S BEEN A SERIOUS ROBBERY... IT'S NO TIME FOR CLOWNING!
I DON'T KNOW WHAT YOU'RE TALKIN' ABOUT!
3-26
Copr. 1942, Walt Disney Productions
World Rights Reserved

COME! COME! A MINUTE AGO YOU TOLD US YOU WERE A MONKEY!
I DID NOT! WHY SHOULD I SAY ANYTHING AS SILLY AS THAT?

...WHEN EVERYONE KNOWS I'M A KANGAROO!
WALT DISNEY

YIPPEE! I'M A KANGAROO FROM TIMBUCTOO!
CUT THE CLOWNING, MOUSE... I'VE GOT WORK TO DO!
HE'S NOT CLOWNING ...THERE'S SOMETHING WRONG WITH HIM!
3-27

BUT WHAT'VE KANGAROOS GOT TO DO WITH IT... WHAT ABOUT THE ROBBERY?
MICKEY! TAKE ME HOME ...RIGHT AWAY!

YOU'VE GOT TO SEE A DOCTOR, MICKEY... YOU'VE BEEN ACTING VERY QUEER!
ME... ACTING QUEER! HA! HA! THAT'S FUNNY, COMIN' FROM YOU!
Distributed by King Features Syndicate, Inc.

NEXT MORNING.
FUNNY, I CAN'T REMEMBER MUCH ABOUT THE PARTY LAST NIGHT! SEEMS TO ME THERE WAS A ROBBERY... OR WAS THERE?
3-28

WHY, SURE! I ACTUALLY SAW MINNIE GIVIN' JEWELS TO THE "GLEAM"! OR DID I?
R-RRRING!!

OH, HELLO, MR. O'HARA!
I THINK YE BETTER TAKE A REST, M' BOY... THIS CASE HAS GOT YOUR NERVES!
BUT... THERE'S NOTHIN' WRONG WITH ME!

...FROM WHAT THEY TELL ME OF LAST NIGHT, YOU'RE IN PRETTY BAD SHAPE AND...!
BUT... I DIDN'T DO A THING!

JUST WHAT MINNIE TOLD ME! ARE THEY ALL GOIN' CUCKOO?

EVERYBODY INSISTS I ACTED CUCKOO AT THAT PARTY LAST NIGHT, BUT I SURE CAN'T REMEMBER IT!
3-30

IF IT WAS MINNIE, I COULD BELIEVE IT! SHE'S BEEN DEFINITELY SICK FOR A LONG TIME, POOR KID!
MINNIE MOUS

HELLO! HOW DO YOU FEEL TODAY?

BUT, MINNIE...!
NOW, DON'T TIRE YOURSELF, TRYING TO TALK...JUST REST AND BE COMFY!
WALT DISNEY

BUT, I TELL Y', I'M NOT SICK!
YES, I KNOW! JUST KEEP QUIET AND TAKE A NICE REST!
3-31

IT'S THESE JEWEL ROBBERIES! YOU'VE BEEN WORRYING TOO MUCH AND...!
PHOOEY! THERE'S NOTHIN' WRONG WITH **ME**!

LISTEN, MINNIE! AREN'T WE INVITED TO ANOTHER PARTY TOMORROW NIGHT?
YES, WE ARE! BUT **YOU'RE** NOT GOING... YOU'RE NOT WELL ENOUGH!

I'M NOT WELL! I'M GOIN' TO THAT PARTY AND I'LL GET TO THE BOTTOM OF THIS MYSTERY, IF IT'S THE LAST THING I DO!

ONCE AGAIN A RITZY PARTY IS IN FULL BLAST! MICKEY HIDES OUTSIDE THE HOUSE, HOPING TO GET ANOTHER CHANCE AT THE MYSTERIOUS "GLEAM"!

DOGGONE IT! LOOKS LIKE THIS IS **ONE** NIGHT HE'S NOT SHOWIN' UP!
4-1
Copr 1942, Walt Disney Productions World Rights Reserved

HELP! POLICE! ROBBERS!!
OOPS! I SPOKE TOO SOON!

BUT DARN THE LUCK, I MUST'VE BEEN HIDIN' IN THE WRONG PLACE!

HERE, OLD PAL...PUT THESE WITH YOUR COLLECTION!
WALT DISNEY

DID YOU CATCH SIGHT OF THE GLEAM AT ALL, MICKEY?
NO, HE DIDN'T COME BY WHERE I WAS HIDIN'!
4-2

CASEY'S OUT THERE SOMEWHERE ...OH, MAYBE THAT'S HIM, NOW!

GOOD GOSH! HE'S GONE CUCKOO!
ERK! ERK! ERK!

CUCKOO? DUMB-BELL.... DON'TCHA KNOW A CUCKOO FROM A TRAINED SEAL? ERK! ERK! ERK!
CLAP! CLAP! CLAP!
WALT DISNEY

WELL, I'LL BE...THE INSPECTOR'S BLOWN HIS TOP! THINKS HE'S A TRAINED SEAL!
EEEK! SOMEBODY DO SOMETHING!
?
SURE! DON'T I RATE A FISH? ERK! ERK!
CLAP! CLAP!
4-3

NOW, IF YOU'LL JUST COME QUIETLY, SIR, WE WON'T SEND FOR THE STRAIT-JACKET!
ERK...EH? WHAT'S GOIN' ON HERE?

WHY, YOU...CALLIN' YER SUPERIOR A TRAINED SEAL! I'LL HAVE YOU BROKE FOR THIS!
Distributed by King Features Syndicate, Inc

DOESN'T REMEMBER A THING... JUST LIKE THEY CLAIM I WAS! WHAT'RE WE UP AGAINST, ANYWAY?

NEXT MORNING, MICKEY IS CALLED TO THE OFFICE OF THE CHIEF OF POLICE!

HELLO, MICKEY! TELL ME ALL YE KNOW ABOUT DETECTIVE CASEY'S ACTIONS LAST NIGHT!
HE THOUGHT HE WAS A TRAINED SEAL...BUT I CAN'T EXPLAIN IT, SIR!
4-4
Copr 1942, Walt Disney Productions World Rights Reserved

BUT WHERE'S THE CONNECTION WITH JEWEL ROBBERIES? YOU THOUGHT YE WERE A MONKEY AND A KANGAROO!

SO THEY SAY! I CAN'T REMEMBER BEIN'...!
WELL, FROM THE WAY THE POLICE ARE BEIN' PANNED, I KNOW WHAT I'LL BE...

WHAT, SIR?
BAA-A-A-A! THE GOAT!
Distributed by King Features Syndicate, Inc.

P.D.
I DON'T BLAME THE CHIEF FOR WORRYIN'! THE GLEAM PUTS IT OVER ON HIS COPS EVERY TIME!
POLICE HEADQUARTERS
4-6

!
IT'S SURE BAFFLING HOW HE.. ..GOOD GOSH! THERE HE IS, NOW... IN BROAD DAYLIGHT!

YOU MISTAKE ME FOR SOMEONE, YOUNG MAN?
WHY, I THOUGHT ...FOR A MINUTE... UH...!

HERE WE GO SCATTERING NUTS IN MAY... ON CHRISTMAS DAY IN THE MORNING!
WALT DISNEY

OH, I AM A GAY BALLERINA! TRA-LA-LA!
MAYBE WE OUGHTA CALL A COP!
THE GUY'S BATS!
4-7

I KNOW THIS YOUNG MAN... I'LL TAKE CARE OF HIM! HE JUST HAS SPELLS!
Y' BETTER PUT HIM IN THE DIZZY HOUSE!

COME ALONG, SON... IT'S UNCLE DUDLEY!
I DON'T CARE WHO Y' ARE... YOU'VE GOT NO RIGHT UP HERE ON THE STAGE INTERRUPTING THE PERFORMANCE!
WALT DISNEY

FEELIN' BETTER, SON?
WHY, SURE, I'M ALL RIGHT... SAY! THIS IS MINNIE'S HOUSE ... HOW'D I GET HERE?
4-8

HAD ANOTHER OF HIS DIZZY SPELLS! I FOUND HIM DOIN' BALLET DANCIN' IN THE STREET!
WHAT DO Y' MEAN, DANCIN'? I JUST LEFT CHIEF O'HARA AND... AND CAME OVER HERE... SOMEHOW!
OH, YOU POOR DEAR! IT'S DREADFUL!

AND, SAY! I MET THE GLEAM! WHY DIDN'T I ARREST HIM, I WONDER?

I LET HIM GET AWAY! WHAT THE DICKENS MADE ME DO THAT?
NOW, NOW, HONEY, YOU'LL BE ALL RIGHT! JUST LET LITTLE OLD MINNIE TAKE CARE OF YOU!

I GUESS I MIGHT AS WELL ADMIT THEY'RE RIGHT... MY MIND'S CRACKIN' UP FOR SURE!
4-9

HI, MICKEY! JEST DROPPED BY TO SEE IF YUH WUZ MAKIN' ANY PROGRESS ON THAT JEWEL CASE!
I'LL SAY I AM! I'M HALF WAY TO THE BOOBY HATCH ALREADY!

I ACT LIKE A MONKEY AND A KANGAROO... AND THEN DON'T REMEMBER A THING ABOUT IT!
SHUCKS, MICKEY! THAT AIN'T NUTHIN' SERIOUS!

NO? I SUPPOSE YOU CAN EXPLAIN IT!
HAW! HAW! WHY, SURE! I SEEN IT ON THUH STAGE YEARS AGO! IT'S CALLED HIPPNERTISM!
Distributed by King Features Syndicate, Inc.

HYPNOTISM! BY GOSH, GOOFY, I BELIEVE YOU'VE GOT THE ANSWER!
'COURSE, I HAVE! AIN'T NUTHIN' TOUGH ABOUT THAT! SHOULD 'A ASKED ME BEFORE!
4-10

THAT WOULD EXPLAIN CASEY'S ACTIONS, TOO ... AND WHY WE COULDN'T REMEMBER ANYTHING LATER!
SURE! THOUGHT YUH KNOWED THAT! WELL, I GOTTA BE GOIN'! S'LONG!

DARNED IF THAT GUY HASN'T SOLVED THE WHOLE CASE! IT'S SIMPLE, NOW...

...EXCEPT...HOW THE HECK ARE Y' GONNA ARREST A GUY WHO CAN HYPNOTIZE Y'?

THERE MUST BE A WAY TO PREVENT BEIN' HYPNOTIZED, IF I CAN ONLY FIND IT!
PUBLIC LIBRARY

HOT DOG! PLENTY OF BOOKS ON THE SUBJECT! I'LL FOOL THAT OLD GLEAM YET!
"H"
4-11

MY, MY! DOES THIS MEAN YOU'RE GOING TO START A NEW CAREER, MICKEY?
NO, MA'AM! AS A MATTER OF FACT...

...I MEAN TO END SOMEBODY'S CAREER ...I HOPE!
WALT DISNEY

CONVINCED THAT THE GLEAM'S SUCCESS IS DUE TO SUPER HYPNOTISM, MICKEY RUSHES OUT AND GATHERS A FLOCK OF BOOKS ON THE SUBJECT!

BOY! ALL I HAFTA DO IS LEARN HOW TO PREVENT BEIN' HYPNOTIZED AND I'VE GOT HIM!
4-13

...MMM-MUMBLE..."STARE FIXEDLY AT THE SUBJECT AND IN A LOW, STEADY VOICE SAY, 'SLEEP...SLEEP'..." NO, THAT'S NOT IT!

"...AND IF PRACTISED FAITHFULLY, CANNOT FAIL! THE SUBJECT WILL BELIEVE HIMSELF A RABBIT OR..." AW, PHOOEY!

EVERY ONE THE SAME! NOT A WORD FROM THE RABBIT'S ANGLE!

LICKED AGAIN! THERE'LL PROB'LY BE A PARTY ANY NIGHT, NOW AND THAT PESKY GLEAM WILL PUT IT OVER ON US AGAIN, AS USUAL!
Copr 1942, Walt Disney Productions World Rights Reserved
4-14

IF ONE OF THESE BOOKS TOLD HOW NOT TO BE HYPNOTIZED! BUT, NO...THEY'RE ALL LIKE THIS...!

...THEY JUST TELL Y'...MMM-MUMBLE ...UMBLE...
HUH??

HOW DID I MISS THAT BEFORE?

BOY-OH-BOY! HAVE WE GOT HIM, NOW! YIPPEE!!
WALT DISNEY
Distributed by King Features Syndicate, Inc.

AT LAST! A WAY TO GUM UP THE GLEAM'S HYPNOTIC STUFF! WILL HE GET A SURPRISE!
4-15

I'LL TELL MINNIE...OR SHOULD I LET HER IN ON IT YET?
RRR-RINNGG!!

OH, HELLO, MINNIE! I WAS JUST GONNA CALL Y'...ER, THAT IS... NO, I GUESS I WASN'T!
MAKE UP YOUR MIND! ANYWAY, WE'RE INVITED TO A PARTY TONIGHT...!

...BUT I DON'T SUPPOSE YOU'RE WELL ENOUGH TO...
SWELL! I FEEL GREAT! WHAT TIME SHALL I PICK Y' UP? HOT DOG!

I DECLARE...THAT MICKEY! NOW, HE'S JUST CRAZY TO GO TO A PARTY!

... I'M SURE I'M RIGHT THIS TIME, MR. O'HARA ... AND TONIGHT MAY BE OUR LAST CHANCE!
HMM... YOUR IDEAS HAVEN'T BEEN SO HOT ON THIS CASE, MICKEY...
Copr. 1942, Walt Disney Productions World Rights Reserved
4-16

... BUT NEITHER HAVE OURS! GO AHEAD, SON, AND TRY OUT YOUR PLAN!
THANKS, MR. O'HARA!

YUH WANTED TO SEE ME, MICKEY?
YEH! HERE'S WHAT YOU'RE TO DO TONIGHT!

BZZ-BZZ-Z ...BZZ-BZZZ...!
IZZAT SO? SAY! I DIDN'T KNOW I WAS SMART LIKE THAT! THAT'LL GIT 'IM SURE! UH-HAW! SOME SURPRIZE!

COMES NIGHT... AND THE FATEFUL PARTY IS IN FULL SWING!

NOW, MICKEY, WHERE ARE YOU WANDERING OFF TO SO MYSTERIOUSLY?
NOTHIN' MYSTERIOUS! FELLA HAS TO ...HO-HUM.. HAVE A BREATH OF AIR NOW AND THEN!
4-17

WHOO-O-O-O-O-O... WHOO-O-O...!

WHOO-O... WHOO-OO...!
WHOO-OO..!
WHOOT WHOO-O!
WHOOT!

WHOO! WOO! THIS HERE OWL'S ALL READY, MICKEY!
WALT DISNEY

GOSH, IT'S GETTIN' LATE! DON'T TELL ME THE GLEAM'S NOT GONNA SHOW UP, AFTER ALL MY PLANS!
4-18

EEEEEEEK! HELP! POLICE!
HOT DOG! THERE HE IS! AND MINNIE'S HANDING OUT THE JEWELS... FOR THE LAST TIME ...I HOPE!

PSSST... GOOFY! GET GOIN'! DO YOUR STUFF!

PURDON ME, MR. GLEAM, BUT YOU'RE UNDER ARREST! JEST COME QUIETLY AN' SAVE BULLETS FER THUH WAR!
WALT DISNEY

YOU HEARD ME... YOU'RE UNDER ARREST! AND HAND OVER THEM JOOLS!
THERE MUST BE A MISTAKE, MY FRIEND! YOU SEE NO JEWELS!
4-20

DON'T GIMME THAT HIPPNERTISM STUFF... IT WON'T WORK! I GOT A SPESHUL KIND O' MIND!
BUT THERE ARE NO JEWELS! YOU CAN'T SEE A THING!

HOT DOG! WE'RE GETTIN' AWAY WITH IT! HE CAN'T HYPNOTIZE GOOFY!

YOU FOOL! THERE ARE NO JEWELS! YOU'RE... YOU'RE A SQUIRREL! GO CLIMB A TREE!
AW CUT OUT THUH HORSE-PLAY, DOC! DON'TCHA RECKO'NIZE SUPERIOR INTELLECK WHEN YUH SEE IT? I AIN'T LIKE ORDINARY FOLKS!

THERE HAS BEEN NO ROBBERY... THERE AREN'T ANY JEWELS! AND YOU ARE A SQUIRREL... CAN'T YOU UNDERSTAND?
OH, SURE! SURE! THAT'S FER ORDINARY FOLKS! BUT I TOLE YUH I GOT A SUPERIOR KINDA INTELLECK!
4-21

HE'S BREAKIN' HIS NECK, TRYIN' TO HYPNOTIZE GOOFY AND HE CAN'T DO IT!

I KNOW YER STUFF, DOC, SO QUIT WASTIN' MUH TIME! HAND OVER THEM JOOLS!

ALL RIGHT, YOU'RE TOO SMART FOR ME! I GIVE UP! BUT COULD I ASK A SMALL FAVOR?
ANYTHING WITHIN REASON, DOC! YOU'LL FIND I AIN'T HARD-HEARTED!

AHEM! WHUT'S THIS HERE FAVOR YUH WANT ME TO DO DOC B'FORE I TURN YUH IN?
I'VE AN ACCOMPLICE WAITING OUT IN THE CAR FOR ME AND... WELL HE DOESN'T KNOW I'M ARRESTED AND...
4-22

...IT ISN'T QUITE CRICKET TO LEAVE HIM SITTING OUT THERE ALL NIGHT... ..DO YOU THINK?
HMM... GUESS YOU'RE RIGHT! AND I AIN'T ONE TO USE UN-FAIR TICTACS! OKAY ...TELL HIM TO GO ON HOME!

BUT MAKE IT SNAPPY! DON'T TRY TO PUT ANYTHING OVER ON ME!
NO, SIR! THANK YOU, SIR! I'LL BE RIGHT BACK!

OMIGOSH! GOOFY'S LETTIN' HIM GET AWAY! SOMEP'N'S GOTTA BE DONE QUICK!
WALT DISNEY

MR. CASEY! QUICK! THE GLEAM IS GETTIN' AWAY!
STOP HIM! HEAD HIM OFF!
4-23

WHY GIT SO HET UP? DON'T THEY KNOW HE'S COMIN' BACK... THET HE'S SKEERED TO DEATH O' ME?

STICK 'EM UP, MUGG!
YEH ...WE GOTCHA!
WELL, HOW INTERESTING... TOTEM POLES THAT CAN TALK!

NOT BACK YET! COULD HE BE TRYIN' TO SLIP A FAST ONE OVER ON ME?

SO! THAT GOLDURNED JOOL-THIEF TURNS OUT TO BE A CROOK! PLAYS ME FER A SUCKER!
4-24

I TREAT HIM FAIR AN' SQUARE AN' HE PULLS A FAST ONE ON ME! THUH NEX' TIME I... OH-OH!

EXTREMELY INTERESTING TOTEM POLES... IN FACT, THE BEST I'VE EVER SEEN! SORRY I MUST LEAVE, BUT...

OH, NO, YUH DON'T, YUH DOUBLE-CROSSER! GIT BACK AN' UN-HIPPNERTIZE THEM GUYS 'FORE I BLOW YER BRAINS OUT!

UN-HIPPNERTIZE THEM GUYS PRONTO! I GOT AN ITCHY TRIGGER-FINGER!
BUT CAN'T YOU SEE? THEY'RE ONLY TOTEM POLES?
4-25

DON'T GIMME THAT GUFF! SNAP 'EM OUT OF IT... AND FAST!

YES SIR, IT TAKES A MASTER MIND TO NAB A MASTER CROOK! AND WON'T THUH FOLKS INSIDE GIT A BIG SUPPRIZE!
AND THEY'RE NOT THE ONLY ONES WHO WILL GET A SURPRISE, OLD BOY!

HERE HE IS, FOLKS... HIS JEWEL-SNATCHIN' DAYS ARE OVER!
SHUCKS! WARN'T NUTHIN' TO IT, ONCE THEY GOT **ME** ON HIS TRAIL!
GREAT SCOTT! THEY'VE CAUGHT THE GLEAM!
HOW **EVER** DID YOU DO IT?
4-27
Copr. 1942, Walt Disney Productions World Rights Reserved

STOP THAT WOMAN! SHE'S THE GLEAM'S ACCOMPLICE!
SIR? I BEG PODDEN... THE LADY IS THE GUEST OF HONOR!
WALT DISNEY

THAT'S WHAT I SAID...SHE'S THE GLEAM'S ACCOMPLICE!
IT'S **OUTRAGEOUS!** I NEVER SAW THE MAN IN MY LIFE!
THIS IS A SERIOUS CHARGE, MOUSE! CAN YOU PROVE IT?
I SURE CAN! GOOFY, YANK THAT TURBAN OFF THE GLEAM!
HUH? WHUT'LL **THAT** DO?
Copr. 1942, Walt Disney Productions World Rights Reserved
4-28

EEEEEK! **UNCLE DUDLEY!**

IMAGINE, DUDLEY MOUSEGOMERY BEING THE GLEAM!
ASTOUNDING!
AHH... BUT HE'S **NOT** YOUR UNCLE, MINNIE!
MY OWN UNCLE... A **JEWEL THIEF!** OHHHHHH...!
4-29

BUT... I DON'T...
NO, YOU WON'T REMEMBER, BUT THE GLEAM, HERE, HYPNOTIZED YOU MAKING YOU BELIEVE YOU HAD AN AUNT AND UNCLE "MOUSEGOMERY" BEFORE HE AND HIS WIFE ARRIVED!

OKAY...SNAP OUT OF IT, SISTER! NO NEED LEAVING YOU IN A FOG, NOW THAT THE JIG'S UP!
OHH...
OHHHHH...!

YOU...YOU **IMPOSTOR!** USING **ME** TO MEET THESE NICE PEOPLE, SO YOU COULD **ROB** THEM!
DECEITFUL, TOO!
THAT'S... SPLUT..T.TT. ...IT'S... DIS-HONEST!
WALT DISNEY

YOU IMPOSTOR! POSING AS MY UNCLE!
YOU HYPNOTIST ...YOU... YOU JEWEL THIEF...!
AND THAT'S NOT ALL, MINNIE! HE HYPNOTIZED YOU INTO SNATCHING THE JEWELS WHEN THE LIGHTS WERE OUT! YOU WERE HIS ACCOMPLICE!
4-30

JUST AS HE HYPNOTIZED ME... AND MADE INSPECTOR CASEY THINK HE WAS A TRAINED SEAL, WHEN WE TRIED TO CAPTURE HIM!
I DON'T REMEMBER A THING!

BUT HE CAN'T HYPNOTIZE ANY MORE POLICE AGAINST THEIR WILL WITHOUT THAT ELECTRIC JEWEL IN HIS TURBAN!

AND EVEN THET FAILED AGAINST A SUPERIOR INTELLECK! I, A. GOOF, HE COULDN'T HIPPNERTIZE!

LOOK HERE, MOUSE, WHAT MADE YOU SUSPECT THAT THE GLEAM AND DUDLEY WAS ONE AND THE SAME PERSON!
WHEN HE HYPNOTIZED ME ON THE STREET I SMELLED GREASEPAINT ON HIM! A SHORT TIME LATER HE RESCUED ME WITHOUT HIS DISGUISE AND I COULD STILL SMELL IT! SO I JUST PUT TWO AND TWO TOGETHER!
2X2 =4
WHUT'S FOUR GOT TO DO WITH IT!
5-1
Copr. 1942, Walt Disney Productions World Rights Reserved

OH, MR. GOOFY, HOW WONDERFUL! THE ONLY MIND IN TOWN THAT COULDN'T BE HYPNOTIZED
YOU'RE A HERO!
AWW... 'TAIN'T SO MUCH!

PROBERLY ALL CAUSED BY INHERITANCE!
WALT DISNEY

I THOUGHT HIS HYPNOTIC ABILITY HAD US LICKED, TILL I READ IN A BOOK THAT A CERTAIN TYPE OF...ER...INTELLECT COULDN'T BE HYPNOTIZED! UH...I REALIZED GOOFY HAD THAT TYPE MIND!

OKAY, YOU TWO, YOU GO ON ICE FOR THE NIGHT!
NICE WORK, MOUSE! SEE Y' TOMOR-ROW!
WAIT A MINUTE! IF THOSE CROOKS ARE NOT MY RELATIVES, THEY OWE ME FOUR MONTHS' BOARD BILL! I DEMAND AN ACCOUNTING!
WHOA, MINNIE! THEY'RE INTERNATIONAL JEWEL THIEVES AND THERE'S A REWARD THAT OUGHT TO EVEN EVERY-THING UP!
5-2
Copr. 1942, Walt Disney Productions

I'VE GOT A HUNCH WE'LL FIND ALL THE STOLEN JEWELRY AT MINNIE'S HOUSE, SO NOBODY'LL LOSE ANYTHING!

I'M AWFULLY SORRY I'VE CAUSED SUCH A FLURRY IN THE SOCIAL WORLD MRS. RHINE-STONE!
SORRY? MY DEAR, YOU'VE GIVEN US THE MOST EXCITING SEASON I'VE EVER KNOWN! WE'LL NEVER FORGET IT!
Distributed by King Features Syndicate, Inc.

IMAGINE! THE ONLY MIND IN TOWN THET COULDN'T BE HIPPNERTIZED! WHO'D EVER SUSPECTED THET I HAD SUCH A SUPERIOR INTELLECK?

THE GOTTFREDSON ARCHIVES

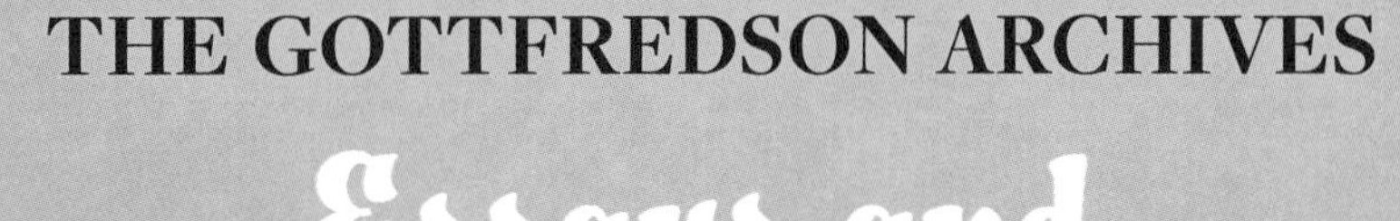

Essays and Special Features

The Cast: PETE (…AND SHYSTER?)

One day in the depths of the Great Depression, a rotten-hearted crook became an honest man overnight.

Wait… *what?*

Nothing's ever that simple—except, perhaps, in an animated cartoon. And indeed, that is where Pegleg Pete made the transformation in question. The formerly criminal cat was now a law-enforcing sheriff in the Mickey Mouse film short *Moving Day* (1936). To make matters knottier, Mickey—squatting in an unpaid-for house—was effectively a lawbreaker!

We could shrug *Moving Day* off as a film role played by Pete the actor; as a work with no relation to the *Mickey Mouse* daily strip continuity. Yet *Moving Day*, through its vestment of Pete with legal authority, foreshadowed a major comics development. Pete was scary as a villain and as a menace; but he was arguably scarier in a position of unimpeachable power. Mickey could beat a semi-powerful mob boss, as Pete had been in Floyd Gottfredson's "Editor-in-Grief" (1935); but Mickey couldn't beat *lawman* Pete—only flee, as Mickey did at *Moving Day*'s end. The more legitimate authority Pete had, ipso facto, the more of a challenge he presented.

While Gottfredson never cited *Moving Day* as an inspiration, his Pete stories began to follow a similar path. The more power Pete was able to aggregate, the more interesting he got. As early as 1936, in "Mickey Mouse Joins the Foreign Legion," Pete was suddenly Mickey's Legionnaire sergeant: still a crook whose crimes put his status at risk, but also an official with authority to abuse while he had it. When Mickey became Pete's formal subordinate, it made their usual clash of personalities that much more vibrant.

By 1940, and the tales in this volume, authority came so naturally to Pete that he wielded it, on some level, even in more traditional crook roles. Bandit Pete in "The Bar-None Ranch" can flee, guns blazing, from farms he has raided; but he flees home to a private underground kingdom—where a hired (or captive?) scientist enables him to control the very sky above. In "Mystery at Hidden River," Pete works for his old boss Sylvester Shyster, but spends more time on his own, running a logging camp as a fiefdom with Mickey as his serf. All the better for more "Foreign Legion"-like feuding: it's hard for Mickey to unseat an enemy who effectively rules his world.

"Hidden River," as noted elsewhere in this book, was based on a Donald Duck screen short—*Timber* (1941)—in which Pete also played the boss, in this case Donald's. Later Duck cartoons would also dote on the conceit, even making Pete Donald's recurring military sergeant: a callback to "Foreign Legion," if an unintentional one. By now, an authoritarian Pete seemed so natural that he could turn up anywhere.

"Hidden River" was the last Pete adventure plotted by Floyd Gottfredson alone. When Pete returned in 1943's "Mickey Mouse on a Secret Mission," scripter Bill Walsh was co-plotter as well; soon afterward, the plots would become all Walsh's. Notably, "Secret Mission" was the only Walsh-era serial to show Pete as another villain's partner. Apart from it, the big cat reappeared almost exclusively in positions of unrivaled clout: a future-world emperor, a pirate king, even a high-ranking Soviet apparatchik.

The mature Gottfredson Pete had become a power broker first—and everything else second. So what of former boss Sylvester Shyster? Even in "Hidden River," we note, Shyster only gives orders to Pete when both are safely ensconced in Shyster's hideout. Pete rules his own timber fields with an iron fist; and significantly, Shyster never visits him there. Maybe he didn't dare? [DG]

ABOVE: Power broker Pete looms over the gang in a 1938 *Mickey Mouse Magazine* feature drawn by Tom Wood. Image courtesy Walt Disney Photo Library.

Gottfredson's World: THE BAR-NONE RANCH

Every country that loves Mickey Mouse has had its own edition—or editions—of Floyd Gottfredson's epics. And each country's Disney comics publisher has tried to make its own version unique, usually by asking homegrown talent to create their own covers or vignettes based on the stories.

In this series we're proud to anthologize these images, both foreign and domestic, old and new—and give you a sense of how far Gottfredson's classic adventures have traveled over the years. Saddle up and come along with us... first stop, the Wild West! [DG]

ABOVE FAR LEFT: *Better Little Book* 1471 (1943). Art by Hank Porter; image courtesy Larry Lowery.

ABOVE LEFT: Italian *Albi d'oro* 8 (1946, 2nd series). Art reinked from Gottfredson by Michele Rubino; image courtesy Matteo Sonz.

ABOVE RIGHT: Brazilian *Mickey* 25 (1954). Art by Jorge Kato; image courtesy Arthur Faria Jr.

ABOVE FAR RIGHT: *Gladstone Giant Comic Album Special* 3 (1990). Art by Murad Gumen; image courtesy Thomas Jensen.

LEFT: Italian *Topolino d'oro* 26 (1973). Art by Marco Rota; image courtesy Leonardo Gori.

The Gottfredson Gang in "Their Own" Words

ASK PEOPLE ON THE STREET who Mickey Mouse is, and they'll likely tell you—a cartoon character. A TV host. A theme park mascot. Not a comic strip hero, nor exactly a celebrity, though in his early heyday he was known as one.

Mickey's early 1930s public image—as we have seen in past volumes—evolved directly from press tie-ins with Floyd Gottfredson's comics. Via careful Disney publicity campaigns, Mickey often granted "interviews" to a variety of journalists, using language and attitudes that came not from the screen, but from Mickey's more complex daily strip persona. In essence, the Mickey of the funnies fleshed out the Mickey of other media.

By the early 1940s this was changing. Proof positive is an "interview" created to publicize Disney's feature film *Fantasia* (1940): while Mickey's mood still reflects the gutsy, energetic hero of the past, he isn't the hero now—just the master of ceremonies for other Disney characters. In fact, the central "joke" of the interview is that Mickey, while the speaker, is anything but the subject.

A contrast with a much earlier "interview," excerpted on the opposite page, shows us how much times had changed. In 1930, as exemplified by the vintage publicity piece "My Love Life," Mickey had been a sparkling, dashing adventurer in all media. After World War II, "our" Mickey Mouse—Floyd Gottfredson's cheeky, daring comics Mickey Mouse—would only be found in the comics. [DG]

Mouse Tells All About New Film In 'Interview'

From The Atlanta Constitution, *September 27, 1942*

THIS WAS Mickey Mouse's big moment, and he was making the most of it. The occasion was Mickey's being interviewed in connection with his starring in his first full-length motion picture, Walt Disney's new and exciting "Fantasia."

"Come right in!" squeaked Mickey, his black eyes popping with glee. He tripped over his Magician's robe and nearly lost his wizard's hat, but recovered with a flash of that old Mickey grin.

"I've got all the cast here!" Mickey rushed around herding the temperamental ostrich dancers, the dinosaurs, the unicorns, the centaurs and centaurettes, and all the rest of the five hundred new characters you'll meet in "Fantasia." "Break it up, boys—break it up!" ordered Mickey to the hundred and three musicians who play the score of "Fantasia." They were having a little jam session, in spite of the fact that they supposedly had to maintain their dignity as members of the Philadelphia Symphony orchestra.

Mickey was back at our side. "Have some ambrosia," he said, offering a glass. "Right out of the Elysian fields. We make it ourselves, in the picture, you know."

"Now about your part in the picture, Mickey," we began.

"Wait!" he said. "Here comes little Hop Low, funniest accentric dancer Walt Disney ever drew. "Please," added Mickey, lowering his voice, "please don't mention steaks. Hop Low is a mushroom, you know, and he's afraid of steaks."

We bowed low to Hop Low. He gave a funny little skip and said anxiously, "You don't like steaks, do you?"

"Steak? Steak?" we said. "Never heard of anything called a steak." Hop Low grinned and skipped away happily.

"Thank you," said Mickey. "Gosh, he's funny in the picture!" "Yes, but what about you, Mickey?"

"Wait!" said Mickey, "here's the Sound Track! Is he a scream in the picture! Hey, Mr. Sound Track!" A Bronx cheer replied to Mickey, produced by a long, tall, thin Being who suddenly stretched into a spinning top; at the same time giving off a deep "blue" sound. "That's his saxophone number," said Mickey. "Just wait'll you see him!"

"What about you, Mickey?" We caught him by a flowing sleeve and held him firmly. •

MY LOVE LIFE AND OTHER THINGS

As told by Mickey Mouse

* * * *

To CEDRIC BELFRAGE

Excerpted from Motion Picture Classic, *August 1930*

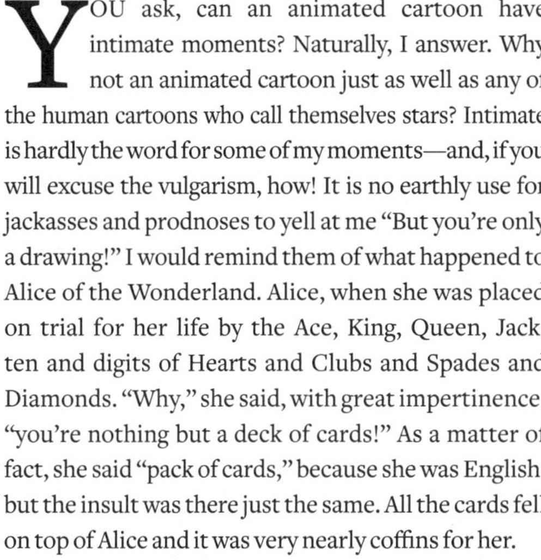

YOU ask, can an animated cartoon have intimate moments? Naturally, I answer. Why not an animated cartoon just as well as any of the human cartoons who call themselves stars? Intimate is hardly the word for some of my moments—and, if you will excuse the vulgarism, how! It is no earthly use for jackasses and prodnoses to yell at me "But you're only a drawing!" I would remind them of what happened to Alice of the Wonderland. Alice, when she was placed on trial for her life by the Ace, King, Queen, Jack, ten and digits of Hearts and Clubs and Spades and Diamonds. "Why," she said, with great impertinence, "you're nothing but a deck of cards!" As a matter of fact, she said "pack of cards," because she was English, but the insult was there just the same. All the cards fell on top of Alice and it was very nearly coffins for her.

First and foremost, of course, in an interview such as this, I have to mention the real love of my life—Minnie Mouse. Minnie, as my vast public knows, works as my leading lady; at least, she says I work as her leading man but that of course is simply a young girl's idle prattle. I may as well confess—for we stars of the screen can keep nothing, not even the holiest things, secret—that ever since the first time Minnie kissed me and blew heart-shaped bubbles into the air as she did so, my heart has not been my own. I gave it then into her keeping, and she still has it. I had been kissed before—what mouse-of-the-world has not? But this, I knew, was something different. Minnie can take my heart and make it dance a jig in thin air as we kiss, or make it stand to attention and then fade from sight just as if she were Houdini. We have tried to show this little trick of Minnie's in my pictures. I have never found anyone else who can kiss like Minnie, and all the most thrillingly intimate moments of my whole life have been with her.

As for the fantastic stories that have been circulated coupling my name with that of Clarabelle Cow, I can only strive to maintain my composure and state in an even voice that they are false. Not that Clarabelle is not an attractive enough animal, as cows go. But Hollywood is like that; if you are seen twice in public with a cow, everybody at once thinks the worst and starts spreading scandalous gossip. What if I did give Clarabelle the lavaliere cowbell which she wears around her dainty neck? And what if I did, on perhaps two or three occasions, take her to lunch at the Brown Derby and to dance at the Roosevelt?

It has been said of me, too, that moments I have spent in Clara Bow's company have been of an intimate character. That is true, and I am proud of it; and anybody who thinks that means what they think it means, can just go run round the block. Few of us young fellows in Hollywood have not at one time or another fallen under the spell of the Divine Clara. I came chronologically between Gilbert Roland and Victor Fleming in the list of Clara's boyfriends. Clara and I used to ride for hours on the rollercoasters at Ocean Park, and while she tenderly tore off the lobe of my ear with her teeth I would slowly throttle her with my tail—which, by the way, she always thought had "It." Ah, happy nights!

Clara had a sweet, soothing way of doing things which was in a class by itself. But she could not juggle with my heart as Minnie Mouse does. Finally, one day, she chewed my ear as we rounded a bend on the rollercoaster, and merely tore out a mouthful of hair. I accused her of having become cool in her ardor, and she could not deny it. I jumped out and quickly disappeared into the crowd, since when I haven't seen Clara again. I tell this story in detail to discount the absurd and libelous rumors which have been circulated about our friendship—another beautiful thing in my life which slanderers have done their best to show in an evil light. •

ABOVE: This iconic "straw hat" pose, drawn by Ub Iwerks, illustrated "My Love Life"—but was first used on various 1929 posters and publicity. Image courtesy Walt Disney Archives.

RIGHT: Clarabelle Cow: Mickey's onetime fling? Publicity drawing for *The Shindig* (1930); art attributed to Floyd Gottfredson, image courtesy Walt Disney Archives.

Who's Heyudi? Floyd Gottfredson never quite figured it out—but the Liberty Belle Hotel's house ghost(s) still did an amazing job of haunting our *Mickey Mouse* monthly comic book in 1989. As the issues of a "Bellhop Detective" serialization progressed, the cover logo got spookier and spookier! [DG]

ABOVE: *Mickey Mouse* 251–253 (1989). Art by Murad Gumen; images courtesy Thomas Jensen.

RIGHT: New title vignette from reprint in *Walt Disney's Comics and Stories* 30–35 (1943). Art by Dan Noonan; image courtesy Thomas Jensen.

MICKEY MOUSE ON CAVE-MAN ISLAND. Painting by Floyd Gottfredson, November 1978 (illustrating this volume's "Land of Long Ago"). Image courtesy Malcolm Willits. 249.

Behind the Scenes: MICKEY'S DINOSAUR

Nothing says "animation" like dinosaurs—because animation is one of the only ways we can *see* dinosaurs on film. From Winsor McCay's *Gertie the Dinosaur* (1914) right up to the present day, animators have been recreating the extinct reptiles with paper, cels, clay, and computers. The "Rite of Spring" sequence in *Fantasia* (1940) was just the first of many Disney dino tales.

But dinosaurs have never encountered Disney's icon, Mickey Mouse, in an animated film—or have they? Floyd Gottfredson's Mickey comic strips often reflected cartoon projects in the planning stages; and "Land of Long Ago" (1940) was no exception. Surviving storyboards for "Mickey's Dinosaur," in development contemporaneously with the comic, show us that Disney did have a Jurassic Mouse cartoon in mind. The plot finds caveman Mickey hunting a dino egg for breakfast: shades of the "fried egg au giganticus" that he cooks in the Gottfredson strip!

When the egg hatches a baby bronto, Mickey tries to exile him, then to train him—without success. Alas, just then the egg's monster mama shows up... with designs on Mickey as a midday meal. But thanks to a rescue by Mickey's baby buddy, our cavemouse hero stays safe.

"Mickey's Dinosaur" died out around the time that World War II cut down Disney's production of shorts—but we can play paleontologists and enjoy this fossilized story just the same. All images courtesy Walt Disney Animation Research Library; special thanks to Fox Carney. [DG]

HEY!

Gottfredson's World: LAND OF LONG AGO 

Strange, but true: the Gottfredson story set farthest in the prehistoric "past" was also the most *recent* Gottfredson story—chronologically speaking—to be serialized in our modern-day *Mickey Mouse* comic book. Or… as Doc Dustibones' Pleistocene buddy, Oompa, would say: "Gub kabibble *many covers*! Countum goob, toob, throob… uh, foob… uggle *real hard*!" [DG]

TOP LEFT: Italian *Albi d'oro* 31 (1946, 2nd series). Art by Michele Rubino; image courtesy Matteo Sonz.

TOP RIGHT THREE: *Mickey Mouse* 247–249 (1989). Art by Daan Jippes (247, 248) and Murad Gumen (249); images courtesy Thomas Jensen.

BOTTOM LEFT: Dutch *Mickey Maandblad* 1977–05. Art by Daan Jippes and Danny Wanner; image courtesy Roy Kooijman.

RIGHT: Italian *Topolino Collezione ANAF* 40 (1984). Art by Romano Scarpa; image courtesy The Walt Disney Company.

MICKEY MOUSE IN LOVE TROUBLE. Painting by Floyd Gottfredson, March 1981. Image courtesy Malcolm Willits.

♣ *Gottfredson's World:* WOOERS OF 1941 ♣

How much of Mickey's 1941 was spent trying to win reluctant hearts? The ridiculous romance of "Love Trouble" was followed almost immediately by a different kind of pursuit—art director Mickey's efforts to woo reluctant ad clients in "Mickey Mouse, Supersalesman." [DG]

TOP LEFT AND MIDDLE: Italian *Topolino collezione* ANAF 42 (1984), illustrating "Supersalesman." Art by Romano Scarpa; image courtesy The Walt Disney Company.

TOP MIDDLE: Italian *Albi d'oro* 49 (1947, 2nd series), illustrating "Supersalesman." Art by Michele Rubino; image courtesy Francesco Spreafico.

TOP RIGHT: Dutch *Mickey Maandblad* 1976-04, illustrating "Love Trouble." Art by Daan Jippes; image courtesy Roy Kooijman.

BOTTOM: New title vignettes from reprints in *Walt Disney's Comics and Stories* 36 (1943, left) and 91 (1948, right). Images courtesy Thomas Jensen.

Behind the Scenes: THE GOTTFREDSON REDRAWS

IT ALL BEGAN WITH scissors and paste. Floyd Gottfredson's *Mickey Mouse* newspaper serials were among the most popular stories told in their medium—so why not move them to a slightly different medium? As early as 1933, Disney comic strips were being sliced, glued, and physically rearranged to retell their stories in children's storybooks, such as Western Publishing's *Big Little Books*. In 1937, the strips moved into Western's monthly protocomic *Mickey Mouse Magazine*. Color was added for magazine publication; shading, now arguably superfluous, was sometimes erased.

And the end results were evidently huge successes. All the way up to 1948, Gottfredson strip-stories were a mainstay of Western's Disney publications. Mickey serials, broken over several months apiece, became one of *Walt Disney's Comics and Stories'* biggest draws.

But then something happened. Or rather, several "somethings."

First, in the wake of Carl Barks' Donald Duck comic book sagas, Western began assembling talent to create original Mickey comic book material: stories that appeared from 1943 in Western's *Four Color* one-shots. Many of these stories' Mouse artists, like Bill Wright and Dick Moores, had started out as Gottfredson's inkers on the newspaper strips.

Second, for reasons now lost to history, Western began to regard serialized daily comic strips—both Disney and non-Disney—as unusable for the magazine format. Newspaper cartoonists were drawing postwar funnies in a tighter aspect ratio; perhaps it was not cost-effective to revamp these narrower panels for standard comic book pages.

Rather than use current Gottfredson material, then, Western decided to recycle the old—sort of. In February 1949, two "new" Mickey stories debuted in Western's pages: "Mickey Mouse and His Sky Adventure" in *Four Color* 214, and "Mickey Mouse Outwits the Phantom Blot" in *Walt Disney's Comics* 101–106. The former was drawn by Wright, the latter by Moores and Wright—but neither story was really all-new. Instead, they were direct redraws of past Gottfredson serials, now updated to feature 1949 character models and—in Wright's case—action that read right-to-left instead of left-to-right, apparently by editorial fiat.[1]

For better or worse, readers seemed to accept these "new" stories as they had the earlier remounts. And thus it was that—continuously through 1951, and occasionally thereafter—Western had many Gottfredson tales redrawn, with the full roster of their regular Mickey artists taking part. While Wright and Moores were most common, Paul Murry, Al Hubbard, and others gave their own fascinating, unique reinterpretations of Gottfredson's staging and design.

Later, Gottfredson's writing was also reinterpreted. "The Bar-None Ranch" (original 1940, redraw 1959) and "An Education for Thursday" (1940/1960), two of the last stories redrawn, were also partly rescripted to give Mickey and other characters less dialogue, less edge, and arguably less personality. By this time, Western's Mickey had solidified as a no-nonsense detective/homeowner; perhaps 1930s street slang was considered beneath him. Whether a less colorful Mickey was a better Mickey, of course, remains open to question.

On the following pages, let's take a look at some redraws and... er, draw our own conclusions. [DG]

The author wishes to thank Michael Barrier for invaluable assistance.

ABOVE: Excerpt from the comic book remount of Gottfredson's daily strip serial "Mickey Mouse Joins the Foreign Legion" (1936; version from *Walt Disney's Comics and Stories* 9, 1941). Awkwardly extended crosshatching attests to the difficult work involved in turning comic strips into comic books.

1 Bill Wright paraphrased in Don Thompson, "Obituaries: Bill Wright." *The Comics Buyers' Guide* 585 (February 1, 1985), p. 46. Wright recalled being asked to flip the action horizontally in every panel; the finished product suggests he obeyed most of the time. The reason for the rule is unclear; other artists seem not to have been subject to it.

"Island in the Sky": Gottfredson daily strip for February 27, 1937; redraw by Bill Wright from *Four Color* 214 ("Mickey Mouse and His Sky Adventure," February 1949).

"Mickey Mouse Outwits the Phantom Blot": Gottfredson daily strip for June 13, 1939; redraw by Dick Moores from *Walt Disney's Comics and Stories* 102 (March 1949).

"The Seven Ghosts": Gottfredson daily strip for September 30, 1936; redraw by Dick Moores from *Walt Disney's Comics* 109 (October 1949).

"Mystery at Hidden River": Gottfredson daily strip for October 28, 1941; redraw by Bill Wright from *Walt Disney's Comics* 112 (January 1950).

"The Miracle Master": Gottfredson daily strip for January 10, 1940; redraw by Al Hubbard from *Walt Disney's Comics* 151 (April 1953).

"The Bar-None Ranch": Gottfredson daily strips for May 30 and June 1, 1940; redraw by Paul Murry from *Walt Disney's Comics* 229 (October 1959). Great horny toads, what happened to Mr. Hawkins' Wild West drawl? •

Somebody hid Hidden River! No, not really; the waterway is visible enough for Mickey to tumble into a few times. But the story still seems to have been hidden from *cover artists*. While "Mystery at Hidden River" headlined various Disney comic books around the world, it was only ever a front-page feature in Italy. As such, it anticipated many later Gottfredson serials—which, despite their popularity, rarely got covers to themselves. [DG]

LEFT: Italian *Albi d'oro* 53 (1947, 2nd series). Art reinked from Gottfredson by Michele Rubino; image courtesy Matteo Sonz.

RIGHT: Italian *Topolino collezione ANAF* 43 (1984). Art by Romano Scarpa; image courtesy The Walt Disney Company.

Bing! You're hypnotized! You're now in several countries at once! And in one of them, the larcenous Gleam has brainwashed some local comic book editors—and invaded a Disney magazine that's no place for mice. Can you spot it? (Actually, the real story is that—with a certain Disney TV series off the air—non-TV Disney characters were brought into the magazine to keep sales up. But we prefer our first explanation.) [DG]

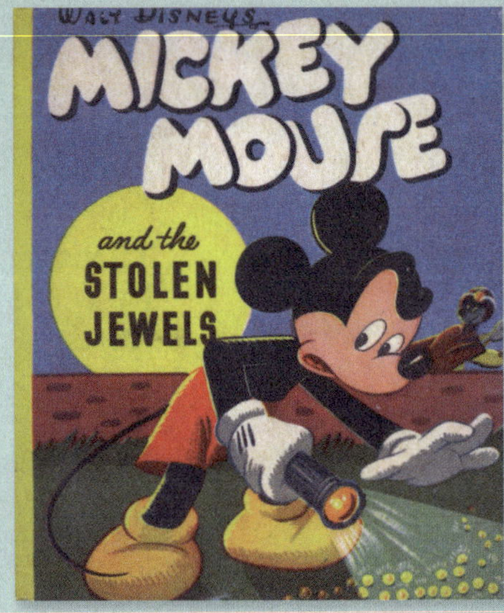

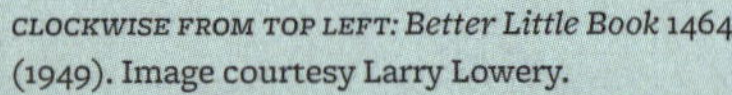

CLOCKWISE FROM TOP LEFT: *Better Little Book* 1464 (1949). Image courtesy Larry Lowery.

Brazilian *Mickey* 24 (1954). Art by Álvaro de Moya; image courtesy Arthur Faria Jr.

Dutch *DuckTales* 50 (1997). Art by Daan Jippes; image courtesy Roy Kooijman. Racecars, lasers, aeroplanes; it's a... mouse blur?

Dutch *Mickey Maandblad* 1981-09. Art by Marco Rota; image courtesy Roy Kooijman.

ABOVE: At a commemorative Christmas dinner in 1982, Carl Barks (left) and Floyd Gottfredson compare their "Duckster" and "Mousecar." These award statuettes were given by the Disney Studio for distinguished service to the company or community. Photo courtesy Malcolm Willits.

THE HEIRS OF GOTTFREDSON:

CARL BARKS

» BY DAVID GERSTEIN

NOW AND THEN A PUPIL becomes more accomplished or better-known than his teacher. While protégé Carl Barks (1901–2000), creator of Uncle Scrooge McDuck, hardly outpaced Floyd Gottfredson in quality, "Duck Man" Barks did surpass his inspiration in terms of fame.

This event came about for several reasons. Firstly, the Barks canon consisted of relatively short stories made for color comic books, historically allowing for easier reprint than Gottfredson's wide-format, super-long serials. Secondly, discounting short gag pages, Barks created almost twice as much content as Gottfredson, with twice as many milestones by nature.

And third: Mickey Mouse, due mainly to his later 1940s animated output, spent years popularly misperceived as a dull goody-goody. While Scrooge built a reputation that preceded him—based on his wild heroism and volcanic temper—the comics Mickey was preceded by an undeserved bad rap. It was no small irony; given that, had Gottfredson never grown his Mickey, Barks' Scrooge, Gyro, Magica De Spell, and other great characters might never have been hatched.

Barks, of course, hatched first. Born in Merrill, Oregon, the young man was an errand boy, lumberjack, and railroad repairman before becoming a cartoonist. Throughout the late 1920s and early 1930s, Barks picked up income drawing for the *Calgary Eye-Opener* and similar adult humor magazines. Then in November 1935, while living in Minneapolis, Barks applied to work at Disney—but not as a Duck man. Barks' new career started with a Mouse.

"When I first started noticing the *Mickey Mouse* strip, [Gottfredson] leaned toward western adventures," Barks later recalled. "You had stagecoach robberies and rubber-legged horses and so on, always very funny..."[1] Inspired by these tales, Barks submitted two large Wild West–themed Mickey publicity drawings to Disney. The Studio bought the drawings and hired Barks on the spot.[2]

Moving to California for his new job, Barks started as an animation inbetweener; but the young talent had loftier goals. In 1936, in his spare time, Barks storyboarded a long gag sequence pitting Donald against a robot barber chair: a sequence, used in the cartoon *Modern Inventions* (1937), that mightily impressed Walt Disney. Barks could tell a gag; could Barks tell a full-length story? To find out, Barks picked up a shelved Mickey plot idea and spent several weeks expanding it into a storyboard.

The result was "Northwest Mounted," a highly elaborate adventure cartoon. The style of Gottfredson's Westerns impacted everything but the setting: while staged in snowy Canada, Mickey's adventure as a Mountie pitted him against Pete as a gruff gold mine bandit—and co-starred Tanglefoot the horse, a Gottfredson character who had never appeared in animation.

POW

Alas, "Northwest Mounted" was "pretty wild and too illogical for Walt's taste," Barks remembered, "so [story editor Dick Creedon] put me into a story room with Harry Reeves. Harry had much experience in what could and couldn't be used in animation comedy."[3] Harry was also a Donald Duck story man.

Over five years, Barks matured in a story unit that contained Reeves, Chuck Couch, and Jack Hannah at various times. Most of their output starred Donald—and his nephews, girlfriend Daisy, and gluttonous cousin Gus Goose, all of whom Barks developed significantly. Soon Barks became a story director within the unit. Cartoons he helmed, like *Fire Chief* (1940), explicitly establish Donald as his nephews' underqualified boss: a likeable braggart with dreams of glory.

It was this incarnation of Donald that Barks brought to print. Moonlighting with his colleagues in 1941, Barks had begun to dabble in comic books: helping to write Western Publishing's "Pluto Saves the Ship" (*Large Feature Comics* 7, 1942), then joining Jack Hannah to draw "Donald Duck Finds Pirate Gold" (*Four Color* 9, 1942). Work on these tales led Barks to an important decision. He was tired of the Studio's lack of privacy; the office's air conditioning units bothered his sinuses. In 1942, Barks left Burbank, moved to San Jacinto—and launched into thirty years of Disney comics freelance work.

While Donald was Barks' star, Mickey remained influential. Gottfredson inspired Barks' art: "It was the *Mickey Mouse* strip he did that influenced my drawing more than anything else," Barks recalled. "Roy Crane, [Hal Foster's] *Prince Valiant*, [E.C. Segar's] *Popeye*... contributed small things to my drawing style. But it was all to help me adapt myself to Floyd's way of drawing."[4] Gottfredson also shaped Barks' writing style: "I was trying to follow [his] format... having Mickey and the other guys involved

OPPOSITE: One of the two sample publicity drawings Carl Barks drew for Disney in 1935, at the start of his job with the Studio. Drawn with pen and ink and blue wash on board, it illustrates Gottfredson's Mickey Sunday serial "Lair of Wolf Barker," reprinted in Volume 1 of our companion Sunday strip series (see that volume for Barks' other publicity drawing, also illustrating "Wolf Barker").

RIGHT: The Barks Ducks in microcosm, from "Race to the South Seas" (*March of Comics* 41, 1949). Six highly character-driven panels encapsulate irony, jealousy, realistic fear—and not one, but *two* family feuds.

in funny situations at the same time they were having serious problems."[5]

Gottfredson even helped Barks discover the limits of the medium. As Barks remembered:

> You could draw just so much violent action in a comic book before it got tiresome. Floyd Gottfredson put his finger on it... He says, "In the strip, the reader can hold it up, and he looks at it for a long, long time, but when it's on the screen, he sees it for a twenty-fourth of a second, and it's gone."... I toned down my action a little bit after having talked with him.[6]

OPPOSITE: Mickey Mouse in "The Riddle of the Red Hat" (*Four Color* 79, 1945). Story and art by Carl Barks; cover (presented afterward) by Carl Buettner; new color by Susan Daigle-Leach.

ABOVE: Barks' early Disney comics were heavily inspired by Gottfredson. Two panels from Barks' "Taming the Rapids" (*Walt Disney's Comics and Stories* 58, 1945) feature Mrs. Van Astorocks, a Gottfredson bit player; compare with her appearance in the June 17, 1941, *Mickey* daily.

RIGHT: Another view of Gottfredson and Barks at the 1982 Christmas dinner. Photo courtesy Malcolm Willits.

Barks traded his early Duck slapstick for more cerebral themes: battles of wits, the dark humor of conservative cynicism, and the debut of strong new personalities, who could play off of Donald and each other. Just as earnest Mickey could be goaded by a windy Horace or struggle to outwit a powerful Pete, ne'er-do-well Donald could flinch under Scrooge's authority and strain to humble a smug Gladstone Gander. Foils for a risk-averse Duck came as easily as those for an adventure-seeking Mouse.

Barks created Scrooge in 1947; in 1952, the "skinflintillionaire" got his own comic book. Over time, Barks developed a richer environment for Scrooge and Donald than had been seen in any other medium. Barks' Duckburg cast, which grew to include the Junior Woodchucks and the nefarious Beagle Boys, became a distinctive contribution to modern folklore.

Like the best folklore, the Barks canon always featured a highly distinctive attitude. A dark view of human nature—with the odd redemption—characterized stories like "Lost in the Andes," with its naïve race of square-edged Incas, and "The Golden Helmet," in which Donald's effort to save the world from an autocrat devolves into a plan to rule it himself. In the 1970s, retiring from comics, Barks began painting the Duck characters in oils; in time, he would rule his own world of international fans and admirers.

In 1945, Barks drew "The Riddle of the Red Hat," his one and only *Mickey Mouse* comic book tale.[7] It was an awkward fit for the Duck Man: by this time, Barks felt, Mickey was not "my cup of tea."[8] But if Gottfredson Mice could inspire Barks Ducks, they could also inspire Barks Mice. Gottfredson's "Love Trouble," reprinted in this volume, directly

influenced numerous Mickey and Minnie poses in "Red Hat": compare them and you'll see.

"Through this portal pass the fastest mice in the world," Barks' Mickey puffs as he escapes Pegleg Pete. A little Barks wit is there, too. •

1 Carl Barks to Floyd Gottfredson, *Mickey Mouse in Color* deluxe edition (Prescott: Another Rainbow, 1988), p. 106.

2 This and other details of Barks' Disney studio period: Thomas Andrae, *Carl Barks and the Disney Comic Book: Unmasking the Myth of Modernity* (Jackson: University Press of Mississippi, 2006), pp. 30–60.

3 Carl Barks to Geoffrey Blum, *Mickey Mouse in Color*, p. 8.

4 Carl Barks to Bruce Hamilton, *Mickey Mouse in Color*, p. 100.

5 Carl Barks to Donald Ault, Thomas Andrae, and Stephen Gong, *Carl Barks: Conversations* (Jackson: University Press of Mississippi, 2006), p. 92.

6 Carl Barks to Michael Barrier, *Carl Barks: Conversations*, p. 66.

7 Barks' records show that he submitted the story as "Mickey Mouse and Hat Trouble"; the published title appears to have been added by editor/cover artist Carl Buettner.

8 Carl Barks, letter to Michael Barrier, June 9, 1966.

WALT DISNEY PRESENTS
MICKEY MOUSE and THE RIDDLE of the RED HAT
OOOH! LOOK AT THE BEE-YOOTIFUL RED HAT, MICKEY!
Ritzee hat Shoppe
IT LOOKS SORTA SILLY TO ME!
EXCLUSIVE MODEL
W OS 79-01

YOU MUST NEVER CRITERCIZE A GIRL'S HAT! YOU'VE GOTTA APOLOGIZE TO HER!

YEAH, I S'POSE SO!
A NICE BOX O' CANDY WOULD HELP WITH THE APOLOGIZIN', MICKEY! US GIRLS ALL HAVE SWEET TOOTHS!

THANKS FOR THE ADVICE! I'LL DO IT! S'LONG, CLARABELLE!

THE COLOR'S TOO BRIGHT, AND IT...
YOU JUST DON'T KNOW A GOOD-LOOKING HAT WHEN YOU SEE ONE!

BESIDES, IT'S AN EXCLUSIVE MODEL, SO NO ONE WILL HAVE ONE LIKE IT!

I'M GOING IN AND BUY IT! YOU WAIT THERE, MICKEY!
YOU'RE MAKING A BIG MISTAKE, WASTING GOOD MONEY ON THAT RED HORROR!

NOW TO FIND MINNIE! BUT I CAN'T MISS HER WITH THAT HAT!

THERE ARE MINNIE AND THE HAT NOW... GOIN' INTO THAT BUILDING!

A FEW MINUTES LATER
THERE! ISN'T IT SUPER?
GOSH!

WHAT ARE YOU LAUGHING AT?
I HATE TO SAY IT, MINNIE, BUT YOU LOOK EXACTLY LIKE A COMIC VALENTINE!

YOU'VE INSULTED ME, MICKEY MOUSE! DON'T EVER SPEAK TO ME AGAIN!
BUT... BUT... MINNIE... I...

SHE'S GETTIN' INTO THE ELEVATOR!

SURPRISE! HERE, I AM!

AW, MINNIE... WAIT A MINUTE! I DIDN'T MEAN...
DON'T SAY ANOTHER WORD! OUR FRIENDSHIP IS ENDED FOREVER!

WHATSA MATTER, MICKEY? YOU LOOK SORTA SAD!
I AM SAD, CLARABELLE! MINNIE'S MAD AT ME BECAUSE I DIDN'T LIKE HER NEW HAT!

SHHH! NOT SO LOUD, YOU DOPE!
???

BUT....
QUIET! WAIT TILL WE GET THERE!

ROOF, PLEASE!
BUT... BUT...

YOU SHOULDN'T HAVE SPOKEN TO ME DOWN THERE! YOU WERE SUPPOSED TO MEET ME HERE!
BUT...

YOU'RE EARLY! I DIDN'T EXPECT YOU SO SOON!
I'M AFRAID THERE'S SOME MISTAKE... I...

....AND THAT'S THE STORY! HERE'S THE PACKAGE!
OKAY, MICKEY! LET'S OPEN IT AND SEE WHAT'S IN IT!
P.D.

GOSH! A DIAMOND RING!
DIAMOND, MY EYE! IT'S NOTHIN' BUT A HUNK O' GLASS, MICKEY!

THERE'S NO MISTAKE, DOPE! I'M WEARIN' THE RED HAT! YOU'RE CARRYIN' THE BOX OF CANDY!
?

HERE IT IS! YOU KNOW WHAT TO DO WITH IT! TAKE IT TO MISTER WHOOSIT RIGHT AWAY!
WAIT...

BUT IT MUST BE WORTH SOMETHING!
WE'LL CALL THE JEWELRY EXPERT AND SEE!

IT'S ONLY A PIECE OF GLASS! YOU CAN BUY RINGS LIKE THIS FOR A DIME!

HERE'S YOUR DIAMOND RING, MICKEY! GUESS SOMEBODY WAS PLAYIN' A JOKE ON YOU!

I'M NOT WAITIN' FOR ANYTHING! AN' YOU'D BETTER HUSTLE! IF YOU KEEP WHOOSIT WAITIN', THERE'LL BE TROUBLE!

DOWN
HEY!

DON'T COME BACK AND BOTHER US WITH ANY MORE JOKES, MICKEY! WE'RE BUSY AROUND HERE!
OKAY, I WON'T!

HIYA, MICKEY! WHAT YUH GOT THERE?
JUST A CHEAP PHONEY OLD RING, GOOFY!

SORRY, BUB! YOU'LL HAVE TO WAIT FOR THE NEXT TRIP!

I WONDER WHAT.... THERE'S NO NAME AND NO ADDRESS!

THERE'S SOMETHING FUNNY GOING ON! I'D BETTER TAKE THIS TO THE POLICE!
BANK BUILDING

KINDA PURTY THOUGH, AIN'T IT? LOOKS LIKE A REAL DIAMOND... ALMOST!

OOPS! SOMETHIN'S HAPPENED! I MUSTA BROKE IT! THE STONE'S A-MOVIN'!

YOU MUSTA TOUCHED A LITTLE HIDDEN SPRING, GOOFY!
THERE'S SOMETHIN' UNDER THE WHITE STONE! IT'S A RED STONE!

RED STONE, NOTHIN'! THAT'S A REAL RUBY OR I MISS MY GUESS!

IS A RUBY WORTH A LOTTA DOUGH, MICKEY?
I'LL SAY IT IS! AND THIS ONE'S A HUMDINGER!

I KNEW THERE WAS SOMETHIN' FUNNY ABOUT THIS RING! I'LL FIND OUT WHAT IT IS... EVEN IF THE POLICE WON'T!

IF I HADN'T SEEN YOUR RED HAT, I NEVER WOULDA FOUND YOU...
YOU'RE MAKING A MISTAKE.. ..I..

CUT OUT DE KIDDIN', SISTER! HERE'S MY BOX OF CANDY TO PROVE WHO I AM! NOW WHERE'S DE RING?

I HAVEN'T GOT ANY RING! I DON'T KNOW WHAT YOU'RE TALKING ABOUT! LET ME GO!

WHATCHA GOIN' T'DO, MICKEY?
FIRST WE GOTTA HIDE THIS RUBY! YOU TAKE IT, GOOFY! THEY'VE SEEN ME, BUT THEY DON'T KNOW YOU!

I'LL HIDE IT IN MUH SHOE! NOBODY'D EVER THINK O' LOOKIN' THERE FER IT!

TRYIN' A DOUBLE CROSS, ARE YUH? WELL, YOU WON'T GET AWAY WITH IT, SISTER!

I'LL TAKE YUH TO WHOOSIT AN' SEE WHAT HE SAYS ABOUT THIS!

THERE, IT'S HID! NOW WHAT?
NOW WE'RE GOIN' TO FIND A MISTER WHOOSIT! C'MON! WE'LL LOOK IN THE TELEPHONE BOOK!

IN THE MEANTIME!
I GUESS MAYBE MICKEY WAS RIGHT! THIS HAT DOES LOOK SILLY! PEOPLE ARE LAUGHING...

DON'T MAKE ANY NOISE, SISTER, OR YOU WON'T EVER YELL AGIN!

AT THAT SAME MOMENT!
THERE'S ONLY ONE WHOOSIT IN THE BOOK! HE LIVES AT 72 VERBENA BOULEVARD!

WAIT A MINUTE, SISTER! NOT SO FAST!
WH-WHAT? ???

WHAT'S DE IDEA O' BREAKIN' OUR DATE? I BEEN WAITIN' AN' WAITIN' UP ON DE ROOF!
BUT...BUT...

BUT ONLY RICH FOLKS LIVE ON VERBENA BOOLEVARD, MICKEY!
I KNOW! BUT WE'LL TRY THIS WHOOSIT, ANYWAY!

72
HERE'S THE PLACE! SURE A SWELL ONE, ISN'T IT?
YUP! BUT TH' GUY THAT LIVES IN THERE COULDN'T BE NO CROOK! HE MUST BE A MILYONAIRE!

C'MON, MICKEY! LET'S GET OUTA HERE! THEY'LL CALL THE POLEECE IF THEY FIND US A-SNOOPIN' AROUND!
WAIT A MINUTE!

SEE THAT RED THING CAUGHT ON THE BUSHES? IT LOOKS LIKE MINNIE'S NEW HAT!
THAT THING A HAT?

I'M GOIN' TO SEE WHAT IT IS! GOSH! THE GATE'S LOCKED! I'LL HAVE TO CLIMB THE FENCE!
YOU CAN'T DO THAT! THAT'S BURGLARIN'!

OUCH! MUST HAVE SOME LI'L STONES IN MUH SHOES! SURE HURTS WHEN I RUN!

GOTTA HAVE THESE HERE SHOES FIXED SOME DAY!

THAT FEELS BETTER! NOW I CAN MAKE TIME!

IF ANYTHING HAPPENS TO ME IN THERE, GO TELL THE POLICE CAPTAIN, GOOFY!
TELL HIM WHAT?

TELL HIM I NEED HELP! NOW, STAY HERE AND WATCH! AND DON'T LOSE YOUR SHOE!
GAWSH! HOW COULD I LOSE IT? IT'S TIED ON MUH FOOT!

..BUT MICKEY TOLD ME TO TELL YUH! YUH BETTER COME QUICK...
DON'T BOTHER US! WE'RE BUSY! THE FAMOUS FAITH RUBY HAS BEEN STOLEN!
P.D.

AND IN THE HOUSE ON VERBENA BOULEVARD!
WHAT'S THE TROUBLE, PETE?
I CAUGHT DIS FELLA SNOOPIN' AROUND DE PLACE, MISTER WHOOSIT!
I CAN EXPLAIN! I SAW THIS RED HAT AND I...

IT IS MINNIE'S HAT! THERE'S THE NAME OF THE RITZEE HAT SHOPPE INSIDE IT!

WHAT YUH TRYIN' TO DO, PAL? DON'T YUH KNOW YOU'RE TRESPASSIN'?
!!!

HELP! LET ME OUT OF HERE!
MINNIE!
BANG
KNOCK

SO YOU KNOW HER, DO YOU?
SURE! THAT'S MINNIE MOUSE! I'D KNOW HER VOICE ANYWHERE!

I CAN EXPLAIN...
SURE... BUT YOU'LL DO YOUR EXPLAININ' TO DE BOSS!

GAWSH! MICKEY SAID TUH GET THE POLEECE! I BETTER HUSTLE!

THEN MAYBE YOU KNOW WHERE THE RING IS, TOO!
SURE DO! IT'S RIGHT HERE IN MY POCKET! A GIRL IN A RED HAT GAVE IT TO ME!

IT IS THE RING!
OPEN IT UP QUICK, BOSS!

MICKEY! OH, I KNEW YOU'D FIND ME!
I EVEN RETURNED YOUR HAT! HEE! HEE!
THE RUBY'S GONE! GRAB THAT DOUBLE-CROSSER!

NO, YOU DON'T! THROUGH THIS PORTAL PASS THE FASTEST MICE IN THE WORLD!

SLAM

BUP
BUP
BUP
BUP
BUP

COISES! WE MISSED 'EM!

DIVE OVER THAT HEDGE, MINNIE, AND HUG THE GROUND!

KEEP DOWN AND CRAWL AS FAST AS YOU CAN!

NOW WHERE'D DEY GO? ...OH! OH!

SURRENDER, YUH RATS! I SEE YUH BEHIND DAT HEDGE!

EEEK! STOP SHOOTING! WE SURRENDER!
BUP
BUP
BUP
HOW ON EARTH DID HE SEE US BEHIND THIS HEDGE?

OH, I GET IT— THAT HAT!

WHERE'S THE RUBY THAT WAS INSIDE THIS RING?
MY FRIEND GOOFY'S GOT IT! I'LL GET IT FOR YOU IF YOU'LL LET MINNIE GO!

OH, NO! YOU GET THE RUBY AND BRING IT HERE! THEN I'LL LET YOU BOTH GO! IF YOU CALL THE POLICE, YOU WILL NEVER SEE HER AGAIN!

HEY, MICKEY! THE POLEECE..
WHAT...!!
STAND STILL, WHOOSIT! YOU, TOO, PETE! DON'T SHOOT, SERGEANT!

WHO..WHUT... WHERE'S THE..?
STAY WHERE YOU ARE, SERGEANT! KEEP 'EM COVERED!

HOLD YOUR HANDS UP! GET PETE'S GUN, MINNIE!

KEEP YOUR HANDS UP, YOU TWO! SERGEANT GOOF IS THE CRACK SHOT OF THE POLICE FORCE!

C'MON IN, GOOFY! WE'LL TIE 'EM UP WITH THE CURTAIN CORDS!

BUT WHERE'S THE POLEECE, MICKEY? I DON'T SEE NO SERGEANT!
YOU ARE THE POLICE AND THE SERGEANT, GOOFY!
WHAT!!

NO, I AIN'T! I'M JEST GOOFY! THE POLEECE WOULDN'T LISSEN TUH ME! THEY WUZ TOO BUSY HUNTIN' FER SOMEBODY THAT STOLE SOMEBODY'S RUBY!

LATER.. AT THE POLICE STATION!
I APOLOGIZE, MICKEY! WHO WOULDA THOUGHT THAT HARVEY WHOOSIT WAS THE HEAD OF A GANG OF JEWEL THIEVES! NOW, WHERE'S THE FAITH RUBY?
GIVE US THE RUBY, GOOFY!
P.D.

GAWSH! IT'S GONE! I MUSTA SHOOK IT OUTA MY SHOE WITH THEM LIL' STONES THAT WUZ HURTIN' ME!
WHAT??

WHAT'S THAT RED THING CAUGHT IN THE HOLE IN YOUR SOCK, GOOFY?

WAAL, I'LL BE GOLDURNED! THERE IT IS! LUCKY I DON'T DARN MY SOCKS, AIN'T IT?

HERE'S YOUR FAMOUS FAITH RUBY, CAPTAIN!
GOOD WORK! YOU'LL GET A NICE BIG REWARD FOR THIS!
P.D.

DO YOU KNOW WHAT I'M GOING TO DO WITH MY SHARE OF THE REWARD MONEY, MICKEY? I'M GOING TO BUY ANOTHER HAT!
NOT ANOTHER RED ONE... I HOPE!
Ritzee hat Shoppe
EXCLUSIVE MODEL

NO, INDEED! I'LL NEVER BUY ANOTHER HAT THAT YOU DON'T LIKE, MICKEY!

WALT DISNEY'S
MICKEY MOUSE
in the RIDDLE of the RED HAT

"Gottfredson's greatest contribution to comics was quality. He will be remembered for making complex continuities easy to understand and read."

—Carl Barks
to Leonardo Gori and
Francesco Stajano, 1998

LEFT: 1942 birthday card from the Walt Disney Studio to William Randolph Hearst, then the owner of Disney newspaper strip distributor King Features Syndicate. Art by Floyd Gottfredson; image courtesy The Walt Disney Company Italia.

ABOUT THE EDITORS

DAVID GERSTEIN is an animation and comics researcher, writer, and editor working extensively with the Walt Disney Company and its licensees. Gerstein's published work includes *Mickey and the Gang: Classic Stories in Verse*; *Walt Disney Treasures—Disney Comics: 75 Years of Innovation*; and *Walt Disney Uncle Scrooge and Donald Duck: The Don Rosa Library*. He has also worked with Disney to preserve the *Mickey Mouse* newspaper strips seen in this volume.

GARY GROTH co-founded Fantagraphics Books and *The Comics Journal* in 1976. And he is still at it.

THOMAS ANDRAE is an internationally recognized authority on social theory and cultural studies and an instructor at California State University East Bay. He is co-founder and senior editor of *Discourse: Journal for Theoretical Studies in Media and Culture*. He is the author of *Carl Barks and the Disney Comic Book: Unmasking the Myth of Modernity* and *Creators of the Superheroes*, and co-author of Bob Kane's autobiography, *Batman & Me*; Siegel and Shuster's *Funnyman: The First Jewish Superhero* (with Mel Gordon); and *Walt Kelly: The Life and Art of the Creator of Pogo* (with Carsten Laqua).

STEPHEN DeSTEFANO has drawn comics for DC, Marvel, Fantagraphics, and King Features. He has also worked extensively in animated cartoons as an art director, a voice and story artist, and a background and character designer on such productions as Sony's *Hotel Transylvania* and the original *Ren & Stimpy Show*. He published his first graphic novel, *Lucky in Love*—co-written by George Chieffet—in 2010. He currently resides in Hoboken, NJ, with his cats Mia, Mona, Lila, and Ollie.

BYRON ERICKSON has spent the last 28 years of his life editing and writing Disney comic books, first for Gladstone and then for Egmont in Denmark. Some wags claim he's best known as Don Rosa's Disney editor, but he prefers to be remembered for the over two dozen Mickey Mouse stories he's written, most of which were drawn by Cèsar Ferioli.

LEONARDO GORI is a comics scholar and collector specializing in Italian Disney authors and syndicated 1930s newspaper strips. With Frank Stajano and others, he has written many books on Italian "fumetti" and American comics in Italy. He has also written thrillers, which have been translated into Spanish, Portuguese, and Korean.

FRANCESCO "FRANK" STAJANO was imprinted on Disney comics at preschool age and never grew out of it: the walls of his house are covered in bookshelves and many of them hold comics. He has often written about Disney comics, particularly with Leonardo Gori. In real life he is an associate professor at the University of Cambridge in England.

CHRISTOPHER E. BARAT is an associate professor of mathematics at Stevenson University in Stevenson, MD, and a longtime columnist and commentator on comics and cartoons. His work has appeared regularly in *The Harveyville Fun-Times* among other venues, and he coauthored *The DuckTales Index* with Joe Torcivia. He has also provided dialogue for American editions of European Disney Duck comics. He regularly blogs at *newsandviewsbychrisbarat.blogspot.com*.

THAD KOMOROWSKI began his professional association with Disney comics as a teenager, writing character dialogue for American editions of European *Uncle Scrooge* stories. Today a historian and archivist, Komorowski maintains the blog *whataboutthad.com*, devoted to the art of animation, comics, and live-action film. He is the author of *Sick Little Monkeys: The Unauthorized Ren & Stimpy Story*.

JOE TORCIVIA is a comics historian renowned for decades of Disney, Warner Bros, Hanna-Barbera, and DC Comics scholarship. He has also worked as a dialogue writer for American editions of European Disney comics. He maintains the blog "The Issue At Hand" (*tiahblog.blogspot.com*), featuring a light-hearted look at pop culture.

LEFT: Floyd Gottfredson's Comic Strip Department produced this special promotional drawing for the Toledo Community Chest in 1940. William Block, editor of the *Toledo Blade*, sent a special thanks to the Disney Studio. "I cannot tell you how much I appreciate this—and I know I am speaking for several thousand voluntary chest workers." Image courtesy Walt Disney Photo Library.